THE BOOK OF
WHAT?

A THESAURUS OF THINGS EVERYDAY AND ESOTERIC

Compiled and edited by
Rodney Dale

COLLECTOR'S
REFERENCE
LIBRARY

To my wife, family and friends

This edition first published in 2004 by CRW Publishing Limited,
69 Gloucester Crescent, London NW1 7EG

ISBN 1 904919 19 7

Typeset and designed in Bliss by Bookcraft Limited, Stroud, Gloucestershire
Printed and bound in China by Imago

Contents

CONTENTS

Introduction

I keep six honest serving men
(They taught me all I knew);
Their names are What and Why and When
And How and Where and Who.

Rudyard Kipling

The Book of What? is the last in the present series, following as it does *When?*, *Where?* and *Who?* All gradually came into being when I was in that delightful garden at Probus in Cornwall, contemplating the raised Cornwall-shaped bed on whose surface are laid geological specimens from various parts of the Duchy. I envisaged an account of the materials from which matter, and hence the universe, is made; then the universe itself, then the earth, then its peoples, and so on and so on, until *The Book of What?* emerged as part of the Grand Scheme.

The book is in two Parts. Part 1 is the A to Z, listing things (in the widest sense) in alphabetical order. This section also directs the seeker to Part 2: the tables, where the information is arranged in categories. By this arrangement, I intend to guide the seeker towards the information sought. The scope of such a work is enormous, but one purpose to inform my selection has been to help those solving crosswords and other types of quiz (again in the widest sense).

No doubt the book will be used in many different ways for many different purposes, and I will welcome comments and feedback – preferably by e-mail.

Rodney Dale
Haddenham, Cambridgeshire 2004
info@fernhouse.com

Acknowledgements

Many people have helped to bring this book into being, but I would particularly like to thank Meredith MacArdle whose research has been all-important in gathering the material in Part 2 of this book.

I am also deeply indebted to Charlotte Edwards in my office for her crucial part in marshalling the computer files and keeping everything in order as the project developed.

Others have provided and confirmed information, made comments, and generally facilitated the work: Stephen Adamson, Mags Barrett-Jolley, Anne Challis, Christopher Dunn, Lindsay Goddard, Mark Hatcher, Gina Keene, Michael and Valerie Grosvenor Myer, Georgia Parkes and Steve Puttick, and Nick and Sue Webb.

A book such as this stands or falls by its design, and I thank John Button of Bookcraft Ltd, and Matt Gavan, for an especially creative relationship. And Graham Frankland's contribution to the reader's wellbeing has been more than helpful – having said which my shoulders accept the usual author's burden as the place where the buck stops.

And for their faith, patience, and ever-cheerful encouragement: Marcus Clapham, Clive Reynard and Ken Webb; in other words, CRW.

Abbreviations used in this book

=	generally indicates a translation
aka	also known as
AS	Australian slang
b	born
BCE	before the common era (aka BC)
BS	backslang
C	century
c	about
CB	citizens' band
CE	common era (aka AD)
cf	compare
d	died
et al	and others
inter alia	among others
LSD	lysergic acid diethylamide 25
PC	political(ly) correct(ness)
pron	pronounced
(*qv*)	which see
RN	Royal Navy
RS	rhyming slang
UK	United Kingdom of Great Britain and Northern Ireland
US(A)	United States (of America)
WW1	World War 1
WW2	World War 2

Part 1   A–Z

A note on alphabetical order
In the following pages and for the purposes of keeping important material together, some of the highlighted panels may be slightly out of alphabetical order with the main text entries.

A

  Amphetamines (speed).

Abbots Bromley (Horn Dance)

One of the rare European animal dances surviving from remote times, it dates back to at least August 1226. Originally danced at the Barthelmy Fair in the Staffordshire village of Abbots Bromley, it now takes place on Wakes Monday: the first Monday after 4 September (unless 4 September is a Sunday, in which case the Dance is on 12 September). The side comprises 12 men: the six Deermen, who carry the reindeer antlers (on iron frames, and weighing between 16 and 25 pounds); the other six are the stock figures: the Hobbyhorse, the Fool, Maid Marian, and the Bowman, and the two musicians who respectively play the melodeon and the triangle. The horns are normally kept in the church, and drawn at 8am on the day of the Dance, which covers some 10 miles and a dozen locations. For nigh on 200 years, the Lead Deerman has been a member of the Fowell family, and he is responsible for choosing the rest of the side.

Abderian laughter
  The scoffing laugh of Democritus of Abdera.

Abe's Cabe
  A five-dollar bill, from the portrait of Lincoln thereon; cabbage = money.

Abergavenny
  Penny [RS].

Ablutions
  Military bathroom accommodation.

Abo
  A native Australian; now un-PC.

Abominable snowman
The elusive yeti of the Himalaya, of whom there have been no authenticated sightings, only questionable footprints.

Abrazo
Greeting of bearhug and back-pat.

Absolutism
See Political -isms.

Abyssinia
Goodbye [a corruption of 'I'll be seeing ya,' to which the answer is 'Ceylon'. 'Sri Lanka' doesn't work half as well].

AC/DC
Hetero/homosexual.

Acapulco gold
High-quality marijuana of that leaf-colour grown there.

Acca
Australian academic.

Acceptional child
One with learning disabilities; One differently abled [PC].

Accidentally on purpose
Drunk driver [CB].

Accommodation collar
A police arrest for the sake of reaching a target.

Ace in the Hole
A surreptitious advantage to be pulled out as necessary.

Ace of spades
AIDS. (RS).

Ace, Ace note
A dollar.

Acerola
See Edible fruits.

Acespay
A space [BS].

Acey-deucey
Curate's eggy, after the two (in this case) lowest cards.

Ache
Rain (RS).

Acid
LSD (lysergic acid diethylamide 25), an hallucinogenic drug.

Acid freak; acid head
A user of LSD.

Acid rain
Rain, snow or solid ash which is actually acidic and, when it falls to earth, damages plants, contaminates water, kills fish and waterlife. It is caused by industrial pollutants such as nitrogen oxides and sulphur dioxide that create weak nitric or sulphuric acid when they combine with moisture in the air.

Acid rock
Style of loud thump-thump music with strobe effects, the whole said to be reminiscent of the effects of LSD.

Ack-ack
Anti-aircraft fire [WW1 phonetics].

Ack emma
Air Mechanic [RAF]; AM [in the morning – WW1 phonetics].

Ackamarackus, The old
Claptrap.

Acker
Milk [RS].

Ackers
Money [Arabic *fakka* = change].

Acne
Rough road [CB].

Acorn Academy
Mental hospital.

Acres, Bob
A coward, named after a character in Sheridan's *The Rivals*.

Acts of the Apostles
See Books of the Holy Bible.

Adam
1   Adam Faith – Safe [RS].
2   MDMA (methylenedioxymethamphetamine), an hallucinogenic drug.
3   See Who's who in the world's major religions.

Adam and Eve
Believe > 'Would you Adam and Eve it?' [RS].

Addled Parliament
Sat in the reign of James I from 5 April to 7 June 1614; so called for its sterility (as in addled egg), as it was dissolved without passing a single Act; for other Parliaments, see Parliament.

Adept
1   A guru (Hindi), fundi (Swahili), or maven (Yiddish); one who knows what he's doing; see Expert.
2   Originally, one who has reached proficiency in alchemy; nowadays one who is good at anything.

Admiral's watch
A good night's sleep.

Adonis Garden
A short-lived pleasure, a display of cut flowers, named from the cultivated fennel and lettuces grown by the Greeks for the Festival of Adonis and then discarded.

Adrian Quist
Pissed [RS an Australian tennis-player].

Adventists
Those Protestants that expect the Second Coming at any minute. The movement was founded in the US (1831) by William Miller, and in England in the following year. The present-day followers are the Seventh-Day Adventists.

Adverbially premodified adjectival lexical unit
A phrase designed to upset no one, such as 'politically correct' [PC].

Advertising
Marked police car with lights on [CB].

Adzuki
See Vegetables.

Aeolus, Ball of
The first steam turbine, supposedly invented by Hero of Alexandria.

Aerial ping-pong
Australian rules football [from its high kicks].

Aerial torpedo
Finned mortar-bomb dropped from an aircraft [WW1].

Afghanistanism
Concentration on far-off events to divert attention from problems nearer home.

Age of Enlightenment

Or, in Britain, Age of Reason; the C18 rise of a broader and more questioning philosophy based on reason and scientific enquiry, rather than on authoritarian orthodoxy gave rise to the Enlightenment. The seeds were sown in C17 as the understanding and acquisition of scientific knowledge gained pace, and scholars such as Descartes, Newton and Pascal began to question the established order of things. In England, it was intertwined with the Industrial Revolution. Some well-known British figures from the Age of Enlightenment:

1642–1727	Sir Isaac Newton (physicist)
1650–1715	Thomas Savery (steam engineer)
1663–1729	Thomas Newcomen (steam engineer)
1674–1741	Jethro Tull (agriculturalist)
1677–1717	Abraham Darby (ironmaster)
1693–1776	John Harrison (chronologist)
1704–1780	John Kay (weaving engineer)
1709–1784	Samuel Johnson (man of letters)
1711–1763	Abraham Darby II (ironmaster)
1711–1777	David Hume (philosopher)
1716–1772	James Brindley (civil engineer)
1720–1778	James Hargreaves (spinning engineer)
1723–1790	Adam Smith (economist)
1724–1792	John Smeaton (civil engineer)
1728–1779	James Cook (explorer)
1728–1799	Joseph Black (physicist)
1728–1808	John Wilkinson (ironmaster)
1728–1809	Matthew Boulton (engineer)
1730–1795	Josiah Wedgwood (potter)
1731–1802	Erasmus Darwin (physician)
1732–1792	Sir Richard Arkwright (spinning engineer)
1733–1804	Joseph Priestley (chemist)
1734–1794	Edward Gibbon (historian)
1736–1803	Francis Egerton, 3rd Duke of Bridgewater (engineer)
1736–1819	James Watt (engineer)
1748–1814	Joseph Bramah (engineer)
1749–1823	Edward Jenner (physician)
1750–1791	Abraham Darby III (ironmaster)
1753–1827	Samuel Crompton (spinning engineer)
1754–1839	William Murdock (civil engineer)
1757–1834	Thomas Telford (civil engineer)
1771–1831	Henry Maudslay (engineer)
1771–1833	Richard Trevithick (engineer)

African music

Made by *filimbi* (traditional flute), *ilimba* (thumb piano), *izeze* (one-string fiddle) and *nguga* (ankle bells).

Afro

Someone from Africa, or a tight hair-style perhaps reminiscent of a cauliflower.

Age set

Many primitive societies are ordered so that groups of people (usually males) pass through a procession of grades in each of which they are expected to perform various tasks reflecting their abilities such as physical strength, experience and wisdom. There may be 'streams' of warriors, and of elders with political or ritual specialities. Compare this with the introduction of managerial and technical 'ladders' in industry which recognised at last that not everyone worthy of promotion has to be 'manager material'.

Ageism

Discrimination against one age-group by another [PC].

Agricultural

Adjective describing a batsman's playing, supposedly reminiscent of a village cricket match.

Ain't she

Seat [RS]

Air bear

Police helicopter [CB].

Airbrain; Airhead

A nincompoop.

Airmail

Dispose of rubbish on to road from a moving vehicle by perfenestration.

Airplane

A device for smoking a questionable cigarette to the end.

Airs

Faces; braces [RS].

Airtights

Canned food.

Aisle surfing

Controlled (or reckless) trolley riding around the supermarket gondolas.

AKA, aka
Also known as.

Akee
See Vegetables, and Edible fruits.

Akubra
Australian hat [maker].

Alakeefic
Indifferent to one course of action as opposed to another [Army slang; supposedly from Arabic].

Alans
Knickers [RS].

Alastor
A house demon; the skeleton in the cupboard that torments a family so burdened.

Albert
A watch chain as sported by Prince Albert (1819–61), Queen Victoria's consort.

Albert Hall
Wall [RS].

Albondiga
Meat/fish ball [SP].

Alcatraz
Spanish = pelican; an island in San Francisco Bay, west California, on which was a federal prison ('The Rock') used between 1934 and 1962.

Alchemical theory

Everything is a combination of various amounts of the four 'elements' air, earth, fire, and water. Lead combines all four; thus by removing the appropriate amounts of its constituents, it may be transmuted into any other material, particularly gold. Alchemy (the forerunner of chemistry) brought into play the alkahest (the universal solvent), the elixir of life (preventing the user's death), the panacea (a cure for all ills) and the philosopher's stone (whereby baser metals might be turned to gold – overlooking the possibility that, by its profusion, it would then become valueless).

Alf
Australian unsophisticate, an ocker. Opposite: Roy.

Alfalfa
See Vegetables.

Alice Ann
Sorrel horse [*alazan* = sorrel SP].

Alice in Wonderland
A confused driver [CB].

Alky, alkie
Alcohol; One who drinks too much of it.

All the flowers you can handle
Best wishes [CB].

All the monarch's personnel
PC version of 'all the king's men'.

Alley apple
Horse dung; Sockful of stones for use as a cosh.

Alligator
Non-playing jazz aficionado; 'See ya later, alligator;' 'In a while, croco-dile'.

Alligator pear; pepper
See Vegetables.

All-originals scene
A Blacks-only occasion.

Ally Pally
Abbreviation for Alexandra Palace, North London's 1871 answer to the Crystal Palace, which was moved to Sydenham after its work for the Great Exhibition (1851) in Hyde Park. The Crystal Palace having burned down (30 November 1936), Ally Pally experienced its own trib-ulations, but still stands proudly on its north London eminence. See Television.

Almonds
Socks [RS].

Alphonse
Ponce – Pimp, or less-specific freeloader [RS].

Alternatively schooled
Illiterate; uneducated [PC].

Altruism
See Political -isms.

Alvin
A mark, patsy or sucker, the prey of the amster, or ram.

Alyo
A short trip [CB].

Am(p)ster
Secretly in league with the snake-oil vendor [Amster dam = Ram [RS]].

Amaranth
See Vegetables.

Amateur night
Professionals behaving like piss-artists.

Amber fluid, liquid, nectar
Australian beer.

Ambulance
Youngsters who spy such a vehicle may, with appropriate actions, say: 'Hold your collar | And don't swaller | Until you see a four-legged animal,' or variant thereof.

Ambulance chaser
A less-than-ethical lawyer who persuades accident victims to sue for damages (sometimes for an exorbitant cut of any award). The result of the 'compensation culture' has been a huge increase in insurance premiums (or sometimes a dearth of insurers), and people afraid to do anything which might result in their being sued – and, worse, employers who prevent their employees from exercising common-sense and humanity lest *they* should be sued.

American persimmon
See Edible fruits.

Amniomancy
See Fortune telling.

Amped
High on amphetamines.

Amscray
Scram! [BS].

Anachronism
Something in the wrong chronological relationship with other things and events as depicted in fiction or inaccurate historical accounts. An oft-quoted anachronism is 'The clock hath stricken three' in the Scottish Play by Shakespeare, but television docudramas offer examples by the shedload, especially in the nuances of the dialogue.

Analemma
A graduated scale shaped in a figure of eight that indicates the daily declination of the sun; hence analemmatic sundial, as set up in the market square at Ely, Cambridgeshire, where the on-stander acts as the gnomon.

Anarchism
See Political -isms.

Anato
See Vegetables.

Anaxaridian trousers
See Fashion.

Anchor bodies
Family [CB].

Andrew, The
The Royal Navy [from a feared press-gang master].

Angel
A financier, especially one bankrolling an entertainment; Snake-oil vendor's generic codename for an Alvin, mark, patsy or sucker.

Angel buggy
Badly-loaded truck [CB].

Angel dust
Phencyclidine.

Angel face special
Wife [CB].

Animal entrails
See Fortune telling.

Ankle-biter
A less-well-behaved child.

Annie Oakley
Free admission ticket to sport or entertainment [from the holes as crack shot Phoebe Anne Oakley Moses (1860–1926 (of *Annie Get your Gun* fame)) might have made].

Annual Shareholders' Meeting
A traditionally silly set piece where a few eccentric private shareholders have an opportunity of addressing pertinent questions to a supercilious chairman on a remote dais, only to receive unsatisfactory and patronising answers.

Antsy
Jittery; sexually aroused [ants in the pants].

Anniversaries

Certain materials or artefacts are traditionally (or commercially) attached to particular wedding anniversaries, as follows:

1 Cotton, Paper, Plastics, Clocks
2 Paper, Cotton, Calico. China
3 Leather, Glass, Crystal
4 Fruit, Flowers, Linen/Silk, Appliances
5 Wood, Silver
6 Iron, Sugar, Sweetmeats
7 Wool, Copper, Brass, Desk Sets
8 Bronze, Pottery, Appliances, Linen
9 Copper, Pottery, Willow, Leather
10 Tin, Aluminium, Diamond
11 Steel, Jewellery
12 Silk, Linen, Pearl
13 Lace, Textiles, Fur
14 Ivory, Gold
15 Crystal, Timepieces
20 China, Platinum
25 Silver
30 Pearl, Diamond
35 Coral, Jade
40 Ruby, Garnet
45 Sapphire
50 Gold
55 Emerald, Turquoise
60 Diamond, Gold
70 Platinum
75 Diamond, Gold

In the above list, the traditional materials are on the left, and more modern introductions (which embrace specific artefacts as well as the material from which they might be made) as you move to the right. In general, it appears that the longer whatever it is has been going on, the more expensive the material associated with it; however, values of materials change and, relatively, some have increased (leather, wood, copper, tin) and others decreased (sugar, wool, china) in value. Presumably the category '(electrical) appliances' was introduced by the Electrical Appliances' Manufacturers' Association or some such. As for the desk set …

Apples, Everything's
In good order, under control *cf* Cactus (AS).

Appliqué
A technique used for decoration, involving cutting out pieces of coloured fabric and applying them to a contrasting fabric.

Apricot
See Edible fruits.

Arbalest
A steel crossbow.

Arcadenik
One whose life is arcade games and the like; the suffix -nik denotes a follower of the practice that precedes it: beatnik, peacenik, spacenik and so on.

Armageddon
According to the Revelation of St John the Divine (16:14) the site of the last great battle of that great day of God Almighty ... (16:16) at the place that in Hebrew is called Harmagedon (*ie* the mountain district of Megiddo). The concept has been widened to embrace any great slaughter, such as World War I.

Armani suit
See Fashion.

Arrowroot; Artichoke; Arugula
See Vegetables.

Arvo
Australian slang for afternoon, usually elided to 'the sarvo'.

Ash glaze
A glaze for pottery, that includes a proportion of vegetable or wood ash. Different ashes give different colours and textures to the glaze.

Asparagus
See Vegetables.

Aspirin
Acetylsalicylic acid presented as an analgesic in various forms; based on natural chemicals from bark and leaves of the willow (*Salix* species), whose properties were rediscovered by Revd Edward Stone of Chipping Norton in mid-C18.

Assume
Smart Alec marketing tutor: 'Never ASSUME; it makes an ASS of U and ME.

Astragalomancy; Astrology; Astromancy
See Fortune telling.

Aubergine
See Vegetables.

Australian salute
The movement of the hand brushing away flies.

Authoritarianism
See Political -isms.

Avocado
See Edible fruits.

Awkward age
Epithet adduced for the transition from child to adult, especially by
parents as an excuse for any embarrassing behaviour; better perhaps
to remember the adage 'never apologise; never explain'.

Axminster (carpet)
A type of patterened carpet traditionally made at Axminster, in Devon.
See Gripper and Spool.

Azuki
See Vegetables.

Babalaas
South African hang-over.

Back end
A term for Autumn used in northern England.

Bael
See Edible fruits.

Bagman
An itinerant carrying his possessions with him. This is the broadest
sense of the word, covering both the tramp and the traveller on horse-
back.

Balolo moon
The annelid balolo (or palolo or paolo) worm (*Eunice viridis*) flourishes
among coral reefs in the Pacific; its sexual activity, when its rear end
containing sperm or ova detaches and swims to the surface to release
the gametes, is governed by the phases of the moon. There is a small
rising in October (Vula i balolo lailai), and a much larger one in
November (Vula i balolo levu), when the islanders put to sea to collect
the delicacy.

Bamboo shoots
See Vegetables.

Banana
See Edible fruits.

Bandana
See Fashion.

Bannock
Round, flat griddle cake of oatmeal or barley eaten in Scotland around May Day; originally 'Bannoch Belltainn' baked in the Beltane fire, it later shed its knobs and acquired a cross on one side like a hot cross bun; moreover, Scottish children took to rolling the bannock down hill-sides in the manner of an Easter egg.

Barberry
See Edible fruits.

Bardie
An edible wood grub [*Bardistus cibarius*] (AS).

Barebones Parliament
That of 140 godly members approved by Oliver Cromwell which sat between 4 July and 11 December 1653; it was named (happy coincidence) after one of its members, Praise-God Barebon; for other Parliaments, see Parliament.

Barley
See Edible grasses.

Bartholomew Fair
An annual fair held at Smithfield on St Bartholomew's Day (24 August), from 1133 to 1752, and then (after calendar reform) on 3 September until its last year: 1855. It moved from Smithfield to Islington in 1840; its successor was the Caledonian Market ('The Stones') which closed in 1939, but lives on as the New Caledonian Market in Bermondsey, South London.

Baseball cap
An item of headgear that some find extremely unbecoming, and believe that, when it is worn back to front, it symbolises a complete absence of brain.

BASIC
See Some computer programming languages.

Basket Vine
See Vegetables.

Bastille Day
Commemorates 14 July 1789, when the French Revolution began with the storming of the Bastille fortress in Paris, built in C14, used as a state prison in C17 and 18, and seen by the mob as a symbol of the incompetent, corrupt and despotic Bourbon monarchy.

Bats, Parliament of
See Club Parliament.

Batty riders
See Fashion.

Bazaar Malay
A pidgin used in that country in those days.

BCPL
See Some computer programming languages.

BDMLR
British Divers Marine Life Rescue: unbeaching stranded whales and the like.

Beam
In weaving, the cylinder at the rear of the loom on which the warp threads are wound; the width of the beam determines the width of the cloth.

Bean
See Vegetables.

Bearberry
See Edible fruits.

Beer
A traditional British beverage made from barley, yeast and hops. Brewers use hop cones – the mature female flowers – dried in a kiln (oast) for 12 hours and then compressed into bales for storage or transport. The barley is 'malted' by being allowed to germinate, then 'kilned' (dried) and 'mashed' (heated with water). The 'wort' is boiled with the hops to concentrate it and obtain the flavour. The yeast is used to break down the sugars in the wort to produce alcohol and carbon dioxide gas. Hops not only give the beer its flavour; they also help to preserve it.

Beetroot
See Vegetables.

Bel and the Dragon
See Books of the Holy Bible.

Bells

On board ship, a system of announcing the time in half-hours for all to hear. Eight bells, sounded as four paired chimes, represents 4, 8, and 12 o'clock both day and night. The next half-hour – 4.30, 8.30, and 12.30, am and pm – is one bell; the following half-hour – 5, 9, and 1 o'clock – is two bells; and so on.

In this way, the hours are immediately audible as complete pairs of chimes; half-hours always have one final unpaired chime.

The Watches are as follows:
1200–1600 Afternoon Watch
1600–1800 First Dog
1800–2000 Last Dog (not Second Dog)
2000–0000 First Watch
0000–0400 Middle Watch
0400–0800 Morning Watch
0800–1200 Forenoon Watch

	Morning	Forenoon	Afternoon	First Dog	Last Dog	First	Middle
1 bell	0430	0830	1230	1630	1830	2030	0030
2 bells	0500	0900	1300	1700	1900	2100	0100
3 bells	0530	0930	1330	1730	1930	2130	0130
4 bells	0600	1000	1400	1800	2000	2200	0200
5 bells	0630	1030	1430			2230	0230
6 bells	0700	1100	1500			2300	0300
7 bells	0730	1130	1530			2330	0330
8 bells	0800	1200	1600			0000	0400

All Watches are of four hours, except for the two Dog Watches of two hours each, a system designed to obviate the same people taking alternate Watches from being on the same Watch every day ('dog' is derived from 'dodge'). As the New Year dawns, 16 bells (rather than eight) are struck to usher it in.

Belembe
See Vegetables.

Bell-bottoms
See Fashion.

Belomancy
See Fortune telling.

Bent Ball, Sir Charles
(1st Baronet), Hon Surgeon to Edward VII in Ireland (1904–10).

Benthamism
See Political -isms.

Bhindi
See Vegetables.

Bib and brace
See Fashion.

BIBLE
Basic Instructions Before Leaving Earth.

Biedermeier Period
Of or suggesting a style of furniture and interior decoration popular among the middle classes in Austria, Germany and Scandinavia in the 19th century (*fl* 1816–1848). The fictional character Gottlieb Biedermeier, master of bourgeois bad taste, was created by the German poet Ludwig Eichrocht (1827–92). Biedermeier painting aimed at naturalism, apparently reflected by the English Pre-Raphaelite Brotherhood who – wittingly or no – took over when Biedermeier ended.

Big Brother
An all-encompassing, seemingly benevolent but in fact oppressive and authoritarian government which is constantly monitoring its citizens. Invented by George Orwell (1903–50) in his novel *Nineteen Eighty-Four* (1949). Also an inexplicably phenomenally successful television show placing a group of strangers in a house where their interactions are continuously televised.

Big five
On safari: buffalo, elephant, leopard, lion, rhino.

Big Sea Day
Old-time custom in New Jersey when, on the second Saturday in August, the farmers and their families drove to the sea-shore to picnic and to bathe in their everyday clothes.

Bikini
See Fashion.

Bilberry
See Edible fruits.

Billabong

A waterhole; On the billabong = out of work (and camping by a waterhole – AS).

Biorhythms

In the 1970s–80s, the 'newest scientific discipline' of Biorhythmics came to the fore: 'the computerised study of biological clocks – built-in natural cycles that powerfully influence our behaviour.' According to the theory, there were three chief co-existing rhythms that swung from positive to negative about a time axis in the manner of sinewaves. The *physical* wave has a frequency of 23.5 days, the *emotional* 28 days and the *intellectual* 35 days. If all these cycles start on day zero, they will not all reach zero again for 6,580 days, or just over 18 years. During that period, there will be every combination of the three rhythms relative to one another, and hundreds of examples were gathered demonstrating the apparent relationship between events in the lives of the famous and infamous and the states of their biorhythms. The chief application seemed to be to demonstrate the power of the computer to open-mouthed visitors to exhibitions, and to sell books about Biorhythms. The whole 'discipline' seems to have today fallen by the wayside, and Biorhythms are no longer a central topic of conversation.

Bird chili pepper

See Vegetables.

Bishop (Barker)

A long glass of beer (Frederick Barker, Bishop of Sydney 1845-81, was 6′ 5″ tall – AS).

Birth stone

A gemstone associated symbolically with the month of one's birth:

January	Garnet
February	Amethyst
March	Bloodstone or Aquamarine
April	Diamond
May	Emerald
June	Pearl, Agate, Moonstone or Alexandrite
July	Ruby or Cornelian
August	Sardonyx or Peridot
September	Sapphire or Chrysolite
October	Opal or Tourmaline
November	Topaz
December	Turquoise or Zircon

Bitter greens; Bittergourd; Bittermelon; Black Eye Bean; Black gram
>See Vegetables.

Bixfu
>An example from W M Saunders' *Everybody's Pocket Code* meaning 'At what rate can you engage a carriage with two horses and a coachman?'

Blackberry; Blackcurrant
>See Edible fruits.

Black Parliament
>That which sat between 1529 and 1536, in the third decade of the reign of Henry VIII, when the Church of England came into being; for other Parliaments, see Parliament.

Blamey
>Drinking vessel made from the body of a beer bottle, cutting off the top by tying a kerosene-soaked string round the body, setting it alight, and plunging the whole into cold water (AS).

Blog
>= Web log; an on-line diary.

Blood
>See Fortune telling.

Bloomsday
>16 June 1904, the day on which Stephen Dedalus and Leopold Bloom wander round Dublin and finally meet, in James Joyce's *Ulysses* (1918). It was the very day on which Joyce and Nora Barnacle (later Mrs Joyce) first walked out together.

Blouson
>See Fashion.

Blue
>See Some computer programming languages.

Blue heeler
>An Australian cattle dog.

Blueberry
>See Edible fruits.

Bog in
>Attack food with gusto (AS).

Bok choi
>See Vegetables.

Bolshevism
See Political -isms.

Bombast
See Fashion.

Bone needles
A feature of the Stone Age; see Fashion.

Book, opening at random
See Fortune telling.

Boot cut
See Fashion.

Boshes
The widest part of a blast furnace, where the tuyères – for introducing the blast – are located.

Botanomancy
See Fortune telling.

Bottle
1   Radio valve or vacuum tube (slang; see output bottle).
2   Negative quality: 'It's not a lot of bottle'.
3   Bravery: 'You got the bottle to do that?'.

Bottle gourd
See Vegetables.

Bottle kiln
An early kiln for firing pottery, shaped like a bottle.

Boxer Rebellion
The Boxers (properly Fists of Righteous Harmony) were a secret society in China in the late C19 with two aims: the overthrow of the Imperial Qing or Ch'ing dynasty, and the expulsion of foreigners. At that time, several European countries – Austria, France, Germany, Great Britain, Italy, as well as Japan and Russia, had forced China to accept humiliating and unwelcome trading concessions. The USA was also trying to acquire trading rights in the country. In 1898 the Dowager Empress Isu Hsi managed to turn the Boxers' revolutionary tendencies to violent attacks on foreign religious and trade missions, and the uprising culminated in mid-June 1900 with the Boxers besieging the foreign legations' compound outside the Forbidden City in Beijing (Peking), the capital of China. 45,000 foreign troops, from all the besieged nations as well as the USA, fully equipped with the most modern weapons, invaded China and raised the siege on 14 August. They went on to sack the Forbidden City, forcing the court to flee. The Dowager Empress was humiliated further when the foreign nations

then enforced an 'open door' trading policy, giving them huge trading concessions.

Boy bishop

St Nicholas of Bari was reckoned to be pious from his earliest days, and was so named; a custom arose as a result that on his day (6 December) a boy should be chosen from a local or cathedral choir to act as a mock Bishop for three weeks, until Holy Innocents' Day (28 December); this practice was followed also at some public schools. Henry VIII abolished the custom in 1541, revived under Edward VI in 1552, and abolished for ever by Elizabeth I (she thought). The custom has been revived; at St Nicholas's Church, Tuxford, Nottinghamshire, on 6 December 2002, retired Bishop John Finney 'enthroned' nine-year-old Louis Maybe as boy bishop 'to help young people feel more included'. Louis Maybe handed his regalia on to 11-year-old Amanda Brewer the following year, making her the first girl bishop.

Braai

South African barbecue; Afrikaans braai vleis = meat cooked over a fire.

Braies

See Fashion of the Middle Ages.

Bramble

See Edible fruits.

Brassière or Bra

See Fashion.

Breadfruit

See Edible fruits; Vegetables.

Breechclout

See Fashion.

Brolly

British slang for umbrella; see bumbershoot.

Buckley's (chance)

(AS) no hope at all; never; possibly from:
1   William Buckley, a convict who absconded from Port Philip and went native between 1803 and 1835 when he gave himself up; he died in 1856.
2   Possibly from the Melbourne firm of Buckley and Nunn.

Buffaloberry

See Edible fruits.

Bull nettle

See Vegetables.

Bumbershoot
US slang for an umbrella for over a century, perhaps from a corruptive combination of 'umbra' and 'parachute', in much the same way as the British 'brolly' has emerged.

Bumps on the head
See Medical specialities.

Burning branches
See Fortune telling.

Burns Night
The Anniversary of Robert (Rabbie) Burns's Birthday on 25 January 1759. Burns Night celebrations have assumed a set form the world over; a meal is served consisting of cock-a-leekie soup, and haggis with champit neeps and bashit tatties (chicken and leek broth, and haggis with mashed turnip and mashed potatoes). The haggis is 'piped in' (escorted to the table by someone playing the bagpipes) and Burns's *To a Haggis* is recited.

Butter bean; Buttersquash
See Vegetables.

Buzzkill
A spoilsport or party pooper.

Byzantine dress
See Fashion.

Cab(b)ala(h)
See Kabbalah.

Cabal
1 A group of often political intriguers.
2 By a happy coincidence, the initials of Clifford, Ashley, Buckingham, Arlington and Lauderdale, ministers in the government of Charles II 1667–73.

Cactus
The direction of failure, *cf* apples.

Caff, Ace, with a rather good museum attached
That at the Victoria and Albert Museum, South Kensington (see Sir Henry Cole); the first Caff was set up by William Morris in 1865.

Caftan or kaftan
See Fashion.

Calabash
See Vegetables.

Calabaza
See Vegetables.

CamuCamu
See Edible fruits.

Cantaloupe
See Edible fruits.

Cantoris
In a church choir, the side on which the singers take the lower part in antiphonal singing; *cf* Decani.

Cape gooseberry
See Edible fruits.

Capitalism
See Political -isms.

Capnomancy
See Fortune telling.

Capri pants
See Fashion.

Carambola
See Edible fruits.

Cardoon
See Vegetables.

Carrot
See Vegetables.

Cartomancy
See Fortune telling.

Cassava
See Vegetables.

Castrato
See Singing voice types.

Causalism
See Political -isms.

Causimancy
See Fortune telling.

Cayenne
See Vegetables.

CBRN
Chemical, biological, radioactive or nuclear incident.

Ceci beans
See Vegetables.

Cee gwa
See Vegetables.

Celeriac; Celery
See Vegetables.

Centrism
See Political -isms.

Cep
See Vegetables.

Ceroscopy
See Fortune telling.

Ceylon spinach
See Vegetables.

CFCs or chlorofluorocarbons
CFCs are not only one of the major 'greenhouse' gases contributing to global warming, they also destroy the ozone layer around the earth. The ozone layer blocks a great deal of the ultraviolet radiation from the sun and, as it thins, more of this harmful radiation gets through to earth, damaging crops, wildlife, sealife and human skin. A 'hole' in, or thinning of the ozone layer was first observed over the Antarctic in 1977. In 2000 CFCs were completely banned in the developed world.

Chanterelle; Chaya; Chayote
See Vegetables.

Chempedak; Cherimoya; Cherry
See Edible fruits.

Cheongsam
See Fashion.

Chickpea; Chicory
See Vegetables.

Chiku
See Edible fruits.

Chili leaves
See Vegetables.

Chinese cabbage
See Vegetables.

Chinese gooseberry
See Edible fruits.

Chinese hexagrams
See Fortune telling.

Chinese jujube
See Edible fruits.

Chinese leaf
See Vegetables.

Chinos
See Fashion.

Chiromancy
See Fortune telling.

Chiton
A feature of Classical Greek fashion; see Fashion.

Chokeberry
See Edible fruits.

Chow-chow
See Vegetables.

Christophine
See Vegetables.

Chronicles
See Books of the Holy Bible.

Chronotype
Factor in one's make-up that determines whether one is a lark (early to bed, early to rise) or an owl (late to rise, late to bed), or somewhere in between.

Cinque Ports
Although cinque is French for five, this confederation of five English ports – Dover, Hastings, Hythe, Romney and Sandwich – is pronounced 'sink' not 'sank'. The five created an informal confederation in C11 to regulate the wealth-producing herring fairs, but since they sit strategically on the south-east coast overlooking the English Channel, the medieval kings found it expedient to gain the ports' support. In 1260 the first known formal charter was issued acknowledging their joint rights over the herring fairs and giving the ports freedom from taxes and the right to raise their own local taxes. In

return the ports supplied ships for the Royal fleet, both for war and for general transport of the monarch. Rye and Winchelsea later joined the list, as did a number of others on the same coast. The post of Lord Warden of the Cinque Ports has been filled by the Duke of Wellington, Sir Winston Churchill, and Queen Elizabeth, the Queen Mother.

Citron; citrus fruits
See Edible fruits.

Clementine
See Edible fruits.

Clepsydra

A water clock: a device for measuring the passage of time that relies on the constant flow of water (or occasionally some other liquid, rarely mercury) through a stricture. Even the Ancient Egyptians had some device of this kind. The term is the Latin form of the Greek for 'water clock'. The clepsydra measures time as a constant flow, rather than variably as a sundial does. The ancient Egyptians were preoccupied with death and resurrection, and the behaviour of the Sun (dying each evening) provided constant work for their priests who wished to ensure its continuing morning reappearance. During the day, the Sun itself could cast a shadow to mark the passage of time; in the hours of darkness the clepsydra performed that function. The principle of the clepsydra is simple: water flows (or drips) from a hole in a reservoir. The level of the water drops, and the passage of time can be read from marks inside the reservoir. Alternatively, the water flows from the reservoir into another vessel, and the passage of time is read from the rising level of the surface. Another method is to place a perforated bowl in the reservoir, and observe the bowl sinking as the water leaks in; alternatively, a calibrated air-filled vessel may sink as the air leaks out.

Cloche hat
One shaped like a bell, with little brim, a favoured fashion for the 20s and 30s.

Clock
An old name for church bells; more usually, a device for measuring time. The origins of the first mechanical clocks in Europe are not known, though it is likely that they were devised to mark the Divine Offices in monasteries. This may have led to some confusion, since the word 'clock' is derived from the root we see in French 'cloche', a bell,

reflecting the early 'clocks' in which a bell marked the passage of time. Equally, when the Latin word 'horologium' is used in a medieval text, it might mean a clepsydra, sundial, mechanical clock or bell. However, the bell of the reported 'horologium' or 'clock' may have been struck by a monk watching a clepsydra, hour-glass, candle or other measuring device, and thus the description was not necessarily of a wholly-automatic device. It has been suggested that a dearth of reliable human timekeepers may have spurred the development of the mechanical clock; on the other hand, there must always have been those keen on research and invention, and devising a means for mechanical timekeeping is an ideal task for exercising ingenuity. The birth of the mechanical escapement clock is unrecorded, though it is likely that many craftsmen were experimenting with such devices in various centres of the 13th century. A mechanical clock is said to have been built by the monks of Dunstable Priory, Bedfordshire, in 1283. This predates other recorded clocks by several decades. An astronomical clock with automata and a dial set up in Norwich Cathedral is recorded in the Sacrist's Rolls for 1325.

Clock tax
In 1797, the British Government sought to raise money by imposing an annual clock tax – five shillings for public and domestic clocks, ten shillings for watches carried on the person, and two shillings and sixpence for timekeepers falling outside of the first two categories. The difficulties of collecting the tax are obvious, and it caused such a decline in the clockmaking industry that thousands were put out of work. Fortunately, good sense prevailed; the tax was repealed in 1798, and some compensation paid to the industry. The legacy of the clock tax is the 'Act of Parliament Clock', a large-faced timepiece widely bought and displayed by hoteliers and innkeepers of that time for the benefit of their customers.

Cloudberry
See Edible fruits.

Coat hanger
Sydney Harbour Bridge (AS).

COBOL
See Some computer programming languages.

COBRA
Cabinet Office Briefing Room A.

Coconut
See Edible fruits.

Cocoyam
See Vegetables.

Coke (*pron* Cook)

On 17 December 1849, William Coke of Holkham (pron hokum) in Norfolk took delivery of a felt hat from Lock & Co of St James's (London), designed and manufactured by Thomas and William Bowler. Coke stamped on it twice, pronounced it acceptable and paid 12/- for it. Lock's still call the bowler hat a 'coke'.

Cole, Sir Henry

(1802–82) English civil servant with a flair for design and entrepreneurship who was largely responsible for the Great Exhibition of 1851, under the patronage of Prince Albert. He later became the director of London's South Kensington Museum (now the Victoria and Albert), set up to house many of the artefacts from the Great Exhibition.

Collectivism

See Political -isms.

Colocassi

See Vegetables.

Coloratura soprano

See Singing voice types.

Colossians

See Books of the Holy Bible.

COMAL

See Some computer programming languages.

Communism

See Political -isms.

Conchomancy

See Fortune telling.

Conservatism

See Political -isms.

Corinthians

See Books of the Holy Bible.

Corn

See Edible grasses.

Corn on the cob

See Vegetables.

Cornelian cherry

See Edible fruits.

Corrector, The

Alexander Cruden (1701–70), Scottish bookseller and compiler of the *Concordance of the Holy Scriptures* (1737) who, uncertain in his mental health, assumed that title and went about the country denouncing Sabbath-breaking and profanity.

Corset; Costume; Cotton

See Fashion.

Council of Nicea

The first Ecumenical Council of the Christian church held under Constantine the Great in 325 at Nicea in Bithynia, Asia Minor, primarily to deal with the Arian heresy, which it condemned. The second Council of Nicea (787), the seventh General Council of the Church, was summoned by the Empress Irene to end the Iconoclastic Controversy.

Council of Ten

A secret tribunal exercising unlimited powers in the old Venetian republic. It was instituted in 1310 with ten members. The number was then increased to 17 and it continued in active existence until the fall of the republic in 1797.

Council of Trent

The nineteenth general council of the RC Church held in Trento (Northern Italy) summoned by Pope Paul III to strengthen the Church in the face of Protestantism by clarifying doctrines and instituting reforms held in three sessions: 1545–47; 1551–52; 1562–63.

Covenant

A term applied to those Scottish Presbyterians subscribing to various bonds or covenants for the security and advancement of their cause. The first was entered into by the Lords of the Congregation in 1557 and another was made by ordinance of James VI in 1581. In 1638 the National Covenant was directed against the Laudian prayer book imposed by Charles I. In 1643 a Solemn League And Covenant pledged the Scots and their English Parliamentarian allies to preserve Presbyterianism in Scotland and to establish it in England and Ireland.

Cowboy hat

See Fashion.

Cranberry

See Edible fruits.

Cranberry hibiscus

See Vegetables.

Credit creep

Film credits run longer and longer, now including producer's cat's vet's sister and the like; *Nosferatu* credits (1922) run 82 seconds; those for *The Return of the King* (2003) run 573 seconds.

Creeping peperomia

See Vegetables.

Creole

1   A language developed by interaction between two native languages from which a third language develops.
2   A name given to native-born inhabitants of French ancestry living in Louisiana and other nearby States
3   Other peoples speaking Creole languages.

Cress

See Vegetables.

Croissant

A flaky bread roll made in a crescent shape of a yeast dough similar to that for puff pastry; heart of the 'continental breakfast', and invented after the Siege of Vienna to celebrate the defeat of the Ottomans (hence the shape).

Crook

Unwell (AS).

CROW

Countryside and Rights of Way Act 2000.

Crowberry

See Edible fruits.

Crumbles, The

A stretch of shingle between Eastbourne and Wallsend on Pevensey Bay.

Crystal ball gazing

See Fortune telling.

CTRL

Channel Tunnel Rail Link (through Kent); CTR1 via Tonbridge; CTR2 via Sevenoaks; CTR3 via Redhill.

Cubomancy

See Fortune telling.

Cucumber

See Vegetables.

Cultivated mushroom
See Vegetables.

Currant
See Edible fruits.

Curtain call
After the play proper has ended, the cast reappears to acknowledge the audience's applause; if ever there's a time to judge nicely when to leave 'em howling for more, this is it.

Custard apple
See Edible fruits.

Dagwood
Enormous multilayered sandwich (AS).

Daikon
See Vegetables.

Daks
Trousers (AS, after a manufacturer); also keks.

Dalen, Gustav
A blind Dane who invented the Aga cooker (1925); Aga = Amalgamated Gas Accumulator.

Damson
See Edible fruits.

Daniel
See Books of the Holy Bible.

Darkie Day
A Christmastide custom in Padstow, Cornwall, when fishermen and their wives black up and sing plantation songs to raise money for charity; an obvious target for those who believe in Political Correctness.

Dasani
Apparently tap water at about £1 per bottle, marketed in the UK by Coca-Cola™ in February 2004.

Dasheen
See Vegetables.

Date
See Edible fruits.

Daun salam
See Vegetables.

Deasil
To travel round in the direction of the sun; clockwise; *cf* widdershins.

Decani
In a church choir, the side on which the Dean's stall stands, and the singers take the higher part in antiphonal singing; *cf* Cantoris.

Decoration and body adornment
See Fashion.

Dehumanisation suit
Baggy white clothing worn by behavioural zoologists in an attempt to stop their subjects 'imprinting', or becoming attached to an identifiable individual.

Dendrochronology
The study of the growth of tree rings, each of which gives information on a tree's growth and hence the environmental conditions during the associated solar year. The growing bank of dendrochronological information, and the assistance of the computer, provide another dating weapon in the armoury of the archaeologist and the historian.

Denim
See Fashion.

Depression, manic
See bipolar disorder.

Derby
See Fashion.

Despotism
See Political -isms.

Determinism
See Political -isms.

Deuteronomy
See Books of the Holy Bible.

Devil's Picture Book
The name given to playing cards by Puritans during the English Civil War 1648–51.

Dewberry
See Edible fruits.

Dhoti
See Fashion.

Dice or knucklebones
See Fortune telling.

Dials at Whitehall

How King Charles II's timekeeper, set up in 1669, worked, is not clear. Britten writes: 'This curious erection had no covering; exposure to the elements and other destroying influences led to its speedy decay and subsequent demolition.' However, it is elsewhere reported that this fancy construction of glass globes became the focus of the well-known rake John Wilmot, 2nd Earl of Rochester, and his companions as they returned from some drunken gathering. Stung by the impudence of the multiphallic construction ('What? Dost thou stand here to f*ck time?'), they laid about it with their sticks and smashed it to smithereens. The king was not amused.

Dietl's crisis

A painful renal condition where the ('floating') kidney shifts and kinks the ureter to obstruction; the one contribution to medicine of the Polish physician Josef Dietl (1804–78), who maintained that doctors could describe and diagnose diseases, but not cure them.

Disorder, bipolar

Current name for the erstwhile manic depression.

Divine Offices

0300 Nocturns; 0600 Matins; 0645 Prime: 0900 Terce; Noon Sext; 1330 None; 1615 Vespers; 1815 Compline; and so to bed.

Doc(tor) Martens

See Fashion.

Dordogneshire

Area of the Dordogne favoured by the British.

Domesday

(or doomsday = a day of reckoning); hence the Domesday (or Doomsday) Book, a record of a survey of English lands made by order of William I in the year 1086, so that he could assess the extent of his possessions and the value for taxation purposes of those of his tenants in chief. Royal commissioners collected details of each manor, shire by shire, giving an almost complete (and historically invaluable) picture of the England of the time.

Doublethink

Acceptance or promotion of conflicting ideas. Words take on the opposite meaning so that the Ministry of Peace wages war. Invented by George Orwell (1903–50) in his novel *Nineteen Eighty-Four* (1949).

Dragonfruit

See Edible fruits.

Drawing lots

See Fortune telling.

Dreams

See Fortune telling.

Dreamtime

Native Australian term for the forgotten days of their ancestors. A golden age recorded in the legends of certain Australian Aboriginal peoples as the time when their first ancestors were created (alcheringa); now used colloquially to denote something remote, or out of touch with the present.

Drumstick fruit

See Vegetables.

Dudi gourd

See Vegetables.

Duku

See Edible fruits.

DUKW

(pron Duck) An amphibious WWII US Army vehicle, happily named from its factory code letters D = boat, U = lorry, KW = lorry chassis.

Dungarees

See Fashion.

Dunmow Flitch

The expression 'eating Dunmow bacon' was formerly used of happily married couples, especially those who had lived long together and never quarrelled. The allusion is to a custom said to have been instituted by Lady Juga Baynard in 1104 and restored by Robert Fitzwalter in 1244. It was that any person going to Dunmow, in Essex, and humbly kneeling on two sharp stones at the church door, might claim a flitch (side) of bacon if he could swear that for 12 months and a day he had never had a household brawl or wished himself unmarried. Allusions to the tradition are frequent in literature from C17 and the custom was revived in the second half of C19. Today the Flitch Trials are held at Little Dunmow (Essex) in mid-June every Leap Year.

Durex
1 in Australia, Sellotape™.
2 in Britain, a make of contraceptive.

Durian
See Edible fruits.

-easte
Suffix denoting an enthusiast for something, as in 'cineaste'

Easy-peel
Greengrocers' descriptive name for a small citrus fruit such as a tangerine or satsuma.

Eclipse
By a dispensation of providence, the Sun and the Moon appear from the Earth to be very similar in diameter. If the Moon, therefore, is interposed between the Earth and the Sun, the latter is eclipsed, partially or totally. On the other hand, if the Earth is interposed between the Sun and the Moon, it's more than big enough for an eclipse of up to 104 minutes totality. Eclipses of the Sun and Moon are measured by their duration (how long the eclipse lasts) and their extent (what proportion is eclipsed). The duration of a partial eclipse may be no more than a few seconds; a total eclipse may last for more than 28 minutes from start to finish, with totality for a maximum of 7 minutes 31 seconds. The extent of occultation of a partial eclipse is measured in 'digits'; a digit is half the apparent diameter of the Sun or Moon.

Eddoe
See Vegetables.

Egalitarianism
See Political -isms.

Eggplant
See Vegetables.

Ego(t)ism
See Political -isms.

Elderberry
See Edible fruits.

Elitism
See Political -isms.

Elychnious
Like a lamp-wick.

Emmets
1   Archaic or dialect word for ants.
2   Cornish term for tourists; *cf* Grockles.

Emoticon
Texting symbol made from standard characters, such as :-) [smiley] ;-) [winking] :-o [surprised] :-([sad] >:-([angry] 8-) [someone who wears glasses] o-> [a flower] @-> [a rose] < :o) [clown] :-p [cheeky; protuding tongue] q:-) [wearing a baseball cap].

Emulsifier
An additive added to foods to bind together the water and fat which would normally separate. Emulsifiers keep bread soft and prevent fat from separating from processed meats. There is a natural emulsifier – lecithin – in egg yolk, and there are also chemical emulsifiers.

Empire Day
Instituted after the South African War, to focus schoolchildren on their duties and responsibilities (would that it were now so), particularly their role as citizens of the British Empire. 24 May was chosen to remember the birthday of Queen Victoria who had died the year before.

Empty nester
One of a couple whose children have (at last) left home.

En-dash
Longer than a hyphen (-); shorter than an em-dash (—); used as a parenthetic dash – instead of parentheses – or for connecting two items of equal importance (French–German border); the growing trend for using an en-dash where a hyphen is correct is abominable.

End grain
The grain in a piece of wood that shows at the end of a cut-off length. Fixing to end grain can cause problems because the fibres of the wood lie parallel with the nail or screw and therefore the friction relied on to keep them in place is much reduced.

Endive
See Vegetables.

Entre-Deux-Guerres
The period between the two World Wars; *cf* Entre-Deux-Mers.

Entre-Deux-Mers
Any wine produced in the Gironde area between the rivers Dordogne and Garonne in the south of France.

Entryism
See Political -isms.

Erlang

Or Traffic Unit; in telephony, a unit of traffic density $e = CT$, where C is the number of calls per hour and is the average time of each call. The unit was adopted in 1946, named after the Danish mathematician A K Erlang (1879–1924).

Eureka

Greek = 'I have found it', supposedly exclaimed by the mathematician/scientist Archimedes (287–212 BCE) in his bath when he suddenly realised that the volume of an irregularly-shaped solid object could be measured by the water it displaces.

Eutrapely

The Aristotelian virtue of being easy in conversation.

Exonym

What a place abroad is called in English; hence Lodz (rather than Wutsh), Paris (to rhyme with Harris), Tiflis rather than Tiblisi, and so on.

Expert

Some suggest a derivation from x = the unknown quantity and spurt = a little drip. There do seem to be far too many 'experts' issuing 'good advice' these days, for example: 'don't dip your hands into boiling water'; it's a consequence of the compensation culture.

Eyes

Holes in Swiss cheese.

Face

See Fortune telling.

Factotum

Latin = do everthing; someone employed to do just that.

Fairs

At one time, there were great periodical markets upon which people would converge from miles around; the annual Bartholomew Fair (*qv*), or the horse fairs and goose fairs still remembered in certain parts of the country. The word now usually conjures up a travelling amusement fair, or perhaps a trade fair (which is really an exhibition directed at encouraging orders associated with a particular trade).

Fall

A descriptive English term for the time of year when leaves fall from the trees, now supplemented on the east side of the Atlantic Ocean by the word Autumn, but retained on the west side.

False beard

A feature of Egyptian Fashion; see Fashion.

Film speed

The H&D system was proposed in 1891 by F Hurter (1844–98) and VC Driffield (1848–1915) who established a graph of density against the relative logarithm of the exposure time; the central part of the curve is linear, wherefrom the H&D speed is found.

The Weston number, the ASA system, and the BSI speed number use the same principle as the H&D system.

The ASA (American Standards Association) speed is defined as 0.8/E, where E is the exposure of a point 0.1 density units greater than the fog level on the characteristic curve of the emulsion. It has superseded the BSI (British Standards Institution) system.

The DIN (Deutsche Institut für Normung) system gives an indication of speed in degrees based on the minimum exposure needed to form a detectable image on the emulsion.

The Scheiner scale was devised by J Scheiner (1858–1913) in 1898, and taken up by the Secco Film Company of Boston MA the following year. There are two versions, the European and the American.

Comparative film speeds

ASA	B-W	DIN	ES	GE	H&D	I	USS	W
2.5		5	16	3	75		11	2
auto3		6	17	4	100	A	12	2.5
4	1/3	7	18	4.5	125		13	3
5		8	19	6	160		14	4
6		9	20	8	200	B	15	5
8	1/6	10	21	10	250		16	6
10		11	22	12	320		17	8
12		12	23	16	400	C	18	10
16	1/12	13	24	20	500		19	13
20		14	25	24	640		20	16
25		15	26	32	800	D	21	20
32	1/24	16	27	40	1000		22	24
40		17	28	50	1300		23	32
50		18	29	64	1600	E	24	40
64	1/48	19	30	80	2000		25	50
80		20	31	100	2500		26	64
100		21	32	125	3200	F	27	80
125	1/96	22	33	160	4000		28	100
160		23	34	200	5000		29	125
200		24	35	250	6400	G	30	160
250		25	36	320	8000		31	200
320		26	37	400	10000		32	250

400	27	38	500	H	33	320
500	28		640			400
640	29		800			500
800	30		1000	I		640
1000	31		1250			800
1280	32		1600			1000
1600	33		2000	J		1250

ASA = American Standards' Association
B–W = B-Weston
DIN = Deutsche Institut für Normung
ES = European Scheiner
GE = General Electric
H&D = Hurter and Driffield
I = Ilford
USS = US Scheiner
W = Weston

False roselle
See Vegetables.

Fascism
See Political -isms.

Fastest bird
A peregrine falcon in a dive was measured at 225mph / 363kph.

Fastest land animal
Cheetah at 60mph / 96.56kph, though it can maintain this speed only for short distances.

Fastest sea creature
Sailfish at 68mph / 109kph.

Fava bean
See Vegetables.

Fedora hat
See Fashion.

Feijoa
See Edible fruits.

Felt
A non-woven fabric produced simply by matting fibres of woollen yarn together under compression and heat, to cause the fibres to lock together.

Fennel; Fenugreek; Fiddleheads; Field bean; Field mushroom
See Vegetables.

Fig
See Edible fruits.

Filigree
A method of applying a design to gold and silverware surfaces by attaching thin wires that form the pattern.

Fimbulwinter
Norse = winter of winters; followed by Ragnarok = end of the world.

Fire
See Fortune telling.

FIRKO
Fat-specific Insulin Receptor Knock-Out.

First foot
The first visitor at a house, after midnight has ushered in New Year's Day, especially in Scotland; it is considered lucky if the first footer is carrying symbols of warmth, wealth and food (a handsel), usually a piece of coal, some salt (once more valuable than today) and cake; he or she is rewarded with refreshment such as the Het Pint (a mixture of beer, whisky, eggs and sugar). There are local names for first footing, such as the Yorkshire Lucky Bird, and the Manx Quaaltagh.

First World War
Between 28 June 1914, when Archduke Ferdinand was assassinated at Sarajevo, and 11 November 1918. Britain entered the conflict on 4 August 1914. It took the lives of nearly 10 million people, and more than twice as many were wounded.

Fitweed
See Vegetables.

Five Ks
Central to Sikhism: *kangha* (comb), *kacch* (shorts), *kirpan* (sword), *kara* (steel bracelet), and *kes* (uncut hair and beard).

Flash memory
An electronic non-volatile memory device that retains data without a power supply or back-up battery.

Flax fibres
See Fashion.

FLED
Facility Licence Eligibility Date, when a prisoner has served 3/8 of his sentence.

Fluffer
A tunnel cleaner on the London Underground.

Fly Floor or Tower

The space above a stage from which (usually) scenery may be lowered to the view of the audience, and raised again ('flown').

Foaf

Friend of a friend; the subject of countless urban legends, a term introduced by your compiler in *The Tumour in the Whale* (1978) the world's first published collection of urban legends (then such a new concept that I called them 'whale-tumour stories').

Foreigner, Doing a

Also, a Home Office job; working on a personal project in the firm's time.

Forging

A process of heating and then hammering hot metal into different shapes. The process also helps refine the grain flow, thus strengthening the molecular structure of the metal. The heat source is a forge, traditionally fuelled by coke blown by bellows; more commonly nowadays by gas. Working takes place on an anvil, on which the metal is beaten and shaped. The shape of the anvil has been developed so that every part has a use – the top flat surface is the working face, this has a radiused edge for bending the metal over. There is also a soft cutting face on which metal can be cut, and a beak, or bick, for forming curves. On a larger scale, the work may be forged by a steam hammer, with shaped surfaces to form the desired shape.

French revolutionary calendar

Adopted by the French National Convention on 5 October 1793, retrospectively as from 22 September 1792, and in force in France till 1 January 1806. It consisted of 12 months each of three 10-day weeks, with 5 intercalary days between years (6 after a leap year), initially called Sans-Culottides (after the extreme republicans) in Years I and II, but Les Jours Complémentaires from Year III onwards. The calendar came to an end at midnight on 10 Nivôse XIV, or 31 December 1805, by the decree of the self-crowned Emperor Napoléon Bonaparte. It must have taken a dogged revolutionary spirit to put up with 10-day weeks, and their absence of an obvious day of worship did not appeal to the Church. It was partly to appease the Catholics that Bonaparte reverted to the conventional calendar, no doubt with enormous sighs of relief all round. Notwithstanding that, the FRC was briefly resurrected during the Paris Commune of 1871, but most people carried on as if nothing had happened.

Friday the 13th

A particularly unlucky Friday. In fact, any month beginning on a Sunday must contain a Friday 13th and, as you would expect, there are as many Friday 13ths (48) in the 28-year cycle as any other specified day. There are various theories as to why the day has been thought to be unlucky, but different cultures have different opinions on such superstitions. Perhaps the best that can be said about it is that when the papers have column inches to fill, there's always someone who stays in bed on Friday 13th to keep out of harm's way, only to suffer a collapse of the ceiling, or a runaway lorry ploughing through the wall.

Fringes

A feature of Ancient Assyrian Fashion; see **Fashion**.

Front of House

(FoH) The part of the theatre for greeting and seating the audience; the audience is also known as 'the house', and is lit by the house lights.

Fundi

1 Slang for Fundamentalist.
2 A skilled mechanic (from Swahili); hence someone skilled in any art.
See **Adept**.

Fur

See **Fashion**.

Furry Dance

Part of the spring festival held at Helston, Cornwall, on 8 May. The name has been incorrectly rendered as the 'floral dance', and thus perpetuated by the popular song with the curious drone.

Fuse

A short length of thin wire used for safety in electrical circuits. If the current in the circuit exceeds a certain value, the wire melts and breaks the circuit (the fuse has 'blown'). Cartridge style fuses are used in plugs, and must be replaced when 'blown'. Fuses come in several different ratings, depending on the current to be drawn. It is important to make sure that a fuse is of the correct 'rating' for its purpose.

Futharc (futhark, futhork)

The Runic alphabet, so called from its first six characters (f, u, th, a, r, k) – compare our 'alphabet', so called from its first two characters.

Fynbos

See **Thars**.

Galo

See **Edible fruits**.

Galton's quincunx

Dots in a quincunx are arranged so that there are four, one at each corner of a square, and a fifth in the centre of the square. In one embodiment of Galton's quincunx, an array of horizontal pegs in that pattern between two face-plates is set up, and balls dropped in at the top. A given ball will, if the apparatus is accurately constructed, have to make a left-or-right? decision every time it falls on a peg. Emerging at the bottom of the array, the balls collect in vertical channels, where, because of their passage, their pattern (heights of the columns) exhibits the bell-shaped Gaussian probability curve.

Gamp

British slang for an umbrella, particularly a less-than-pristine one, after Sarah Gamp, the nurse in Charles Dickens's *Martin Chuzzlewit* (1844) who had such an umbrella; see also bumbershoot.

Garbanzos

See Vegetables.

Garbo; garbologist

Municipal garbage collector (AS).

Garlic

See Vegetables.

Gateway drug

An illicit substance that moves the user on to something worse.

Gematria

A technique whereby the (Hebrew) letters of a word are replaced by corresponding numbers, which are then 'interpreted' to reveal 'hidden messages' and the like, or to show that one word or phrase is 'numerically equivalent' to another.

Genip

See Edible fruits.

Getter

A substance (such as titanium) evaporated in a vacuum tube during the final stages of pumping down, in order to absorb any remaining gas – hence the silvery coating inside such tubes.

Ghan, The

North–South Australian railway, 1,851 miles.

Girole

See Vegetables.

Generation

The people in a family or group that were born, raised and educated at roughly the same time. But since people are not born in clumps, there is a gradation of generations in the general population, and generations are best thought of within families, though even then they may become disjointed when siblings' birth dates become widely spaced. Generations generally advance at between three and four per century.

The population of England has grown roughly as follows:

1600	4.8m
1700	6.0m
1800	8.9m
1900	32.5m
2000	49.9m

At any given time, the foundations for the future population are being laid down. So consider a child born in the year 2000, who will have, at four generations per century:

1900	16	great-great-grandparents
1800	256	6 x greats grandparents
1700	4,096	10 x greats grandparents
1600	65,536	14 x greats grandparents

If we treat everyone as coming from a unique line, today's population of 49.9m would imply a 1600 population of 49.9 x 65,536 = 3,270,196.5m. This is clearly an absurd calculation, and the apparent discrepancy is explained by couples having more than child, cousins marrying, and so on.

We can get some idea of the rate of procreation over the years by assuming (somewhat breathtakingly) that the total population at any given time is half male and half female, and that each couple bears children, all of whom go on to have children of their own. This yields the (simplistic) information that the progress of average number of children per family was as follows:

C17	2.12 children
C18	2.22
C19	2.78
C20	2.24.

Glacial rebound
When the glacier melts and flows away, and the ground recovers from the compression of its mass.

Glasnost
Russian = 'speaking aloud'; the name given to the domestic political reforms instituted by Soviet president Mikhail Gorbachev (1931–) from the mid-1980s, allowing freedom of expression in politics, literature and the arts.

Glass blowing
A 'gather', or gob, of molten glass is taken from the furnace on the end of a hollow metal tube, and is then be transferred to a clay mould, and blown so as to fill the shape of the mould. The glass worker keeps the glass turning all the time so that the shape is not distorted. The product is allowed to cool slowly in an annealing furnace or 'lehr'. To be correct, distinguish between glass 'blowing' and glass 'working'.

Glass ceiling
The invisible upper limit on women's salaries in professedly equal opportunity organisations. In the Church, it has been described as the 'stained-glass ceiling'.

Globe artichoke
See Vegetables.

Gobo
A thin metal plate with a design cut in it placed in a lantern so that the shape is projected on to scenery *eg* a moon or stars.

Godot, Waiting for
The name of Samuel Beckett's character is said to have come from Roger Godeau, a French demi-fond (cyclist paced by motorcycle) specialist of the 40s and 50s.

Go-faster Dust
Royal Marines' slang for curry powder, carried as an extra to standard rations.

Going a-corning
See Mumping.

Golden afternoon
4 July 1862 when Revd Robin Duckworth (then a fellow of Trinity College, Oxford) and Revd Charles Lutwidge Dodgson (1832–98; *alias* Lewis Carroll), the Oxford mathematician, rowed a boat in company with the ten-year-old Alice Pleasance Liddell and her sisters Lorina Charlotte (13) and Edith (8) up the River Thames from Folly Bridge

(near Oxford) to the village of Godstow, upon which trip the foundations for the classic that emerged as *Alice's Adventures in Wonderland* (1865) were laid.

Golden gram
See Vegetables.

Golden mean or Golden section
A line AB divided by a point P so that the ratio of the smaller length to the larger is the same as that of the larger to the whole: AB:AP::AP:AB. A rectangle whose sides are in that ratio thought to be the most aesthetically pleasing, and much effort has been expended measuring Classical buildings and Renaissance paintings to demonstrate the wide use of the Golden Section by their architects and artists. The ratio, τ, is $(\sqrt{5} + 1)/2$, which = 0.618034, and you will notice the relationship of its convergent fractions: 1/1, 2/1, 3/2, 5/3, 8/5, 13/8 ... to the Fibonacci series, whose numbers are supposed to relate particularly to the geometry of plants; the fractions of a turn on the stem between leaves. τ-related measurements will be found in 5-related figures and solids; the pentagon, decagon, dodecahedron and icosahedron. For example, the ratios of elements of a pentagram, where the sides of a regular pentagon are produced until they meet at five points, are in the golden ratio.

Good Parliament
That assembled in the last year of his reign by Edward III (1376), which pursued the unpopular Lancastrians, who nevertheless made it to the throne in 1399; for other Parliaments, see Parliament.

Goog
An egg (AS).

Googlebombing
Persuading the search-engine Google to promote your website.

Googlewhack
A Google search producing a single result.

Googol
10^{100}, so named by Milton Sirotta, 9, nephew of the mathematician Edward Kasner.

Gooseberry
See Edible fruits.

Gossima

The original name for table tennis bestowed on it by its inventor (c1889) James Gibb, and so manufactured by Jaques & Son and marketed by Hamley Bros in 1898. It was slow to catch on until its name was changed to the onomatopoeic *Ping Pong* in 1901, when it became the first Edwardian craze.

Goths

See Fashion.

Granny-farmer

One who cultivates the widow of an antique collector in order to relieve her of valuable items at knock-down prices; even more despicable than a knocker (*qv*).

Grape

See Edible fruits.

Grapefruit

See Edible fruits.

Grass skirt

See Fashion.

Grattan's Parliament

The free Irish Parliament (1782–1800) wherein Henry Grattan's machinations led to the Act of Union between Great Britain and Ireland (1800), an arrangement that lasted until 1922, and whose repercussions show no signs of abating; for other Parliaments, see Parliament.

Great Dying, The

When the land-masses of the earth were united as Pangea, in the End-Permian Period 250 million years ago, the 'Great Dying' took place; 90 per cent of marine life and 80 per cent of terrestrial life was wiped out as a result, it is thought, of a meteoric impact in the area now found off the north-west coast of Australia.

Grecian bend

A peculiarly serpentine posture, supposed in its time to be the height of fashion, as depicted on Grecian urns and the like.

Green gram

See Vegetables.

Greengage

See Edible fruits.

Greenwich Mean Time

(Also Universal Time since 1928); a mean time based on noon determined as the mean sun passing over the 0° meridian through Greenwich. It is the standard time adopted by astronomers and was used throughout the British Isles until 18 February 1968, when clocks were advanced one hour and Summer Time became 'permanent'. The new system was designated British Summer Time (as from 27 October 1968), but the arguments against it duly prevailed and the country reverted to Greenwich Mean Time on 31 October 1971. BST, British Summer Time, one hour in advance of Greenwich Mean Time, is kept between 0200hrs on the day following the third Saturday in March and 0200hrs on the day following the fourth Saturday in October. Other countries adjust their clocks in this way; the shift is called Summer Time (*qv*), or Daylight Saving Time. The idea is to make the times by which we live from day to day more in keeping with changing daylight hours.

Greenhouse effect

Greenhouse glass has the effect of trapping warm air inside the greenhouse, since ultraviolet radiation will pass through glass, but infrared won't. Similarly, heat is trapped near the earth as benzine, carbon dioxide, chlorofluorocarbons (CFCs), methane, nitrous oxide, and other pollutant gases build up in the atmosphere since, like glass, they are more transparent to incoming solar radiation than they are to outgoing infrared radiation. In other words, they allow the heat of the sun through to the earth, but trap it there, a major contribution to global warming.

Gregorian chant or plainsong

A style of unaccompanied male vocal music used in the medieval Christian church.

Grey pound

That which marketing people seek to separate from those with grey hair.

Grey Surfer

A mature explorer of the web.

Gripper Axminster

A type of patterned carpet where the yarns of various colours that make up those needed for a given row of the pattern are presented by carriers controlled by a Jacquard mechanism that raises and lowers each carrier to the appropriate height for presenting the desired colour. The ends are then gripped by elements resembling birds' beaks, pulled from the carriers, cut, and woven into the carpet. See also **Spool Axminster**.

Gripping

A National Service practice of comparing release groups; one whose release group is earlier than another's can 'grip' the other.

Grockles

Devonshire term for tourists; *cf* Emmets.

Guy Fawkes' Day/Night

Commemorates 5 November 1605 when it appeared that Catholic conspirators planned to blow up James I and the Houses of Parliament in London. The plot was discovered, the men apprehended and tried for treason, and executed. 5 November was set aside as 'a day of thanksgiving to be celebrated with bonfires and fireworks', possibly taking over the pre-Christian fires once lit at Hallowe'en. This would have extra meaning if, as now seems likely, the 'plot' was an elaborate charade designed to discredit Rome. The leader was Robert Catesby (1573–1605), but the name of one of the others – Guy Fawkes (1570–1606) – seems to have caught the public fancy: 'Remember, remember, the fifth of November, | Gunpowder, treason and plot. | There seems no reason why gunpowder treason | Should ever be forgot.' Until recently, children made Guy Fawkes' Day an excuse for trundling round stuffed effigies (Guys) on broken-down prams demanding 'a penny for the Guy', but this custom seems to have died out since universal paedophilia and H&S paranoia took over, not to mention the urban legend concerning the butcher who was so beset by continual demands for Guy money that he rushed out and stabbed the Guy, which turned out to be a real child dressed in rags. However, the bonfires and fireworks continue to take place, often on a convenient Saturday before or after 5 November, preceded by a parade of Guys, but with the display conducted behind barriers by trained pyrotechnicists, clad in protective clothing, provided that they can find a company to insure the event. Notwithstanding this, the sale of fireworks is not yet properly controlled, and many random explosions take place at around this time (and beyond); presumably the increasing threat of terrorist attack will eventually make all such activity illegal.

Groundhog Day

Candlemas, 2 February, the earliest designation of which appears in 1841 when James Morris recorded in his diary that, according to German immigrants, 'the Groundhog peeps out of his winter quarters and if he sees his shadow he pops back for another six weeks' nap, but if the day be cloudy he remains out, as the weather is to be moderate'. Thus was the imported tradition of Candlemas (from the earlier pagan feast of Imbolc) transferred from the European badger to the American groundhog, aka woodchuck (*Marmota monax*). 'If the sun shines on Groundhog Day; | Half the fuel and half the hay.' I have yet to discover why, in the film *Groundhog Day* (1993), the TV weatherman played by Bill Murray kept waking up to Groundhog Day anew. It was, however, an effective means of popularising the annual re-enactment of Groundhog Day for the commercial benefit of its participants.

G-string

See Fashion.

Guarana

See Edible fruits.

Guava

See Edible fruits.

H&M

Hennes & Mauritz, a Swedish fashion chain.

Habanero pepper

See Vegetables.

Haggai

See Books of the Holy Bible.

Halcyon days

Days of great calm, happiness and prosperity, generally taken to be the seven days on each side of the winter solstice: 14–28 December when, according to an old Sicilian idea, the halcyon bird, or kingfisher, lays its eggs in a nest on the surface of the sea which must, perforce, be calm. The bird family *Alcedinidae* comprises 85 species in two sub-families: the *Alcedininae* (narrow-billed, living near water and feeding on fish) and the *Dacetoninae* (broad-billed and insectivorous). The 'well-known' kingfisher is *Alcedo atthis* – from which 'halcyon'.

Half, The

In the theatre, half an hour before the first actors are due on stage (*ie* 35 minutes before the show begins). All actors must be in by the Half; traditionally, the audience is allowed into the auditorium at the Half; traditionally at the Half the House Manager blows a whistle in the auditorium.

Hand dipping

The traditional technique for producing candles was usually undertaken by the ladies of the household. The wicks are hung from a wire frame, and then dipped into a cauldron of hot wax. By repeatedly dipping, and allowing the growing candles to cool in between, the layers of wax build up, and assume a tapered look. On average, it takes about 40 dips to produce a candle base as thick as a man's thumb. Perfumes and colours are often added to the wax, and elaborate decorative candles are sometimes moulded or carved.

Harem pants

See Fashion.

Harlequin set

In the antiques trade, a tea set whose pieces don't match, but sit more or less easily together.

Haute couture

See Fashion.

Haw, from hawthorn

See Edible fruits.

Heater and cooler

Chasing neat spirits with a draught of beer.

Heath Robinson, W(illiam)

(1872–1944), English illustrator and artist chiefly remembered for his absurd designs for machines – usually strong on knotted string – often for performing everyday tasks. His name has passed into the language to describe any odd-looking 'contraption'.

Heddle

(Heald); carried on a frame or harness, the element of a loom through which a warp thread passes, enabling the position of that thread at the point of weaving (the shed) to be controlled.

Hegira

(Arabic *hejira* = the departure), 16 July 622CE on which day the Prophet Muhammad took flight from Mecca to Medina, and which became the first day of the Muslim calendar – 1 Muharram AH (Anno Hegirae).

Hello work

Japanese for a Job Centre.

Hertz

The SI unit of frequency equal to one cycle per second. Named after Heinrich Rudolf Hertz (1857–94), the German physicist who transformed Maxwell's predictions into the reality of Hertzian – or, as we now call them electromagnetic, or radio – waves.

Hide

In feudal England the amount of land sufficient to support a family, usually varying between 60 and 120 acres (24-49ha) according to the locality and quality of the land. A hide of good land was smaller than one of the poorer quality. It was long used as the basis for assessing taxes.

Highland bagpipe

Bagpipes were played in ancient times throughout the Mediterranean world – the first document linking bagpipes to Scotland dates from C12, and this version of the pipes was simply a pig's bladder inflated by a mouth pipe, with another attached for playing the melody – the chanter. The Great Highland bagpipe as we know it today dates from C18 and was developed by Highland pipers. It has a hide bag, a chanter, and one bass and two tenor drones – long pipes containing vibrating reeds that provide the continuous harmony. The piper first inflates the bag by blowing into it via a non-return valve, and then brings the instrument to life by exerting pressure on the bag with his elbow to make the drones speak and allow him to play the melody on the chanter. The pressure to the instrument is supplied by the elbow, and the mouth replenishes the air in the bag. See also Northumbrian Pipes.

Hipsters

See Fashion.

Hiring fair

A statute fair, once held annually on Martinmas Day (11 November) in most market towns of England and Wales, when labourers and servants were available to new masters and mistresses.

Hognel Time

A widespread English custom, the detail of which is unknown; what is known is that collecting money to celebrate it is recorded in many parish accounts from C14 onwards. At Bolney in Sussex hognel time lasted until 2 February.

Holmes, Mycroft

The brother of Sherlock, who acted as a 'central clearing house' for all police information; with the advent of the computer, it is possible that the police are about to emulate his contribution to solving crime.

Holy dooley!

Australian expression of surprise.

Home Counties banter

A style of conversation sometimes described as a 'Rotarian patois' in which Sunday is 'the Sabbath', drinks are 'tinctures', a wife is 'your good lady' and so on.

Home Office

See Foreigner.

Honeydew

See Edible fruits.

Horn of plenty; Horse bean; Horse mushroom

See Vegetables.

Hot pants

See Fashion.

House, The

Christ Church College, Oxford.

HOV

High-Occupancy Vehicle, for which a lane on a Motorway might be reserved.

Huckleberry

See Edible fruits.

Humanism

See Political -isms.

Hundred Years War

A series of wars fought between England and France between 1337 and 1453, as a result of England's claim to the crown of France; England lost all its French possessions except Calais, and that went in 1558.

Hungry Forties

The 1840s in Great Britain, characterised by poor harvests (and hence expensive bread) and unemployment. With hindsight, we see that the 1820s may have been even worse, the saving grace in the 40s being the development of the railways (providing work), and the repeal of the Corn Laws that had kept prices artificially high.

Ice ages

Term usually applied to the earlier part of the present geological period, when the climate was colder, and the polar ice caps more extensive, than today. It is when the Ice Ages seem to have stopped that the modern geological time – the Holocene epoch – is said to have begun. During each Ice Age much of the sea froze, exposing considerable areas that had previously been seabed. Thus it was that many of the animals of previous millennia managed to become so widespread, crossing land bridges that do not exist today.

I-ching
See Fortune telling.

Icy pole, ice block
Ice lolly, popsicle (AS).

Ides
A day in the calendar of ancient Rome that was about half-way through the month, which it thus divided in two. It was normally on the 13th, but in March, May, July and October was on the 15th.

Immoralism
See Political -isms.

Imperialism
See Political -isms.

Indian jujube
See Edible fruits.

IBM Typewriter

International Business Machines took over a company called Electromatic Typewriters in 1933, and spent a great deal of money in developing a reliable machine which was introduced in 1935. IBM achieved a reliable single-spacing carriage in 1941, and this enabled the production of a 'proportional spacing' machine, so that, for example, narrow letters such as f, i and j occupied two spaces, and wide letters such as M and W occupied five spaces. Other characters were variously three and four spaces wide. This machine, marketed as the IBM Executive, began to dominate office printing after WW2 and, used in conjunction with a small offset litho (qv) machine produced some of the earliest attempts at self-publication. The machine had a two-unit and a three-unit space bar, and it was possible with care to produce 'justified' copy: with all the lines the same length, to heighten the illusion of letterpress printing. The next development was the IBM Scalectric typewriter, whose two main characteristics were the interchangeable near-spherical typeheads, and the absence of a moving carriage – a machine universally referred to as the IBM Golfball. This was followed by the IBM 72 Composer which, hand in hand with associated improvements in printing, sounded the death-knell for letterpress printing (qv).

Incubation period

1 The time that elapses between an organism laying an egg and its hatching. It varies from a few days for a small bird to several weeks for a large tortoise.

2 In medicine, the time that elapses between infection by a bacterium or virus and the onset of the disease (when the first symptoms show). The incubation periods of some common diseases are:

chicken pox	2–3 weeks
common cold	2–72 hours
diphtheria	2–5 days
gonorrhoea	3–9 days
influenza	1–3 days
malaria	2 weeks
measles	8–13 days
mumps	12–26 days
paratyphoid	1–10 days
poliomyelitis	3–21 days
rabies	2–6 weeks
rubella	14–21 days
scarlet fever	1–3 days
syphilis	2–70 days
tetanus	4–21 days
typhoid	1–3 weeks
typhus	7–14 days
whooping cough	7 days

Indian rope trick

An Indian fakir throws a rope into the air; it remains vertical; a boy climbs up the rope and disappears. John Wilkie, a journalist, first described this in 1890 in the *Chicago Tribune* (during its circulation war with the *Herald*) as something witnessed by a Yale man – Fred S Ellmore – (sellmore – geddit?) It's entirely fictitious, though people will still swear that they (or at least a foaf) have seen it.

Individualism

See Political -isms.

Industrial revolution

A term referring to the time of technological and economic changes that transformed Great Britain (and later other countries) from a rural agrarian to an urban industrialised state. It is difficult to pinpoint its start, as it was one of those occasions when there seems to be a sudden and widespread upsurge of something new (*cf* the emergence of Jazz in America at the beginning of C20), and see Age of Enlightenment. The beginnings must have lain in the work of Thomas Savery (end C17) and then Thomas Newcomen, who developed crude but workable steam engines for pumping water from the mines of Cornwall, then from mines further afield to extend their workings, followed by the expansion of the canal system, improved techniques of smelting, the rise of manufacturing, each development pushing the others forward, with the result that people began to move toward conurbations, away from agriculture and into manufacture.

Intaglio printing
A process where a surface is engraved (by hand or photographically – 'photogravure'); ink is then rubbed into the removed areas and squashed out on to the surface of a sheet of paper.

International Date Line
The imaginary great semicircle running from the North Pole to the South Pole that represents the end of one day and the beginning of another. The line of longitude defined as the Greenwich meridian is the line of 0°; the date line is for the most part accordingly the line of 180° Thus, 12 noon on Sunday at Greenwich corresponds just to the west of the date line to the time of 12 midnight at the end of Sunday, almost the first thing Monday morning; and just to the east of the date line to the time of 12 midnight at the end of Saturday, almost the first thing Sunday morning.

Internationalism
See Political -isms.

Invar
An alloy of 63.8% iron, 36% nickel and 0.2% carbon devised by M Guillaume in 1896; because of its low co-efficient of thermal expansion, it is used in accurate measuring and timekeeping devices.

Irish fact
An anecdote so good that it deserves to be true.

Iron and plonker
Used by tailor to shape and finally press a suit. The iron is heavy, and each stroke of the iron is followed by a dab with the 'plonker' – a wooden block – this sharpens the creases and helps to prevent stretching after pressing.

Ja(c)kfruit
See Edible fruits; Vegetables.

Jack plane
A tool used in woodwork and carpentry – a sharp blade a few inches wide mounted in a stock up to 18 inches long to make it easier to plane wood flat and to size.

Jacquard
A device attached to a weaving loom such that each of the warp threads can be controlled individually, An early example of programming using punched cards. See **Dobby**.

Japanese medlar
See **Edible fruits**.

Jazzbo
A low-comedy Vaudeville act

Jeans
See **Fashion**.

Jerusalem artichoke
See **Vegetables**.

Jicama
See **Vegetables**.

Joe Blake
Australian snake (RS).

Jujube
See **Edible fruits**.

Jumbuck
Sheep (AS).

Juneberry
See **Edible fruits**.

Jungle surfing
Activity holiday where participants move along wires connecting platforms suspended high in the trees.

Just now
Phrase which in some communities signifies time past (I did that just now = I've recently done it); in others time present (I'll do that just now = immediately); and in yet others time future (I'll do that just now = very shortly).

Kabbalah
(Hebrew = that which is received); loose name for ancient Jewish wisdom, or by extension any recondite mysticism; more specifically, the neglected books of the *Zohar* (1290), The Greater Holy Assembly,

The Lesser Holy Assembly, The Book of the Mystery and The Assembly of the Tabernacle.

Kangaroos loose in the top paddock
Not bright (AS).

Kanji
A Japanese syllabary based on Chinese characters.

Karel(l)a
See Vegetables.

Katuk
See Vegetables.

Keks
Trousers (AS); see also Daks.

Kembang turi
See Vegetables.

Kerchief
See Fashion.

KGOY
Marketspeak: Kids Growing Older Younger.

Khakis
See Fashion.

Kibla(h)
(Qibla) the direction of Mecca, to which Muslims turn in prayer, indicated in the mosque by the mihrab, a niche in the wall. A prayer-mat embodying a compass has been patented.

Kick flare
See Fashion.

KIPPERS
Kids In Parents' Pockets Eroding Retirement Savings.

Kirtle
See Fashion.

Kiwi fruit
See Edible fruits.

Knitting
A method of producing fabric using a continuous yarn. Warp knitting uses a thread for each stitch and is knitted vertically, whereas weft knitting takes place across the fabric width. One drawback of weft knitting is that the finished fabric is susceptible to stretching and

laddering, whereas warp knitting is firm and strong, and does not ladder. The action of circular knitting produces a tube from a single yarn being fed round and round a frame carrying bearded needles.

Knocker
One who relieves vulnerable people of their antiques, gaining their confidence by offering seemingly huge prices for items that are in reality worth even more; see **Granny-farmer**.

Kolo
A Serbian dance.

Kumquat
See **Edible fruits**.

Kurditcha boots
Worn by a native tracker to simulate the spoor of a chosen animal.

Laa'l Breeshey
In C18 Isle of Man, 31 January was so called for Brigit's Festival.

Lady's finger
See **Vegetables**.

Lakh or Lac
An Indian unit of 100,000, especially of rupees. When, at some VIP university gathering, Harold Macmillan was chatting lightly, he was asked for a collective noun for principals (of colleges), he immediately returned: 'How about a *Lakh* of Principals?' He may, of course, have thought of it as a *lack* of principals, but it's nice to think of the double pun.

Lamb's lettuce; tongue
See **Vegetables**.

Langsat
See **Edible fruits**.

Laras
Indonesian tuning systems for the gamelan; *slendro* offers five fixed pitches to the octave, and *pelog* has seven, which enables a number of pentatonic scales to be played according to the *patet*, which might be translated as 'mode'.

Last trump
The last trumpet call which, some believe, shall awaken and raise the dead on the Day of Judgement, when all earthly things shall finally come to an end.

Lay days

Days allowed for loading and unloading a ship under the terms of a charter party (the contract for hiring the whole or part of a ship for the delivery of cargo).

Lazy Susan

A rotating tray for serving condiments etc at table, or a frame onto which skeins of yarn are draped for further winding.

Lazy tongs

A device of levers so arranged that it can be adjusted by manipulation without the operator (at its proximal end) having to move; it is often furnished with some sort of gripping arrangement at its distal end for retrieving out-of-reach objects and like purposes.

Leek

See Vegetables.

Leftism

See Political -isms.

Lemon

See Edible fruits.

Lemongrass

See Vegetables.

Leninism

See Political -isms.

Lentil

See Vegetables.

Lettuce

See Vegetables.

Levy, Henry Q

See Edible fruits.

Lewis(on)

A device for lifting heavy stones; an x-like arrangement, points on one of whose pairs of ends fit into small depressions suitably cut in the stone so that the action of lifting by the other pair tightens the grip on the stone.

Liberalism

See Political -isms.

Libertarianism

See Political -isms.

Letterpress printing

A raised surface formed by pieces of type or printing blocks is inked, and the ink transferred to the surface of a sheet of paper. In simple letterpress printing, type is set by hand, line by line, in a composing stick adjusted to the specified length (measure) of the lines. Blocks of set type are transferred to a tray (galley) from which so-called galley proofs can be taken by inking the surface and transferring the image to long sheets of paper. When the time comes, the type is transferred to the 'stone', a flat surface on which the forme (ready for the printing machine) is to be built up. After the type, a 'chase' is laid in position; it is this that is designed to be locked into the printing machine. The spaces between the type and the surrounding chase are then packed up with lead 'quads' and wooden 'furniture', and the whole locked up with 'quoins' – in earlier times tapered wedges tightened with a mallet, in later times metal devices expanded with a removable key. If all had been prepared cleanly and thoughtfully, it should be possible to lift even the largest forme without it all falling to pieces. After printing, the forme may be unlocked and the type 'dissed' (distributed back into its cases), or it may be left 'standing' in a rack for future use. Large printers would have small fortunes locked up in standing type.

Lighting-up time

Refers to the period between half an hour after sunset and half an hour before sunrise when it is compulsory for road vehicles in use to show white front and rear red lights. In this context, the law shows rare good sense by recognising local times rather than mean times.

Life sentence

A sentence of imprisonment 'for life'; in Britain, life is the mandatory sentence for murder, and the maximum penalty for certain serious offences such as arson, manslaughter, and rape. People awarded life sentences are normally detained for at least 20 years. If and when they are released, they remain on licence for the rest of their lives and 'are subject to recall if their behaviour suggests that they might again be a danger to the public'; unfortunately, their demonstrable danger may be more than a suggestion. Some say 'life' should mean 'life'.

Line of beauty

A serpentine curve so named by the English artist William Hogarth (1697–1764), similar to, if not exactly the same as, the curve registered by Coca-Cola™.

Lingonberry

See Edible fruits.

Liquorice

See Vegetables.

Lithography

(Litho); depends on the mutual repulsion of oil and water; an image on a plane surface is made ink-receptive, and the rest of the surface water-receptive; when a roller offering ink passes across the surface, it inks the image; the rest of the surface is kept ink-free by means of a roller carrying water. In early lithography (= stone writing) the image was drawn 'on the stone' and, after treatment, transferred to a sheet of paper laid on it and peeled off. Some artists still work this way. The development is offset lithography, where the image is formed on a thin plate attached to a roller, inked (and watered), and transferred (offset) to a rubber blanket, whence it is transferred to a sheet of paper. Because of the double transfer, the original image is the 'right way round', and in early small commercial machines it was possible to type matter on to a paper plate using a special ribbon for reproduction on a 'small offset press'; usually a Multilith 1250 (manufactured by Addressograph–Multigraph); sometimes a Gestelith (manufactured by Gestetner) or the popular Rotaprint machine. It was often difficult to achieve a satisfactory result in the office environment, though commercial machines in a works setting came to dominate printing from the 50s.

Little black dress

See Fashion.

Lock and key party

Icebreaker for singles wishing to date, where the women wear a lock on a ribbon round their necks, and the men are given keys. Finding out whether or not a key fits a given lock provides a means of getting into conversation and may lead to further dating. If the wearer wishes, he or she may apply for a different key or lock. The technique has swept the US, and arrived in the UK at the beginning of 2004.

Loganberry; Longan; Longkong

See Edible fruits.

Longneck

750ml bottle of beer (AS).

Long Parliament

1   That of Henry IV sitting from 1 March to 22 December 1406.
2   That summoned by Charles I, that sat from 3 November 1640 to
    16 March 1660 (the king was beheaded on 30 January 1649).
3   That which sat from 1661 to 1679 in the reign of Charles II; for
    other Parliaments, see **Parliament**.

Loofah gourd

See **Vegetables**.

Looms; Loons

See **Fashion**.

Loquat

See **Edible fruits**.

Loud-hailer

Self-contained battery-operated public address horn introduced by
Pye of Cambridge, memorably used on a beach by Lord Hailsham in
the 60s, and even more memorably described by the *Daily Telegraph*
as 'the Oxford and Cambridge Two-tone Blues Apparatus'.

Love spoon

Often referred to in Wales as the 'poor man's engagement ring'
because it is believed that the girl who accepted a love spoon carved
by her suitor would then consider herself to be 'spoken for'. Little is
known about the craft's history, and many were the work of talented
yet anonymous amateurs, rather than professional craftsmen. It is
believed that the early versions of love spoons were used for drinking
cawl (*pron* cowl, a stew of mutton and vegetables, sometimes made
very thin and with a dollop of mashed potato in the middle of the
plate), a key feature in the diet of those living in Western Wales, and
were simply a development of the decoration of the spoon. Cawl
spoons were generally made of sycamore felled during the winter
when a low sap content reduced blemishes and stains in the wood. The
oldest dated love spoon was carved in 1667. The spoons are made
using a *twca cam*; a long-handled implement with a small curved blade
for scooping out the bowl of the spoon. The designs were made to suit
the receiver, each with a different meaning or purpose. Of the
hundreds of designs, popular ones were anchors (symbolising the hope
of a smooth voyage through life), hearts, locks, keys, lovers' knots,
initials and houses.

Lychee

See **Edible fruits**.

MO – 4

See **Forms of money**.

Mad Parliament

Whose title arose from the adjective *insigne* (distinguished – or notorious) being mistaken for *insane*; it met at Oxford in 1258 to limit the powers of King Henry III; for other Parliaments, see **Parliament**.

Magna Carta

Latin = Great Charter of liberties extorted by church and barons from King John and signed by him at Runnymede, a meadow on the south bank of the River Thames near Windsor, on 15 June 1215.

Maize

See Edible grasses.

Malay apple

See Edible fruits.

Mamihlapinatapai

Fuegian = looking at each other, each hoping that the other will offer to do something that both parties desire but neither is willing to perform.

Mamoncillo; Mandarin; Mango; Mangosteen

See Edible fruits.

Manioc

See Vegetables.

Manteia

See Fortune telling.

Mao suit

See Fashion.

Maoism

See Political -isms.

Marks & Spencer women

See Fashion.

Marrow

See Vegetables.

Martin's Law

The right to protect one's property, named after the Norfolk (England) farmer Tony Martin who was jailed for shooting an intruder in self-defence.

Marxism

See Political -isms.

Masusa

See Vegetables.

Materialism

See Political -isms.

Mauer, Die

German = The [Berlin] Wall erected in 1961 to cut off communist East Germany whence refugees were haemorrhaging to the West. The Wall started to crumble on 8 November 1989 and the world saw powerful images of the event that marked a substantial change in international relationships.

McCarthyism

See Political -isms.

Meatspace

Reality in hardcore geekspeak.

Meal times

There is a case for synchronising meal times in the household, however busy the family, lest manners and good behaviour suffer (assuming that the family is civilised enough to care). 'Break-fast' breaks the fast of the night, and sets the body up for the day ahead, a fact (or fiction) widely recognised by manufacturers of breakfast cereals as a means of selling what may become perilously close to being junk food. Hotels and the like offer the 'full English breakfast' or the 'continental breakfast', both often found in a series of lidded dishes on a central table with hot lights glaring down, the choice for the former to be made from eggs cooked in various ways, bacon (which may or may not be properly crisp), mushrooms, black pudding, tomato (which may or may not be slush from a tin), fried bread, and baked beans; and for the latter simplified to which of the croissants and 'preserves' you pick. It may be served between 0700 and 1000, according to the day of the week and the degree of civilisation of the house. This brings us round to 'elevenses' or docky time as we call it in these parts, although docky, or snap, can be taken at any time. Lunch – which some confusingly call 'dinner' – is served at about 1300, afternoon tea (with crust-off cucumber sandwiches and the best china) at about 1600, dinner (or 'supper' as those who take dinner at lunch time would have it) at about 2000, although some would have 'high tea' somewhat earlier – say 1900. This might precede going to the play or other entertainment, in which case supper would be served later in the evening after the entertainment was over.

Medicinal days

Ancient medicine adhered to an arcane practice of assigning propitiousness or otherwise to certain days; thus it was believed that, in the course of a disease, its 6th, 8th, 10th, 12th, 16th, 18th, etc day were preferable for treatment to the others. There might be some metabolic explanation with certain conditions; in other cases the observer might see what was expected, and the patient react to the placebo effect – provided that he or she had no knowledge of the Unlucky Days (*qv*).

Metrical feet

In poetry, the rhythmic elements upon which a poem is structured; the main ones – in the order shown – are:

iamb(us)	di-dah	guitar
trochee or choree	dah-di	fancy
dactyl	dah-di-di	architect
anap(a)est	di-di-dah	Bucharest
spondee	dah dah	ding dong
amphibrach	di-dah-di	caramba

Others are combinations

amphimacer or cretic	dah-di-dah	fancy that
antibacchius or palimbacchius	dah-dah-di	Tintagel
antispast	di-dah-dah-di	Sir John Gielgud
bacchius	di-dah-dah	it's play time
choreus or tribrach	di-di-di	Zebedee
choriamb	dah-di-di-dah	excellent owl
dibrach or pyrrhic	di-di	silly
diamb	di-dah-di-dah	it's ten to twelve
dispondee	dah-dah-dah-dah	go to your room
ditrochee	dah-di-dah-di	buy some candy
dochmiac	di-dah-dah-di-dah	there's no time for that
epitrite	di-dah-dah-dah	they've all gone home
ionic majore	dah-dah-di-di	long time coming
ionic minore	di-di-dah-dah	Titicaca
molossus	dah-dah-dah	come down here
paeon	dah-di-di-di	owl homily
proceleusmatic	di-di-di-di	Peter Piper

Medicine, early

Until medical science began to advance, it was held that the body was controlled by the four humours – blood, phlegm, bile and black bile – and that keeping healthy was a matter of balancing them.

Medlar

See Edible fruits.

Meliorism

See Political -isms.

Melon

See Edible fruits.

Merciless or Unmerciful Parliament

That which met in 1388 (halfway though the reign of Richard II) to condemn his friends to death or exile; for other Parliaments, see Parliament.

Method, The

1 An acting technique based on Stanislavsky's work where the actor bases his interpretation of a role on the supposed inner motivation of the character played.
2 A set of changes in bell-ringing, though some suggest that those who use the term do so because they think it's an in-word, while those *really* in the know never use it.

Mezzo-soprano

See Singing voice types.

Michaelmas

29 September; the festival of St Michael and all Angels. St Michael was one of the Archangels, the prince of all angels and leader of the celestial armies. He is depicted as a handsome young man with wings, wearing white or armour, holding a lance and shield.

Middle age

If man's span is threescore years and ten, middle age must be around 35 years old; however, it may be thought to encompass the 40s to the 60s, especially if one feels a need to take it seriously. Personally, I've been in my prime since I was 18.

Mihrab

See Kiblah.

Millenarianism

See Political -isms.

Millennium bug

The expected manifestation of the fear that all the world's computers would crash when the year changed from 1999 to 2000. Vast sums of money were spent on (and made by) 'consultants' who sought to prevent aeroplanes dropping out of the sky, public utilities grinding to a halt, governments falling, and whatever else it might be from happening, but in the end very little did, and the media scrambled madly to find examples of the effects of the Bug before it was entirely forgotten.

Millet

See Edible grasses.

MILT

Mothers in leather trousers.

Minden Day

On 1 August 1759 six regiments of the British Army won the most spectacular victory of the Seven Years' War (against the French), sporting wild roses in their caps plucked as they advanced across Minden Heath (north-west Germany). The Day is commemorated by the Minden Regiments (with the exception of the Royal Welch Fusiliers) wearing roses in their caps on 1 August: they were/are The 12th Foot, later the Suffolk Regiment (in which your compiler had the honour to spend his first six weeks of National Service in 1953), later the 1st Battalion Royal Anglian Regiment; The 20th Foot, the Lancashire Fusiliers (the Minden Boys), later the 4th Battalion Royal Regiment of Fusiliers (now disbanded); The 23rd Foot Royal Welch Fusiliers; The 25th Foot, the King's Own Scottish Borderers; The 37th Foot, later the Royal Hampshire Regiment; and The 51st Foot, KOYLI (King's Own Yorkshire Light Infantry, which became the 2nd Battalion the Light Infantry in 1968).

Minneola

See Edible fruits.

Mishnah

(Hebrew = learning, instruction) The collection of moral precepts and traditions that form the basis of the Talmud. It is divided into six parts: (1) Agriculture, (2) Sabbaths, Fasts and Festivals, (3) Marriage and Divorce, (4) Civil and Penal Laws, (5) Sacrifices, and (6) Holy Persons and Things.

Misrule

In medieval and Tudor times the practice of licensed tomfoolery at certain times of the year, of the sort where the roles of servant and master are reversed, was overseen by the Abbot, King, or Lord, of Misrule. Such frivolities may have arisen from long-established events such as the Roman Saturnalia, and took place in the seasons of Christmas, Easter and May. A practice at Hocktide (the second week after Easter) was for the man of the community to capture the women and release them for a forfeit; on the following day, the women would capture the men. Not many such customs survive in these PC days.

Model Parliament

That summoned by Edward I in 1295, the first attempt at gathering a proper selection of representatives; for other Parliaments, see **Parliament**.

Molespud

An essential tool for a molecatcher, the molespud consisted of a wooden shaft with a metal point at one end and a small metal spade, about 3in (8cm) wide at the other. It was used to find mole runs and dig out moles. One of the molecatcher's arts was to ensure that some survived to be caught the following year.

MOMA

Museum of Modern Art, NY.

Momart Fire

When millions of pounds worth of warehoused modern art went up in flames on 24 May 2004, described as the 'biggest "happening" ever'.

Moments

When you suddenly forget where you are and what's going on, variously described as Blonde (non-PC stereotyping), Bristlecone (Bristlecone pine; the oldest living thing), CRAFT (Can't Remember A Flipping Thing), or Senior Moments.

Momo syndrome

Macrocosmia obesity macrocephaly ocular abnormality, an extremely rare genetic condition resulting in rapid weight gain, poor hearing and eyesight, and heart problems.

Monarchism

See Political -isms.

Mongrel Parliament

That summoned to Oxford by Charles II to thwart attempts to allow an RC succession; for other Parliaments, see **Parliament**.

Monkey bread

See Edible fruits.

Monster Mansion

Wakefield Prison, 'a decrepit Victorian prison full of decrepit people who are going nowhere ... unless they leave in a box.'

Montgolfier

French term for a colossal hangover, referring to the hot-air balloon launched by the Montgolfier Brothers in 1783. In 1888, 'Professor' Baldwin, the American aeronaut, came to England and demonstrated parachute jumping from a tethered balloon; Lupin Pooter (in *The Diary of a Nobody* – George and Weedon Grossmith, *Punch* 29 December 1888) referred to his hangover by saying 'my head's as big as Baldwin's balloon'.

Mooli

See Vegetables.

Mop Fair

An English statute or hiring fair taking place in market towns at Martinmas (11 November), when those for hire would line up for inspection, their trade identified by the emblems they bore (such as mops).

Moringa

See Vegetables.

Morris Dance

Summer fetes in England are often graced by a side of Morris Dancers. The dance has been known in England from C15; the dancers often representing characters from the stories of Robin Hood and Maid Marian. Other stock characters included Bavian the fool with his pig's bladder on a stick – licensed misbehaviour – Malkin the clown, a hobbyhorse or a dragon, and foreigners, probably Moors or Moriscos from which the dance takes its name. There are many Morris sides in rural England today giving displays outside village pubs (and afterwards inside); by their bells, beards and beer-guts shall ye know them (unless they be comely young wenches), and by the sound of the accordion or concertina and other folksy instruments.

MP3

Motion Picture Experts' Group audio layer 3; a digital audio compression system commonly used to send files containing music and audio over the Internet.

Muddy

Mud-crab, a great delicacy (AS).

Mulberry

See Edible fruits.

Mullet

A hairstyle described as 'business in front; party in back'.

Mulligan

An illegal golf practice where a mis-hit ball is respotted and reshot.

Music of the Spheres

Interested in music and harmony, Pythagoras discovered that a series of anvils emitted notes when struck whose frequencies were proportional to their masses (as we would say nowadays). (This apparent phenomenon was, however, a curious coincidence.) By a leap of the imagination, he concluded that the planets must make a harmonious sound as they run their courses – the 'music of the spheres'. This inspired Joseph Addison (1672–1719) to write:

The spacious firmament on high,
With all the blue ethereal sky,
And spangled heavens, a shining frame,
Their great Original proclaim,
Th'unwearied sun from day to day
Doth his creator's powers display,
And publishes to every land
The works of an almighty hand.

Soon as the evening shades prevail
The moon takes up the wondrous tale,
And nightly to the listening earth
Repeats the story of her birth;
Whilst all the stars that round her burn
And all the planets in their turn,
Confirm the tidings, as they roll,
And spread the truth from pole to pole.

What though in solemn silence all
Move round the dark terrestrial ball;
What though nor real voice nor sound
Amid their radiant orbs be found;
In reason's ear they all rejoice,
And utter forth a glorious voice,
For ever singing as they shine,
'The hand that made us is Divine.'

This delightful poem was set to music (double long metre) by J Sheeles in 1720, and now appears as No 297 in the *English Hymnal*.

Mulready covers

Prepaid postal wrappers by the Irish artist William Mulready (1786–1863) for letters (1840s) decorated with stirring scenes of the Commonwealth; unfortunately they were much lampooned, and the product soon fell by the wayside.

Mummer

A member of a group that visited houses usually at Christmas-time, performing a stock play about St George and the Dragon with other stock characters such as Father Christmas, the Moor, the Doctor, etc.

Mumping Day

St. Thomas' Day, 21 December, when in some areas the poor would go about 'mumping', or seeking gifts in preparation for Christmas; in Lincolnshire, mumping was a Boxing Day custom; in Warwickshire it was 'going a-corning', since the gift sought was corn.

Mung bean

See Vegetables.

Muskmelon

See Edible fruits.

Mustard greens

See Vegetables.

Mutualism

See Political -isms.

Mystery Play

A medieval religious drama based on episodes from the Scriptures or the lives of the saints.

Nangka; Nannyberry

See Edible fruits.

Nantes, Edict of

Whereby Henry IV of France guaranteed in 1598 Huguenots' rights of worship in certain named towns; revoked by Louis XIV in 1685.

Nationalism

See Political -isms.

Nature strip

Often grassy area between the front of an urban property and the roadway.

Nazism

See Political -isms.

Nectarine
See **Edible fruits**.

Nehru jacket
See **Fashion**.

New style
Denoting dates according to the Gregorian calendar; applied particularly at the time of its introduction to reduce confusion with the Old Style (Julian) calendar, and specified by historians as may be necessary for the avoidance of doubt when citing document dates; abbreviations: NS and OS.

Newspeak
A deliberately contradictory and ambiguous language used by bureaucrats to manipulate and mislead the public and as a form of thought control. Invented by George Orwell (1903–1950) in his novel *Nineteen Eighty-Four* (1949). It also involved reducing the language to a minimum – using only the word 'good' for positive expressions rather than having a wide range such as 'excellent', 'great', and having no negative terms at all, so that 'bad' became 'ungood'. Subsequent Newspeak has resulted in delicate euphemisms where, for example, a bomb capable of destroying the world is described as a 'device', and knocking umpteen bells out of your own forces by mistake is 'friendly fire'. Newspeak is still very much alive and developing, so that adult = pornographic, entry level = the cheapest, incident = any horrific happening and so on.

Nicka-Nan Night
Cornish term for the night preceding Shrove Tuesday.

Nihilism
See **Political -isms**.

-nik
A suffix denoting a state or quality, as in 'beatnik', one who belongs to the Beat Generation, or behaves in that way.

Nine days' wonder
An event on everyone's lips at the time, but then almost completely forgotten, named for the actor Will(iam) Kempe (c1550–c1603), a member of Shakespeare's Company who in 1600 performed a nine-day Morris dance from London to Norwich, and wrote *Nine Daies Wonder* to commemorate it.

Nipper
The name of the dog listening to a phonograph, painted by Francis Barraud, entitled 'His master's voice' (HMV), a name still used by one of the industry leaders.

Nolo episcopari
To refuse the offer of preferment twice is modest; thrice and they believe you.

Northumbrian pipes
Bagpipes usually smaller than the Scottish design, whose air pressure is derived from bellows operated by the player's arm.

Nose art
The practice of painting designs on the nose of an aircraft, for example the likeness of Margaret Polk painted on the Memphis Belle (a B17 'Flying Fortress') by Col Bob Morgan (1918–2004); *cf* Tail Art.

Not the full quid
Not bright (AS).

Oakum
Fibres from unravelled (tarred) ropes, used for caulking seams in wooden ships. A former punishment for prisoners was 'picking oakum', using a fid, or ropemaker's spike, sticking up on the knee.

Oatmeal Monday
The mid-term Monday at Scottish Universities when the father of a poor student would bring him a sack of oatmeal to provide his staple diet for the rest of the term. In the apocryphal tale, the student fills a drawer with porridge, and cuts off a chunk to eat daily.

Obadiah
See Books of the Holy Bible.

Ocker
An uncultivated, boorish Australian (AS). See Alf.

Oddle Poddle
Language invented by Hilda Brabban (neé Wright (1914–2002)), whose brothers Bill and Ben went into greengrocery and served as the inspiration for the Flowerpot Men; younger sister Phyllis became Little Weed. Flobadob was based on farting in the bath; *cf* Alec Guinness on Edward Woodward.

OFSTED
Inspectors of Schools, described as 'the covert enforcers of all fashionable crackpot theories in education'.

-oid
Suffix indicating 'something in the form of', such as android (man-like), factoid (purports to be a fact, but isn't), sigmoid (like a letter S), xyloid (wood-like), and so on.

Oido

(= heard); restaurant kitchenspeak acknowledging orders.

Okinawa spinach

See Vegetables.

Okra

See Vegetables.

Old age

The final period of an average lifespan of that type of organism; hence an old cat or dog might be 20, an old human 90, and an old tortoise 200 years old.

Old style

Refers to dating by the Julian calendar, as opposed to the Gregorian calendar, which was introduced gradually between 1582 and 1923; see New Style.

Oldies; Olds

Parents (AS).

Olive

See Vegetables.

Olivetti Graphika

The only manual proportional spacing typewriter (see IBM) ever produced, introduced in 1957. It was impossible to balance the impact of letters of all surface areas, so that f, i and j tended to cut into the paper, while M and W were weak – hence the lack of competition in the world of manual machines, and the predominance of the IBM models whose electric power could be adjusted to give a much more even result.

Olympiad

A period of four years, particularly that between two Olympic games; hence it was an ancient Greek measure of time dating back to 776BCE.

One of Lewis's

A twerp, after a pre-WW2 naked statue outside the Liverpool department store.

Onion

See Vegetables.

Operation Habbakuk [sic]

See Pykcrete.

Oprah's Law

Named after the American chat-show hostess Oprah Winfrey who used her influence to support a US child protection Bill.

Orange
See Edible fruits.

Ostrich fern
See Vegetables.

Output bottle's gone soft
The thermionic valve that feeds the speaker has lost its vacuum; as a slang saying, transferable to anatomy (and possibly analogous to the 3.5-inch floppy).

Oyster mushroom; plant
See Vegetables.

Pack and Penny Day
The last day of a fair when traders dispose of their remaining goods by selling them cheaply; it saves having to pack them up and take them home, probably in a soiled state. For modern manifestations, witness the last hours of (for example) the London Bookfair and the Chelsea Flower Show.

Pack-Rag-Day
Old May Day, so called in Lincolnshire because servants hired for the year packed up their clothes ('rags') to go home or to seek new employment.

Pak choi
See Vegetables.

Palio
2 July and 16 August, when jockeys dressed in medieval costume honour the Virgin Mary by racing bareback around the main square of Siena, Italy.

Papaya
See Edible fruits.

Parget(ing)
Plasterwork lining flues and rendering walls, the word often denoting decorative work on the latter.

Parka
See Fashion.

Parliaments
See Addled, Barebones, Black, Good, Grattan's, Long, Mad, Merciless, Model, Mongrel, Rump, Short, Useless.

Parsnip
See Vegetables.

Paper production

Paper appears to have originated in China around C2CE, and took another 1,000 years to reach Europe, via Asia and the Middle East. The first paper mills in Europe were set up in Spain in 1150, and in Britain in late C16. Paper was made at first by hand, starting with a pulp of vegetable fibres in water, skilfully scooped on to a wire frame fastened to a wooden frame (mould), shaken to distribute it evenly, and allowed to dry. The wire may incorporate a design to give the paper a 'watermark'. Sizes of paper such as 'crown' and 'foolscap' (now sadly in decline) take their names from their earlier watermarks. The basic raw material has always been vegetable fibre because of its composition and chemical properties; cotton is best because of its long, strong fibres. Handmade paper is still to be found in some communities and at craft demonstrations. The first continuous roll papermaking machine was built in France in 1798, and brought to England in 1803 by the Frenchman Henry Fourdrinier (1766–1854). At the 'wet end' of the machine, pulp is fed on to a wire mesh belt (which may bear a watermark design), where it passes over suction boxes and pressing rolls to become a paper web that can sustain itself after transfer from the wire mesh to the felt belts. The rest of the process consists of drying, calendering and winding the finished product at the 'dry end'. Apart from set-ups comprising a number of machines feeding from one to the next, the Fourdrinier is the longest single-purpose machine made.

Pashmina
See Fashion.

Pass, The
In a restaurant, the counter between the waiting staff on one side, and the kitchen staff on the other.

Passion fruit
See Edible fruits.

Patriotism
See Political -isms.

Pawpaw
See Edible fruits.

PC signs
Sign language for the deaf (or audiologically challenged) is considering replacing, or has replaced, signs for Indians (dot on forehead), Jews

Pendulum

A body suspended from a fixed point so as to swing freely periodically under the action of gravity and commonly used to regulate movements, *eg* of clockwork. Galileo (who made exhaustive studies of phenomena due to gravity) observed a lamp swinging in Siena Cathedral in about 1580, and realised that the period of the swing was independent of the amplitude – that if the swing was greater, the suspended object moved faster to complete its swing in the same period of time. And this, he saw, could be a means of regulating a clock.

The period of swing, in seconds, is equal to $2\pi\sqrt{(l/g)}$ (l = length from suspension point to centre of gravity of bob (pendulum weight); g = acceleration due to gravity; use whatever compatible units you prefer).

The Dutch physicist Christiaan Huyghens designed a pendulum clock in 1656; he found that in fact swings through greater arcs took longer than those through lesser ones, and that ideally the bob should swing in a cycloidal arc. Huyghens achieved this effect by causing the suspension spring to work between cycloidal cheeks, but unfortunately introduced other inaccuracies that mitigated the cycloidal advantages.

(large nose), Chinese (slanting eyes), German (spiked helmet), gay (limp wrist) and others. No westerner, it seems, has objected to depiction by the Chinese deaf sign of round eyes.

Pensioner Parliament
See Cavalier Parliament.

Pe tsai; Pea
See Vegetables.

Peach; Pear; Pear melon
See Edible fruits.

Peasant dress
See Fashion.

Pedal pushers
See Fashion.

Pelisse; Penis hat; Peplos; Peplum
See Fashion.

Pepper
See Vegetables.

Perestroika

Russian = 'reconstruction' or 'reform'. The name given to the economic changes instituted by Soviet president Mikhail Gorbachev (1931–) from the mid-1980s, introducing a free market economy and opening up the Soviet economy to trade, investment and finance with the western world.

Perps and beds

Vertical and horizontal joints in brickwork.

Persimmon or date-plum

See Edible fruits.

Phenakistiscope

A 'magic disc' invented by the Frenchman Joseph Plateau in 1832 with a series of images on one side, alternating with radial slits. The disc is held on its handle so that it can spin freely, with the images away from the viewer, who stands before a looking glass to view the images reflected through the slits. An appearance of motion may be obtained with an appropriate choice of images.

Phishing

Sending e-mail purporting to come from a respectable financial institution in order to extract personal information from unsuspecting recipients.

Phœnix period or cycle

At the end of its life, the legendary phœnix builds a nest of spices in Arabia, sings a melodious dirge, flaps its wings to set fire to the nest, burns itself to ashes, and comes forth with new life, only to repeat the former one. There are various estimates for the life cycle of the phœnix: Tacitus gives 250 years; R. Stuart Poole 1,460 (Julian years, like the Sothic Cycle); Lipsius 1,500 years. However, the phœnix is said to have appeared in Egypt five times: (1) in the reign of Sesostris; (2) in the reign of Am-asis; (3) in the reign of Ptolemy Philadelphos; (4) a year or two before the death of Tiberius; and (5) during the reign of Constantine in 334CE. This suggests that the phœnix cycle is 300 years.

Physalia

The Portuguese Man o'War; a pelagic coelenterate with an air-bladder sail and a powerful sting.

Physalis
See Edible fruits.

Picking
The act of inserting weft by throwing a shuttle across a loom from its shuttle box to the opposite shuttle box, achieved in an automatic loom by the action of a (wooden) picker-stick; loom speed is measured in picks per minute (ppm).

Pidgin
A language developed – mainly for commerce – between two communities, each with a different native tongue. The pidgin draws on both languages; if it then becomes a native language, it is a creole. The word is thought to be a corruption of 'business'.

Pidgin English
A pidgin, one of whose elements is English.

Piker
One who doesn't want to fit in socially (AS).

Pineapple
See Edible fruits.

Pingstorm
Computer sabotage by electronic means.

Pinyin
The modern system of providing a phonetic transliteration (not a translation) of Chinese into English or other Romanised languages. Coming from a Chinese word meaning 'phoneticise' or 'join together', this system was adopted in 1979 by the Chinese government and by the International Standards Organization (ISO), and therefore effectively replaced the previous Wade-Giles system.

Pirn
See Shuttle.

Pitaya
See Edible fruits.

Plantain
See Vegetables.

Platform shoes
See Fashion.

Play-on/play-off
Music to get someone on or off stage; aptly chosen for a chat-show guest, or the signature tune of a professional artist.

PLM

Merging of two Rothschild railway enterprises: Paris–Lyon and Lyon–Marseilles (1857).

Plough Festival

A festival where a plough race is held in the common fields, each contestant being allowed to sow the land he succeeded in ploughing. The modern equivalent is the ploughing match, for both tractor- and horse-drawn ploughs, and a fine sight it is too – especially if there is a plethora of heavy horses and a demonstration of a pair of ploughing engines.

Plum

See Edible fruits.

Poets' Day

Facetious epithet for Friday, especially in the workplace (Piss Off Early, Tomorrow's Saturday).

Poha; Pomegranate; Pomelo

See Edible fruits.

Portland Vase

C1 Roman funerary urn of dark blue glass with white decoration found in a tomb in 1752; bought by Sir William Hamilton: when the Duke of Portland, a British Museum Trustee, became its owner in 1787 he lodged it in the Museum where, in 1845, an educated young Irishman, William Mulcahy, smashed it; it was skilfully repaired, but the positions of a few glass splinters remain unaccounted for.

Portsmouth blockmaking machinery

Originally her husband's invention patented by a widow, Elizabeth Taylor, in mid C18, a set of production-line machines brought to practicality in 1801 by Sir Marc Isambard Brunel (1769–1849) for making the pulley-blocks for which there was an insatiable demand in the days of sail.

Posture, mobile phone

In the early days, those using their mobiles in the street tended to cower embarrassedly in corners; now that the instruments have become smaller, and their users have gained confidence, they strut about without a care.

Potato

See Vegetables.

Porcelain

A white, hard, translucent material made by firing a mixture of china clay (kaolin), feldspar and silica (quartz/flint). Feldspathic rocks (petuntse) are silicates of aluminium, potassium, sodium, calcium or barium. The technique was developed from stoneware manufacture in China between 600 and 900CE. There are three kinds of porcelain: hard-paste, soft-paste and boneware. Hard-paste (true) porcelain is fired to about 2,550°F (1,400°C), and usually glazed with pure petuntse during firing. In soft-paste (false) porcelain, the clay or kaolin is mixed with a flux such as silica, lime, soda etc, and fired at 2,015°F (1,110°C), and the glaze, often glass, is applied for a second firing at 1,835°K (1,000°C). Bone porcelain (bone china) was invented by Josiah Spode in England in C18, using bone ash as flux.

Practical food

Food to be eaten on stage as part of the play, reputedly the saving of many a starving player.

Prayer time

To pray is to speak reverently to a heavenly being in order to express thanks, make a request or deliver a set text by means of a prayer. In Muslim countries or communities, everything stops five times a day for prayers, as signalled from the Mosque. Prayer times vary according to latitude and longitude, and the times of sunrise and sunset. The sequence is: Dawn Prayer, Noon Prayer, Afternoon Prayer, Sunset Prayer and Night Prayer.

Preston Guild, once every

Not very often. Preston Guild meetings have been held every 20 years since 1542 (save that the 1942 meeting was deferred until 1952), on the first Monday after the Feast of the Decollation of St John the Baptist (*ie* the Last Monday in August); the next will be in 2012 'and the inhabitants of Proud Preston, England's newest city, are already looking forward to that day with eager anticipation.'

Prickly pear

See Edible fruits.

Primrose Day

19 April, the anniversary of the death of Benjamin Disraeli (1804–81), Lord Beaconsfield, to whose funeral HM Queen Victoria sent a wreath of primroses from Osborne: 'His favourite flowers'; not true, but the

idea caught on in the name of the Conservative League founded in 1883.

Printing processes
See IBM, Intaglio, Letterpress, Lithography, Xerography.

Props
What is on the theatre stage? Sets, cast and props (properties). Set props are part of the set; hand props are used by the cast as part of the performance, and personal props are carried on actors' persons.

Ptolemaic System

Ptolemy's C2 system to account for the apparent motion of the heavenly bodies. He believed in a geocentric universe with 'the heavens' revolving from east to west, in which there were spheres, each with its own period of rotation, bearing the sun, the planets and the fixed stars. The tenth, outer, sphere was the *primum mobile* that carried all the others. The whole thing was somewhat like a geocentric orrery, and made sweet sounds to boot: the 'music of the spheres' (*qv*). The heliocentric Copernican System, was introduced by Nicholas Copernicus (1473–1543), but was prohibited by the RC church in 1616. Galileo (1564–1642) was no mean astronomer, and affirmed the truth of the Copernican System in 1632; this brought him before the Inquisition which caused him to recant (but uttering under his breath, it is said 'Eppur si muove' = 'and yet it [the earth] moves'). It's this sort of man-delivered short-sightedness that brings God into disrepute.

Punks
See Fashion.

Purple salsify; Purslane
See Vegetables.

Pykcrete
A frozen mixture of about 10 per cent wood pulp in water which is strong enough to be fashioned into aircraft carriers and other vessels, proposed by the now-largely-forgotten lateral thinker Geoffrey Pyke (1894–1948) for naval purposes in WW2 – Operation Habbakuk [*sic*].

Pyromancy/pyroscopy
See Fortune telling.

Qibla
See Kiblah.

Quantum theory
Also known as the observer-related universe, whereby the observer can affect the outcome of a scientific experiment because nothing can be measured or observed without disturbing it.

Quarantine
The period, originally forty days, that a ship suspected of being infected with some contagious disorder is obliged to lie off port. Now applied to any period of segregation to prevent infection, particularly relating to animals.

Quart d'heure, Un mauvais
A bad quarter of an hour. Used for a short, disagreeable experience. In the film *The Prime of Miss Jean Brodie* Miss Mackay, the headmistress of Marcia Blane High School for Girls, summons Miss Brodie to a meeting at quarter to eleven; Miss Brodie observes: 'She seeks to intimidate me by the use of quarter hours;' perhaps she had *Un mauvais quart d'heure* in mind.

Queensborough; Quenepa
See Edible fruits.

Quid, make a
Earn a living (AS).

Quince
See Edible fruits.

Quincunx
See Galton.

Racism
See Political -isms.

Radicalism
See Political -isms.

Radicchio
See Vegetables.

Radish
See Vegetables.

Ragnarok
See Fimbulwinter.

Railway time
As the railways began to spread over the land, they found it necessary to run to a timetable which operated to a standard (railway) time,

rather than to the numerous local times then usual. Fortunately, the developing telegraph made it relatively easy to synchronise time-pieces.

Rank–Xerox platemaking

For about £30 a month in the early 1960s you could rent the complete 1385 Rank–Xerox equipment. Most impressive was the process camera with enlargement or reduction achieved by a bellows-connected camera-front running on a track, and 4 x 500-watt lamps to illuminate the work. Set up the work and adjust its size and sharpness on the ground-glass screen at the back end of the camera, then take a selenium plate in its wooden frame, dust it with grit-free wool, slide it into the charging slot on the xerographic box of tricks, and press the button. An electrically-charged wire moves across the selenium surface, close enough to transfer charge to it. When this is complete, push a dark slide into the frame, transfer the frame to the back of the camera, pull out the slide, and expose the plate to the focused image under control of a timer. Insert the dark slide again, remove the frame and transfer it to a toner tray face downwards, and pull out the dark slide. Turn the tray gently upside down so that the tiny resinous balls coated with toner can cascade over the surface of the selenium plate, adhering to those parts where the electrostatic image has been focused. Turn the tray the right way up, detach the plate, and inspect the image. If all is well, lay a litho plate (for your litho printing machine) on the surface with its toner image, and transfer the toner from selenium to plate by sliding the frame into the charging slot and pressing the button. Then peel off the plate with its exceedingly fragile toner image and inspect it. At this stage, you can 'spot' the plate – removing unwanted spots and the like with a material like Blu-Tack. When (if ever) you are satisfied with the image, you can fix it by baking it (hot-plate provided) and then put it on the litho machine and run it.

That was the process, and those of us who used the equipment remember every little magic shake and shuffle that seemed to improve its seldom-adequate quality. The 1385 equipment (so called because of the foolscap image area of 13" x 8.5") was superseded by the 914 photocopying machine which had a selenium-coated drum and achieved all the manual processes I've just described automatically. The principle has not changed for over forty years, but xerographic photocopiers have become unbelievably reliable compared with their forerunners.

Raisin
See Edible fruits.

Ramadan
The ninth month of the Muslim calendar; that of fasting in honour of Muhammad's flight from Mecca in 622CE. During this month, Muslims do not eat, drink, smoke or take part in sexual activity from dawn till dusk until the Imam announces that Ramadan is over and the festival of *Is-al-Fitr* begins.

Rambutan
See Edible fruits.

Raspberry
See Edible fruits.

Ray-Bans
See Fashion.

Reactionism
See Political -isms.

Red bean
See Vegetables.

Redcurrant
See Edible fruits.

Reed
The element of a loom through which all the warp threads pass so that, after the weft has been thrown across, it may be swung towards the newly inserted weft ('beat up') to form a compact and uniform cloth.

Release Group
A British National Service indication of when one would be discharged after 18 months' or two years' service. There were two intakes every month: on Thursdays, so 5304 would indicate someone serving from Thursday 19 February 1953 to Thursday 17 February 1955. 'Gripping' was the name given to the practice of gloating: 'My release date's earlier than yours,' shortened to 'I can grip you.'

Republicanism
See Political -isms.

Revolutionism
See Political -isms.

Revolve
A turntable on a stage to enable a quick change of scenery or actors.

Rhubarb
See Edible fruits.

Rhythm
1   The pattern of recurrent alternation of strong and weak or long and short elements in the flow of sound, especially in music and speech; rhythm is superimposed on the tempo, or beat.
2   The pace of the interaction of the elements in a play, novel, film, painting etc.

Rice
See Edible grasses.

Ridged luffa
See Vegetables.

Ridgy-didge
Original, genuine (AS).

Rightism
See Political -isms.

Rope making

Rope can be made from many different materials, for example straw, coconut palm and leaf fibres from many different plants such as the abaca, a species of wild banana. The process of rope making is, however, the same no matter what the material being used. First of all the fibres need to be prepared by pulling them through a bed of nails or rods ('hackling'), to make sure they are all running the same way. The next stage is to spin them into a yarn; the third stage is to twist a number of yarns together to form a strand; with hand-made rope this is done using a hook. The number of yarns that are used wholly depends upon the thickness required of the rope. Often three or four strands are twisted, or 'laid' together to form the rope which is usually made in standard lengths of 120 fathoms – 240 yards. Ropes of this length are rarely made by hand any more. To make the usual three strand rope, the ends of the three strands are fixed to three revolving hooks on a mechanism called a jack. The hooks revolve together, driven by gearing or a pulley, and at the other end of the 'rope walk' is a single hook to which the three strands are fixed. As the three hooks turn, the strands twist together to form the rope. A three-strand rope is a 'hawser', and a 'cable' comprises three hawsers. Some ropes may have wire strands around a central hemp core to confer flexibility. Ropes with a central core are said to be 'shroud laid'.

Rinse (v)
To tease.

Robinson, Ralph
Pseudonym of George II writing on agriculture.

Rocker
See Fashion.

Rocket
See Vegetables.

Ropewalk
1   A long, narrow area in which ropes are laid.
2   Barristers' slang for an Old Bailey practice, derived from the murder trials (often ending in 'the rope') that took place there.

Roquette
See Vegetables.

Rosaceae; Rose apple
See Edible fruits.

Roselle
See Vegetables.

Route 66
Santa Monica CA via Arizona, North Mexico, Texas, Oklahoma, Kansas, Missouri to Chicago IL.

Roy
A switched-on Australian; the opposite of an ocker.

Royal styles of address
'My Liege' until the assumption of Henry IV (1399) who was 'Your Grace'; Henry VI was 'Your Excellent Grace'; Edward IV 'Most High and Mighty Prince'; Henry VII 'Your Highness'; Henry VIII 'Your Majesty'; James I 'The King's Sacred Majesty'; Charles II 'Your Most Excellent Majesty'; Queen Victoria 'Your Most Gracious Majesty'; now returns to 'Sir' and 'Madam'.

Rub 'al Khali
Arabic = Empty Quarter, the most forbidding, least known and impenetrable desert in the world, the south area of Saudi Arabia reputedly used for receiving dissidents dropped from aeroplanes; it was, however, investigated by the English explorer Sir Wilfred Thesiger (1910–2003) in 1945–50.

Rucola
See Vegetables.

Rump Parliament

In Cromwell's time, the remnant of the Long Parliament, that abolished the monarchy and the House of Lords; for other Parliaments, see **Parliament**.

Runner bean

See **Vegetables**.

Runnery strips

Strips of land whose use is rotated among farmers so that all share good and bad.

Rutabaga

See **Vegetables**.

Rye

See **Edible grasses**.

Robot

1   Any machine programmed to perform tasks which would otherwise be done by a human being. The word was created by Czech playwright Karel Capek (1890–1938) from the Czech word robota = 'work', in his 1920 play *R U R* (or *Rossum's Universal Robots*). This describes a world in which all drudgery or menial jobs are carried out by mechanical people.
2   In the north of England, traffic lights are sometimes referred to as 'robots', to rhyme with 'oboes'.

Sabbatical year

1   One year in seven, when all the land, according to Mosaic law, was to lie fallow (Exod 23).
2   In education, especially in universities, a sabbatical year gives a member of staff time off to study or travel. The term has now gained wider currency in industry, and has been reduced to 'taking a sabbatical' (*cf* 'an en-suite').

Sack or saque coat

See **Fashion**.

Saffron milk cap

See **Vegetables**

Saguaro

See **Edible fruits**.

Salak

See **Edible fruits**.

Salmonberry

See **Edible fruits**.

Sand glass, hour glass or egg-timer

A device for measuring an exact period of time, involving two glass bulbs connected by a narrow waist through which sand (or other fine granular material) runs from the upper to the lower. In an hourglass, the sand takes precisely one hour to empty completely from the upper bulb into the lower. A sandglass may be timed to last for a longer or shorter duration, and an egg-timer generally has a maximum period of six minutes; usually less. The ancient Greeks used sand glasses as we do today – for measuring cooking times, particularly when boiling eggs. The art of blowing glass was revived at the end of C8 by the monk Luitrand of Chartres, and the sand glass took on a new lease of life. In C14, the practice of paying workmen by the hour was introduced, and hour glasses were again in demand. The particles in the glass must be perfectly dry (powdered eggshell, marble dust or sand) and carefully sieved so that they are all about the same size. The hole through which they flow should be about ten times the diameter of the particles. The rate of flow is irrespective of the amount waiting to pass through, and the air displaced from the lower to the upper chamber finds its way through the particles so that there is no back pressure. The aesthetic properties of the sand glass have also been remarked: its silent running, and the shape of the conical pile below echoing that of the conical depression above.

Salsify
See **Vegetables**.

Samba lettuce
See **Vegetables**.

Samuel
See **Books of the Holy Bible**.

Sanpaku
Japanese = three whites; where the white of the eye is visible all round the pupil, seen in new-born babies; less frequently in adults.

Sapodilla
See **Edible fruits**.

Sari
See **Fashion**.

Sarong
See **Fashion**.

Saskatoon
See **Edible fruits**.

Sastrudi
Rough ice surface at the pole.

Satsuma
See **Edible fruits**.

Scallion
See **Vegetables**.

Schlamperei
A delaying quality of the Viennese civil service 'that makes *mañana* look like greased lightning'.

Scopes and tropes
See **Phenakistiscope, Thaumatrope, Zoëtrope**.

Scorzonera
See **Vegetables**.

Scottish Play, The
Actors' epithet for the name of the play that was thought to be unlucky to utter – *Macbeth*. Nowadays, there is perhaps more emphasis on a thoughtful production than on superstitions to 'explain' why things go wrong.

Screen printing
A method of applying a design to a surface by squeezing ink through a stencil either hand cut or prepared photographically and laid on a silk or polyester mesh stretched over a (wooden) frame; this constitutes the screen. The screen is then placed over the substrate to be printed on – usually paper (for posters and the like) or fabric (for a T-shirt). Dyes or inks are then forced through the areas of the mesh that have not been blocked off by the stencil, using a 'squeegee' with a rubber blade the width of the inside of the frame. The frame is hinged and counterweighted to make the operation more convenient. A different screen is needed for each colour used.

Sculpitecture
Art-form combining sculpture and architecture named by Sir Anthony Caro (1924–), for example 'The Bean', properly Cloud Gate by Anish Kapoor in Chicago's Millennium Park.

Scum of the earth
So Wellington described his men when they embarked on one of the British army's worst-ever atrocities of rape, pillage and murder at Badajoz on 7 April 1812.

Sea kale
See **Vegetables**.

Seaberry
See **Edible fruits**.

Sea-buckthorn
See **Edible fruits**.

Season, The London
The part of the year when the Court and fashionable society generally is (or was) in town – May, June, July.

Second World War
Between 1 September 1939, when Nazi forces entered Poland, and 8 May 1945 (VE- or Victory in Europe Day) and 14 August 1945 (VJ- or Victory over Japan Day). Britain entered the conflict on 3 September 1939, and the US on 7 December 1941 when the Japanese bombed Pearl Harbor, Hawaii.

Segue
(Pron seg-way) a musical production term for the seamless transition from one tune to another.

Segway
Japanese gyroscopically-controlled personal transport.

Sell-by date
A mixed blessing; the date by which a perishable item, such as a food product, must (at least notionally) be sold if it is to be consumed in a fresh or fit state. It is not the same as a use-by or best-before date, which is usually a day or two later, at which time the goods may be reduced in price, or disposed of. The expression has gained a facetious general sense to refer to a person who is 'getting on', so that if one is past one's sell-by date, one is past one's prime.

Semester
(Latin *sex* = six, *mensis* = month) Originally half a year but now, especially in the US, a term of attendance at school, college, or university. Different countries have developed educational terms of differing duration; some have two, some three (as in the UK) and some four. In Germany a semester is a half-year of a school or university course, including any holidays (vacations) within that half-year. Semesterisation is a somewhat clumsy word used to describe playing about with the dates and durations of school or college terms to provide four or even six terms in a year, supposedly preferred (or not) by parents, staff etc.

Sesam

See **Vegetables**.

Settlers' clock

The Laughing Jackass or Kookaburra, the Australian Great Kingfisher; so called because it tends to utter its cry more especially at sunrise and sunset.

Seven ages of man

According to Jaques in Shakespeare's *As You Like It*, II, vii (1599) the seven ages of man are: (1) the infant, (2) the schoolboy, (3) the lover, (4) the soldier, (5) the justice, (6) the pantaloon and (7) second childhood.

Sgraffito

1 A form a decoration of pottery in which a layer of clay slip applied to a clay surface is scratched through so as to reveal the differently-coloured clay beneath.
2 Ware so decorated.

Shaddock

See **Edible fruits**.

SHAZAM

Egyptian wizard who enables Billy Batson to transform himself into Captain Marvel; the wizard in turn is granted his powers by the deities Solomon for wisdom, Hercules for strength, Atlas for stamina, Zeus for power, Achilles for courage, Mercury for speed ...SHAZAM.

Shed

In weaving, the gap between warp threads through which the shuttle is thrown.

Shell suit

See **Fashion**.

Shiitake; Shiny bush

See **Vegetables**.

Shoot through

To depart; Shoot through like a Bondi tram recalls the transport from Sydney to Bondi Beach, discontinued 1961 [AS].

Short Parliament

That summoned by Charles I on 13 April 1640; it lasted but 22 days; for other Parliaments, see **Parliament**.

Short-swing

In commercial transactions (especially in the United States), describes a period for the completion of a transaction of six months or less.

Shuttle

A wooden carrier with pointed metal ends that carries a pirn (package of yarn) through the shed (the space formed by parting the warp threads) across the width of a loom, thus forming the weft ('that which is woven'). In early hand looms, the width was restricted to what the weaver could 'throw' against the frictive resistance of the warp threads upon which the shuttle travelled. John Kay's flying shuttle of 1733 enabled a weaver to throw a shuttle through a wider shed, and to throw it faster (more picks per minute). The use of the flying shuttle was to some extent limited by the amount of yarn available, and this deficiency might have become still more acute after the Revd Edmund Cartwright patented his power loom in 1785, had there not been parallel developments in spinning machinery (*qv*).

Siegfried Line

A line of defence built by the Germans at the beginning of WW2 as an answer to France's Maginot Line. A popular song of the time proclaimed 'We're going to hang out the washing on the Siegfried Line...', but conquering it was no walkover, and the song sank into embarrassed oblivion.

Silk

A natural fibre produced by silk 'worms' (actually caterpillars of the silk moth (*Bombyx mori*, that feeds only on mulberry leaves)) whose existence in China was kept a closely-guarded secret for centuries. The worms' cocoons are carefully soaked and unwound in order to produce the monofilament silk threads, which are twisted together to form a strong yarn, which can then be woven to create fabric. Silk fabrics have a lustrous sheen, are strong, resilient, and warm.

Sissoo spinach

See **Vegetables**.

Sitting by Nellie

Learning on t'job, particularly in t'mill, probably non-PC now.

Six honest serving men

Devised by Rudyard Kipling (1865–1936) for the verse at the end of his *Just-so Story* 'The elephant's child' (1902). It forms a useful checklist in many everyday circumstances:

I keep six honest serving men
(They taught me all I knew);
Their names are What and Why and When
And How and Where and Who.

Sleepyhead Day

In the town of Naantali, Finland, the harvest festival begins with Sleepyhead Day, when anyone who has provided a particular service to the town is honoured by being thrown into the Baltic Sea. It must be a great incentive to doing good.

Slip

Liquid clay, used in pottery-production processes. A pot may be dipped in slip with additives (frits) to form a glaze when fired. A design may be added to a surface by trailing slip across it. Items may be slip cast by pouring slip into a mould with an absorbent surface (eg plaster of paris), and then pouring out the surplus, leaving the raw article to be removed from the mould. Slip cast ware is usually lighter than that produced by other methods.

Sliver

In spinning, the rope of soft fibres ready to be fed forward to the spinning process. In cotton production it is pronounced to rhyme with 'fiver'; in woollen production with 'flivver'.

Skatie

A skateboard (AS).

Skirret

See Vegetables.

Slur and blur

A method of semi-articulate nasal singing that results in phrases such as 'Arm dreamin uvva wy Crizma'.

SMIDSY

The bane of the motorcyclist: 'Sorry, Mate, I Didn't See You'.

Smudger

A 'street, or beach, photographer' (who developed the pictures on site; the title reflects the quality of the pictures). 'On the smudge' – working as a smudger.

Snafu

Situation Normal, All Fouled Up.

Snakefruit

See Edible fruits.

Snake oil

Generic name for any loudly-trumpeted panacea of doubtful benefit.

Snood

See Fashion.

Snubbers, Gabriel

Type of shock-absorber used on some early motor cars. Happily, the firm of Gabriel also made motor horns.

Socialism

See Political -isms.

Socks

See Fashion.

Sorb apple

See Edible fruits.

Sound recording

One of the drivers of development of what was first called the phonograph was not entertainment but the needs of the office; for a dictating machine. In 1877, Thomas Edison devised a means of recording sound by capturing the vibrations of a stylus through its action on a rotating cylinder of tinfoil. When the same stylus was caused to vibrate in the track it had made, some semblance of the recorded sound emerged. Tainter and Bell's Graphophone (1886) was an improvement on Edison's machine, as it used a cylinder of cardboard coated with wax, which proved more biddable than Edison's tinfoil. Edison returned to the charge two years later with a cylinder entirely of wax, so that the surface could be shaved to erase a recording, and another etched in its place. By now, it was beginning to become clear that the principles had some place in entertainment, and Emil Berliner's gramophone of 1888 used a flat rotating disc on whose surface sound could be recorded in a spiral groove, modulated first by its varying depth; later by side-to-side movements. More robust than that in a cylinder, the groove in the disc could unaided move the reproducing stylus; moreover, it was easier to reproduce discs (by pressing) than cylinders. The 'gramophone record' was here to stay. Discs early standardised at 78 rpm; the late 40s saw the emergence of the LP (long play – 33rpm) and the EP (extended play – 45rpm), the latter ready for the emerging 'pop' industry. Reel-to-reel tape as a domestic medium never really caught on, but the tape cassette emerged in the early 70s and became a rival to the disc – as long as nobody wanted to find something on the tape in a hurry. Most of that technology is now in the past, with the development of the CD, and computer techniques for capturing and processing sound.

Sorghum
See **Edible grasses**.

Soursop
See **Edible fruits**.

Soy; Soybean
See **Vegetables**.

SPAD, Spad
(Rail safety) Signal Passed at Danger.

Sparge
To sweep out air from a vacuum tube in manufacture (by filling with nitrogen) before pumping down.

Sparrers
Very early in the morning (from sparrow's fart).

Spats
See **Fashion**.

Speech Day
A School's annual prize-giving day, usually marked by the guest speaker (often an Old Boy – or Girl – made good) asking the Head to grant the pupils a half-holiday amid cheers.

Spencer
See **Fashion**.

Spharistike
The original name for lawn tennis, as opposed to real, or royal, tennis.

Spinach
See **Vegetables**.

Spindle
See **Fashion**.

Spinning
The operation of turning fibres of one sort or another into a yarn suitable for weaving. Natural fibres (cotton, flax, wool) have a minute structure that enables them to provide a very strong yarn when they are properly twisted together, and the art of spinning lies in drawing out and twisting the fibres so as to provide strength and uniformity. (Preparation is all-important, and preparing the yarn by cleaning, combing and carding must be carried out before spinning begins.) Early spinning was achieved by hand using a drop spindle twirled with great dexterity; part of this process was mechanised when the spinning wheel was introduced: C14 in Europe; earlier in India. Both these processes are often demonstrated at craft fairs, where the meaning of

'home-spun' is made clear. Early attempts at mechanising spinning emerged in the 1760s with Hargreaves's Spinning Jenny (named after his wife) and Arkwright's Water Frame, so-called because it was powered by a water wheel. The Jenny alternated the actions of spinning the yarns and then winding them on to bobbins, a process that was later magnified and perfected in the enormous mule-spinning machines that could handle upwards of 500 yarns at a time. Arkwright's method developed into continuous ring-spinning machines in the latter half of C19.

Spiv

A (WW2) dealer on the Black Market, said to be 'explained' as an acronym for Suspected Persons and Itinerant Vagrants, which hardly describes the life of a spiv.

Sponge luffa; Squashes, winter

See **Vegetables**.

Spool Axminster

A type of carpet where the tufts of various colours that make up the pattern for any given row of the carpet are cut from a corresponding spool carrying yarns of those colours wound upon it side by side in order. A set of *n* spools corresponds to the *n* rows in a pattern repeat. See **Gripper Axminster**.

Sprig

A finely modelled 'relief' taken from a mould and added to a clay surface – often seen on pieces of Wedgwood's Jasperware.

Stained-glass ceiling

See **Glass ceiling**.

Stalinism

See **Political -isms**.

Stalker

One who follows a victim all over the place, makes nuisance phone calls, sends endless letters and emails, and makes threats. Stalking in any or all of those manifestations seems to be a part of modern life. Stalkers have been identified as one of three types: *intimate partner stalkers* can't come to terms with the idea that a relationship has come to an end; *delusional stalkers* (often mentally unstable) believe that the victim is in love with them, or might come to love them given time; *vengeful stalkers* seek revenge for some (often imaginary) slight.

Stamps

Useless (RN Slang).

Standard

Something whose misused maintenance leads to dullness, such as a High Street with shops from the same chains in whichever town you are, hospital wards with numbers instead of names, measurements presented in unfamiliar units ... the list is endless.

Star fruit

See **Edible fruits**.

Star Wars

Not the science fiction films made by George Lucas, but America's Strategic Defense Initiative (SDI). Announced in 1983 by then US President Ronald Reagan, SDI was an ambitious plan to create a network of space satellites and ground installations able to use laser-guided missiles to intercept and shoot down any missiles launched at the USA. It has been scaled back again and again and is still not operational in its much simpler, ground-based-only form.

Stickybeak

Nosy parker (AS).

Stirrup pump

A hand-operated water pump that came to the fore for small-scale fire-fighting in WW2, whose body is placed in a bucket of water, and is kept firm by placing the foot on the stirrup.

Stir-up Sunday

The last Sunday after Trinity; it originally took its name from the opening of the collect: 'Stir up, we beseech thee O Lord, the wills of they faithful people' but by a happy coincidence it was a convenient day, falling somewhere between 24 May and 27 June, for making Christmas puddings.

Stockholm syndrome

Where the victim comes to sympathise with the bully, or the hostage with the captors.

Stole

See **Fashion**.

Stone scrapers

See **Fashion**.

Stones, The

The Caledonian Market; see **Bartholomew Fair**.

Stoneware
A hard, opaque pottery, fired at a high temperature.

Stotious
The quality of being drunk (Scottish).

Strawberry
See **Edible fruits**.

Street Users
PC term for tramps, dossers, rough sleepers, homeless people.

Stuffer
In carpet weaving, a thread woven into the backing to give the cloth strength and weight.

Stunt up (v)
Description of process used to prepare faked photographs *eg* the *Daily Mirror*'s Iraqi prisoner abuse pictures.

Sturm und Drang
German (= storm and stress) artistic movement of the late C18, founded in literature, but influencing other arts as well; it soon gave way to romanticism.

Sug (v)
Selling under the guise (of doing a survey).

Sugar cane
See **Edible grasses**.

Sultana
See **Edible fruits**.

Sundial
A means of measuring the passage of time whereby the shadow of a rod or pointer (gnomon), as cast by the Sun, falls on a dial calibrated with the hours of the day. The main disadvantages of this timepiece are that it is impotent without sun, and that as the day lengthens and shortens according to the season of the year, so do the hours as measured. The earliest sundials known date from Egypt in C8 BCE. The latest may be the analemmatic sundial, as set up in the market square at Ely, Cambridgeshire, where the on-stander acts as the gnomon; the analemma is a graduated scale shaped in a figure of eight that indicates the daily declination of the sun.

Sunnies
Sunglasses (AS).

Summer Time

Advancing the clock one hour on GMT in order to make fuller use of the hours of daylight without having to change one's lifestyle. In the UK, Summer Time was introduced by a 1916 Act of Parliament, and then by the Summer Time Acts 1922–25 which laid down that Summer Time begins when the clocks are moved forward by one hour at 0200 (GMT) on the day after the third Saturday in April, but if that Sunday happens to be Easter Day (as in 1965, 1976, 1981, 1990 and 1992) Summer Time will start a week earlier. Statutorily, Summer Time should end by putting the clocks back by one hour at 0200 (BST) on the day after the first Saturday in October. Notwithstanding this, either start or finish date may be varied by the Home Secretary by means of an Order in Council. The earliest onset was on 18 February in 1968. Double Summer Time (GMT + 2 hours) was introduced from 1941 to 1945, and again in 1947.

Year	BST began	BST ended	DST began	DST ended
1935	14 April	6 October	•	•
1936	19 April	4 October	•	•
1937	18 April	3 October	•	•
1938	10 April	2 October	•	•
1939	16 April	19 November	•	•
1940	25 February	31 December		•
1941	1 January	31 December	4 May	10 August
1942	1 January	31 December	5 April	9 August
1943	1 January	31 December	4 April	15 August
1944	1 January	31 December	2 April	17 September
1945	1 January	7 October	2 April	15 July
1946	14 April	6 October	•	•
1947	16 March	2 November	13 April	10 August
1948	14 March	31 October	•	•
1949	3 April	30 October	•	•

From 1948 until 1952, and since 1961, the period of BST was extended, while the Act operated normally between 1953 and 1960.

Supercontinent
In prehistoric times, the two enormous landmasses now called Laurasia and Gondwanaland that together comprised virtually all the present-day continents of the world. Before that, there was a single even greater landmass called Pangaea or Pangea. Laurasia eventually divided to become Asia (without India), Europe, Greenland, and North America; Gondwanaland separated into Africa (and Madagascar), Antarctica, Australasia, India, and South America.

Superstition
An irrational belief originally perhaps founded on ignorance or fear, but now irrationally held by otherwise rational people.

Swag
Bushman's sleeping-bag; hence swagman (AS).

Swan upping
The annual marking of swans on the River Thames, London by nicking their beaks. Since C12, if not before, swans have been royal birds, and every swan in Britain belonged to the Crown. Occasionally a monarch would give a swan to an individual or organisation such as a monastery or guild, and such swans were then marked in a way which would identify the owner. The royal swans were easily identified since they were any unmarked bird. Nowadays the only surviving non-royal swan-owners on the River Thames are two City Livery Companies, the Dyers' Company (received its grant in 1473) and the Vintners' Company (received its grant between 1472 and 1483). Every July representatives of these Companies, together with the Royal Swanherd, row up the River Thames from Southwark to Henley, identifying and marking young swans.

Swandrops
It's commonly, but erroneously, believed that a blunderbuss was loaded with any old iron; in fact the weapon is far more refined than that, and fires specially manufactured pellets: swandrops.

Swede
See Vegetables.

Sweet potato
See Vegetables.

Sweetcorn
See Vegetables.

Syndicalism
See Political -isms.

Synecdoche

A figure of speech where a part stands for the whole: *eg* 50 head of cattle. To this must be added a number of modern sloppinesses: *eg* 'an en suite' for a bedroom with bathroom and lavatory attached, 'a microwave' for a cooking device wherein energy is imparted to the food by means of electromagnetic radiation of very short wavelength, and 'taking a sabbatical' not necessarily one year off in seven.

System X

A comprehensive family of local, tandem and trunk digital exchanges in development by The Plessey Company and STC in the early 80s, designed to be built into existing networks, or to provide new telecommunications systems. As well as speech, System X was to provide a common network for the integrated transmission of data and visual signals. It was in the forefront of technology, and its designers hoped to conquer the world. Unfortunately, the world wasn't ready for it, and its high hopes gradually faded.

Tail Art

The decoration of an aircraft's tail to indicate country of origin or of destination, or to assuage political correctness. See **Nose art**.

Tamarind; Tangelo; Tangerine

See **Edible fruits**.

Tapioca

See **Vegetables**.

TARDIS, The

Time And Relative Dimension(s) In Space; the TV perennial Doctor Who's method of travel (in both time and space); from outside, it looks like an old-fashioned British Police Box 'because the chameleon circuit that allows the TARDIS to appear in any form got jammed on earth in 1963'. Its exterior appearance belied the extensive appointments inside, which are said to include libraries, gardens, swimming pools, and a cricket pavilion, as well as two control rooms, a boot cupboard, a very large costume wardrobe and a pink Zero Room.

Taro

See **Vegetables**.

Tart's handbag

Bikers' name for the Yamaha Virago motorcycle.

Tax year

In the UK, the tax year starts on 6 April and ends on 5 April. In C12, the Church decided that the year should begin on Lady Day, March 25, and this was then the beginning of the tax year. When the Gregorian calendar came into effect in Britain in 1752, the end of that tax year was pushed forward by 11 days to 5 April 1753 to appease those who objected to paying (as they saw it) 365 days' worth of tax on 354 days' worth of income.

Tea and sugar

Weekly train across the Nullabor from Cook SA to Parkeston WA (and back) (AS).

Teenage

Relating to, denoting, or suitable for a teenager or people in their teens. A teenager comes into being on a thirteenth birthday, and ends as the nineteenth year gives way to the twentieth. As for the word, teenagers appeared in the 1940s, teeners having emerged in the 1890s.

Telegony

An outdated belief in the world of animal breeding that a mating with one sire could affect the outcome of a subsequent mating with another; the 'evidence' lay in Lord Morton's foal, born with faint stripes after its mother had previously mated with a quagga (a southern African member of the horse family with a brown coat and stripes on its head and shoulders, now extinct).

Temporary Work at Height Directive

Brussels-inspired nonsense wherefrom some suggest the use of scaffolding for mountain climbing.

Tenpenny nail

In the US, nails (for carpentry and the like) were described by the price for 100 pieces of a given size. 'So I tickled the tail of the great big whale with a tenpenny nail' sang the Bo'sun bold; somewhat dangerous, since the tenpenny nail is only 3 inches long.

Ten-pound Pom

One who spent £10 to emigrate to Australia when that country wished to enlarge its population after WW2.

Terracotta

An ancient unglazed form of red earthenware.

Textiles

Nudists' (Naturists') term for those wearing clothes.

Television

The eccentric Scotsman John Logie Baird is generally thought of as the inventor of television but, without wishing to dismiss him completely, we should remember that he was not alone in devising the proposals that he first turned into a demonstrable system, and that he persisted with developing his mechanically-based system when it was clear that the rival electronic system was set to provide a more satisfactory result. Baird saw that the essence of transmitting an image from one place to another was to scan it point by point, line by line, so that it became a series of signals whose strengths were proportional to the illuminations of the points they represented. This had been described in an enormously comprehensive 1841 patent by a fellow Scot Alexander Bain, who has since been dubbed 'the father of the fax machine'. Baird's machine scanned the image by means of a rotating disc (Nipkow's disc) bearing 30 lenses in a spiral configuration to produce a 30-line image, and reconstructed the image in the receiver with a similar disc which of course had to be synchronised with that in the transmitter. Moreover, the disc rotated only ten times a second; slow for transmitting a respectable image, but quite fast enough for anyone standing nearby. The BBC started test transmissions from its North London Studios at Alexandra Palace in 1936, alternating sessions of Baird signals with those from the competitive EMI system of 405 lines at 25 frames a second. Receiving sets were comparatively expensive, but the annoyance of those who had hitched themselves to the wrong system must have been somewhat mollified by the *schadenfreude* of all transmissions being stopped on 1 September 1939 'for the duration'. WW2 saw great leaps in techniques and understanding of radio transmission, and in the development of systems that would be useful to the post-war resumption of television, particularly high-frequency techniques, and cathode-ray tubes.

Thars

Shaggy-coated mountain goats that live on Table Mountain (over-looking Capetown, S Africa) and are said to upset its delicate ecosystem or fynbos.

Thatcherism

See **Political -isms**.

Thaumatrope

Often manipulated by a string, a card or disc spinning on one of its diameters, with an image on each side; when it is spun, the images appear to merge – thus a bird might be seen in its cage.

The Cross

1   In Australia, the Southern Cross.
2   On British railways, the terminus King's Cross.

Theomancy

See Fortune telling.

Therblig

A modified reversal of the surname of the American engineer Frank Bunker Gilbreth (1868–1924) who invented the term (which it must be said has a somewhat Swiftean appearance) in about 1919 to describe any of the types of action involved in carrying out a task, as a means of task analysis – time-and-motion study. Therbligs include: | Assemble | Disassemble | Find | Grasp | Inspect | Load/unload transport | Position | Release load | Rest (take a break) | Search | Select | Use | Wait (avoidable delay) | Wait (unavoidable delay).

Thermionic valve

((Vacuum) tube); an electronic device whose operation is dependent on its internal vacuum. Early tubes comprised a filament that emitted electrons, and an anode that attracted them. This arrangement of two electrodes constituted a diode, for current could flow from filament to anode, but not in the reverse direction. Diodes were long used for rectifying alternating current to produce direct current; in valve radios, the rectifier diode glows bright and hot to provide the DC needed to drive the rest of the valves. The next stage was the triode where a mesh, or grid, is placed round the filament with the purpose of stopping electrodes reaching the anode. The effect of a small potential on the grid would be multiplied in its effect on the anode, so that the triode became the usual means of amplifying signals (a small variable signal on the grid becoming a larger variable signal on the anode). Early computers were large and not very reliable because they contained thousands of valves; fortunately semiconductor devices (transistors) were invented at about the right time so that they and computers could develop hand in hand. It was later said that, if the thermionic valve had been invented *after* the transistor, it would have been hailed as a breakthrough.

Thessalonians

See Books of the Holy Bible.

Thong

See Fashion.

Three Holy Children

See **Books of the Holy Bible**.

Three-chord trick

So named by the emerging hordes of guitarists in the 50s, whereby most 'ordinary' tunes may be accompanied using three chords; those based on the tonic, sub-dominant and dominant, otherwise the keynote and its fourth and fifth.

Tights

See **Fashion**.

Time

In East Anglian parlance, we append the word 'time' to reinforce our meaning: 'I'll come round yours about quarter past five time'.

Time ball

Knowing the 'exact' time at sea is necessary for fixing one's position. Armed with a sextant, and a chronometer set to the time at the home port, the navigator can work out the position of the vessel. Chronometers of the necessary accuracy were developed from the end of C18, but how to fix the time at one's home port? To avoid ships' timekeepers having to go ashore, a visible time signal was needed, and the first was the 'time ball' which, set on high, drops at a known time each day. This device was proposed by Captain Robert Wauchope of the British Royal Navy in 1824. A manually operated device was first set up at the Royal Observatory, Greenwich in 1833. In due course, time balls were erected in London and in many ports and, in 1862, time balls in The Strand and Cornhill in London, and at the ports of Deal and Liverpool, were dropped by telegraph signals from Greenwich to inaugurate Greenwich Mean Time. In the United States, the Naval Observatory was set up at Washington in 1845; one of first its tasks was to provide a national time service, and it first sent out automatic time signals in 1880.

Time machine

A (hypothetical) device enabling its user to travel forwards or backwards in time. Means have to be incorporated to ensure that, when arriving at some time other than 'real time', the presence of the device does not affect what, at that point, has or has not already happened. This is why time travel often takes place in a different dimension.

Time signal

The 'Six Pips' from Greenwich were first broadcast by the BBC on 5 February 1924, so that 'listeners-in' could use the wireless to adjust their clocks. In 1972 the sequence changed from six short pips to five short pips and one longer pip. The last Greenwich pips were broadcast on 4 June 1990, and the BBC began receiving its signal from atomic clocks, satellite systems, and the 60kHz radio transmitter at Rugby. There is a story concerning the Paris time signal regularly broadcast from the Eiffel Tower; it appears that the Director of the Paris Observatory was making an official visit to the Tower and enquired about the time-signal transmission: 'Tell me, how do you set your clocks?' 'Why, M le Directeur, we telephone your Observatory twice a day and check our clocks against yours. But I've often wondered ... how do you maintain *your* time standards?' After some reddening discussion, it emerged that the Observatory set its clocks by listening to the time signals transmitted from the Eiffel Tower.

Time signature

In music, a character or characters set after the key signature to indicate how many beats of what sort per bar; thus '3/4 time' indicates a waltz ... but does not tell you how fast the piece is supposed to go.

Time value

In music, the relative lengths of notes. Convention provides a series where each type of note lasts half as long as the one before it; the breve (rarely used nowadays); it is the sign whereby an organist triturates the audience with a 64-foot stop); the semibreve (US: whole note); the minim (US: half note); the crotchet (US: quarter note); the quaver (US: eighth note); the semiquaver (US: sixteenth note); the demisemiquaver (US: thirtysecond note); and so on. As an indication of the length of each note, a 'normal' piece of music might be marked at 70–80 crotchets per minute.

Times table

An abhorrent expression meaning 'multiplication table'.

Timing

The art of optimising the effect of a number of actions; the secret of ... er ... comedy.

Timothy

See Books of the Holy Bible.

Tin

A metal with some interesting properties: it emits a strange crackling when a lump of it is manipulated – the 'cry of tin'. It also exists in two allotropic forms and turns from the metallic form to a grey powder when the temperature drops – 'tin pest' – two reported victims of this are the mid-C19 crumbling of organ pipes at a church in Zeitz, and the disintegration of buttons on military uniforms; this occurred in the Crimean War and led, not surprisingly, to some alarm and despondency.

Tinny
Can of beer (AS).

Titus
See Books of the Holy Bible.

Tobit
See Books of the Holy Bible.

Toga
See Fashion.

Tomatillo
See Vegetables.

Tomato
See Vegetables.

Tontine
A form of annuity shared by several subscribers, in which the shares of those who die are added to the holdings of the survivors till the last survivor inherits all; the name is derived from its progenitor, the C18 Neapolitan banker Lorenzo Tonti.

Toshers
Sewer totters of Victorian London.

Totalitarianism
See Political -isms.

Tracksuit
See Fashion.

Trafalgar Day
21 October 1805, when the British Fleet under Admiral Lord Nelson on HMS *Victory* defeated the French off Cape Trafalgar (between Cape Càdiz and Gibraltar), using the daring tactic of attacking the French longitudinally rather than broadside, thus establishing British naval supremacy for over a century. Nelson (*b*1758) was mortally wounded in the battle.

Trainers or sneakers
See Fashion.

Trotskyism
See Political -isms.

Truffle
See **Vegetables**.

Tucker
Food (AS).

Tulipomania
The mania for the purchase of tulip-bulbs that spread from Holland in C17 and was at its greatest height in the mid-1630s.

Tunic
See **Fashion**.

Turban
See **Fashion**.

Turnip
See **Vegetables**.

Tussie mussie
A loving message with the use of flowers.

Tuxedo
See **Fashion**.

Type
A shaped block of metal of accurate dimensions from whose inked face an image of a letter, or other 'sort' is printed. Type (which is unfortunately largely a thing of the past) was cast in typemetal (with an admixture of antimony so that it would expand on cooling to give a sharp image) by hand, or by mechanical means such as the Linotype machine (oft seen in newspaper offices) or the Monotype caster (in the printer's workshop). A set of casting moulds, to make a fo(u)nt of type of a given size was originally made from a set of punches prepared by a punch-cutter, surely one of the most skilled craftsmen ever in any field. So many aspects of printing that were virtually unchanged for centuries are now scarcely remembered, except in words such as 'leading' (to rhyme with shedding) the amount of space between lines of printing, 'pica' (to rhyme with biker) denoting 12-point type, the point measurement itself (properly 72 to 0.9966 inches); upper and lower case (in which the pieces of type were presented to the compositor), and of course the names of many of the typefaces devised by, and remembering, typographical giants such as Baskerville, Bembo, Caslon, Garamond, Gill, Johnston, Plantin and the rest.

Tuyères

The nozzles through which air is injected into a blast furnace; they are located at the boshes, *ie* the widest part of the body of the furnace.

Twinset

See Fashion.

Twirly

Bus Drivers' facetious name for old people with bus passes who, hoping it's time for their concessionary fares, step forward waving their wallets saying: 'Am I twirly?'

Tynwald Day

5 July, Old Midsummer Day, when the proclamation of laws takes place on the Isle of Man, the only place where this old Icelandic custom survives. Officials are sworn in and the laws are proclaimed in English and Manx. All present are charged not to 'quarrel, brawl, or make any disturbance on pain of death'.

Typhoid Mary

A cook and carrier of typhoid disease who infected 47 people with the disease in 1907.

UFO trousers

Those furnished with numerous ribbons that fly out when the wearer twirls at the dance.

Ugli fruit

See Edible fruits.

Umami

The Japanese recognise five basic food tastes: sweet, sour, bitter, salty and umami (tastiness), the latter imparted by MSG (monosodium glutamate).

Umbrella

Arrangement for shading the user from sun or rain; also Bumbershoot, Brolly and Gamp; Dockers' Umbrella: the old Liverpool overhead railway.

Uniform

See Fashion.

United Nations

Formed in 1945 by 50 countries as a 'general organization for the maintenance of international peace and security'. Today practically every sovereign nation in the world is a member. Often more effective on paper than in the real world, it at least provides an ideal to which to work, and is infinitely better than a void.

Unlucky days

According to a record from the time of King Henry VI ...'These under-written be the perilous days, for to take any sickness in, or to be hurt in, or to be wedded in, or to take any journey upon, or to begin any work on, that he would well speed. The number of these days be in the year 32; they be these: January – 1, 2, 4, 5, 7, 10, 15; February – 6, 7, 18; March – 1, 6, 8; April – 6, 11; May – 5, 6, 7; June – 7, 15; July – 5, 19; August – 15, 19; September – 6, 7; October – 6; November – 15, 16; December – 15, 16, 17.' The days seem to have lost their influences after the Reformation, and survived only in a general superstition that fishermen do not set sail, and (especially in the north) that couples are not wed, on a Friday. Analysis of the above list shows that, for a year starting on a Tuesday, there are nine unlucky Fridays, and only four of every other day except Wednesday, of which there are three. Readers may draw their own conclusions.

Unmovic

United Nations Monitoring, Verification and Inspection Committee.

Up-Helly; Up-helly-aa

A fire festival in Lerwick, capital of Shetland, held at the end of January.

Urban streetwear

See Fashion.

USB

Universal serial bus; a high-speed industry-standard connection system for computer peripherals.

Useless Parliament

That summoned by Charles I on 8 June 1625; it spent all its time quar-relling with the king, and was dissolved on 12 August; for other Parlia-ments, see Parliament.

Ute

Utility vehicle (AS) (pron to rhyme with newt).

Utilitarianism

See Political -isms.

Utopianism

See Political -isms.

UYB

Up Your Bum, said to be an arcane correspondence reference used by exasperated Civil Servants.

Vacuum

To achieve a low pressure within an envelope, it is 'pumped down' in two stages. First, the device (or a bank of devices) to be evacuated is connected to a rotary backing pump to reduce the pressure in the system to about one millimetre of mercury; then the low-pressure line is connected to a diffusion pump (using mercury or silicone oil) to reduce the pressure to the desired level. At some time during the process, the system is sparged with nitrogen to reduce the amount of atmospheric oxygen present; the last process before sealing the envelope is to fire the getter to remove any remaining oxygen by combination. The envelope is usually glass, and is sealed by heating the glass connecting tube, which obligingly collapses under atmospheric pressure. The process was developed for manufacturing thermionic valves, television camera tubes, vacuum switches, light bulbs and the like.

VariTyper

This typewriter was originally invented by J B Hammond in 1881, fell into obscurity, and was revived by Ralph C Coxhead in the early 30s, emerging as 'VariTyper, the Office Composing Machine'. The typeface was carried on a semicircular strip, which rotated about the centre of its circle. When the desired character had been positioned, a hammer struck the paper from the rear, pushing it against a carbon ribbon; the image of the character was thus transferred from the ribbon to the paper. In the hands of a patient and skilled operator, it was possible to produce complex (*eg* mathematical) setting, but one error could render the whole sheet useless. The last VariTypers were produced by Addressograph-Multigraph to support their small offset machines, but the whole technology is now in the past.

Verge escapement

By the middle of C14 – perhaps earlier – there were several weight-driven striking clocks in Europe (at Milan and Rouen for example). Their escapement was a *crown wheel*, controlled by *pallets* on a vertical shaft, or *verge*. The verge oscillates about its vertical axis, and the pallets alternately engage with and release the teeth on the crown wheel, allowing it to turn half a tooth at a time. The oscillation of the verge is governed by a *foliot*: an arm with adjustable weights rotating this way and that in a horizontal plane. If the arbor (axle) of the crown (escape) wheel is vertical, the verge may be governed by a (short) pendulum, though the resemblance to the later pendulum whose length regulates the clock with some accuracy is purely coincidental, since the mechanism can be made to go faster by increasing the driving force, or decreasing the weight of the pendulum 'bob'.

VIPER

Vehicle Industry Policy and European Regulation; a steering group on pedestrian-friendly, low-emission vehicles.

VOIP

Voice Over Internet Protocol, enabling you to make phone calls via the Internet.

Volapuk

Artificial language based on English, French, German and Latin devised in 1880 by Johann Schleyer (1831–1912).

Wade-Giles

Named after the two scholars who created it in mid-C19, this was a system providing a phonetic transliteration (not a translation) of Chinese. Developed for specialists in Chinese and phoneticists, it was spectacularly unhelpful to ordinary people struggling to translate Chinese. For example, Wade-Giles led generations of English-speaking people to think that the Chinese capital is pronounced Peking, whereas it always has been pronounced Beijing. Since 1979 Wade-Giles has been replaced by Pinyin (*qv*), which is why Peking has become Beijing.

Walking the Wheat

A Monmouthshire custom – called 'corn showing' in adjacent Herefordshire – when farmers and bailiffs walked their fields on the afternoon of Easter Day, carrying plum-cake to eat and cider to drink to the success of their crops. The practice seems to have died out at the end of C19.

Walpurgis Night

(Ger = *Walpurgisnacht*) The eve of the feast day of the C8 abbess St Walpurga (1 May) when, according to German folklore, witches hold a Sabbath on high ground, particularly the Brocken in the Harz Mountains. Hence the significance of Spectre of the Brocken, seen when one's image is projected on to a screen of fog by the sun at one's back.

Watch

On board ship the 24-hour day is divided into seven watches: five of them are 4 hours long and the remaining two are 2 hours long. The latter two 'dog watches' are from 16.00 (4pm) to 18.00 (6pm) and 18.00 (6pm) to 20.00 (8pm), with the purpose that those who regularly alternate duty on watch automatically get a daily change of hours and at a time when an evening meal is available. The word dog is here a corruption of 'dodge'. The object of these is to prevent the same men always being on duty during the same hours each day.

On British naval ships, the bells (*qv*) that sound the time every half-hour – culminating in eight bells rung in paired chimes at 4 o'clock, 8 o'clock, and 12 o'clock, am and pm – follow the watch system, though with one bell (rather than five) at 18.30 (6.30pm). This practice derives from the time of the naval mutiny at the Nore (1797) when the signal for the mutiny was the five bells at the beginning of the last (second) dogwatch. Five bells at that time of day has since then never been sounded on a British naval ship.

By derivation, however, a watch was a period of duty during the night, when a person had to stay awake (Old English *waeccan* = both 'watch' and '(stay) awake'). The ancient Hebrews had three watches during the night; the ancient Greeks and Romans four, or in some cities five. In England, the night Watch (an early form of nocturnal police force) was introduced in C13, under the control of local Watch Committees, that the streets might be safer at night. 'Period drama' may suggest that the Watch went round crying: 'Three [or whatever] in the morning, and all's well' but it seems unlikely that those sleeping easy in their beds would have put up with such behaviour for long.

Water chestnut; Watercress
See Vegetables.

Waterloo Day
Commemorating 18 June 1815, when British and Prussian forces under Wellington and Blücher routed the French under Napoleon near the Belgian town of Waterloo in Brabant province south of Brussels; on this day, a small flag is presented to the British Monarch as rent for the Strathfield Saye Estate. By cruel fate, the London terminus of the Channel Tunnel Rail Link is at Waterloo.

Watermelon
See Edible fruits.

Well dressing
The custom of decorating village wells with intricate designs or scenes made with flowers is an annual tradition unique to Derbyshire, England. The custom was originally known as Well Flowering, and it consists of decorating wells, or springs – at one time the only source of local water – with botanical material in order to give thanks for their beneficence (though there is a possibility that animal sacrifice once played a part in the custom when it was wholly serious). Nowadays, well dressing plays its part as a fund-raising attraction during the tourist season, lasting as it does from May to September. The decorations are carried on a wooden frame supporting a clay background into which moss, berries, flowers, petals and other botanical materials are pressed. Many themes are religious, though local scenes and commemorations are often chosen.

Wheats
See Edible grasses.

Whiffling
Action of a bird stalling in order to land.

White radish
See Vegetables.

Whitecurrant; Whortleberry
See Edible fruits.

Widdershins
To travel round in the opposite direction to the sun; counterclockwise; see deasil.

Wigs
See Fashion.

Wilton carpet
A type of carpet where the yarns of various colours that will form the pattern are drawn up by heddles from warp level to make the loops that form the pile; the loops may be cut (by withdrawing a 'needle' bearing a blade in the direction of the warp), or left uncut. In face-to-face Wilton, two carpets are woven by passing the tuft yarns between an upper and a lower backing, and cutting the two apart later in the process. The number of colours available for the pattern depends on the number of tuft yarns (frames) the structure of the woven material can accommodate; the more there are, the thicker the backing, for only one yarn is used at any given tuft location. Extra weight may be added to the backing by including stuffers (*qv*).

Wine bottles
Some sizes of larger bottles have names of their own; the initial figure indicates how many 750ml bottles the named size holds. *Bordeaux*: 2 Magnum, 3 Marie-Jean, 4 Double magnum, 6 Jeroboam, 8 Impériale; *Champagne*: 2 Magnum, 4 Jeroboam, 6 Rehoboam, 8 Methuselah, 12 Salmanazar, 16 Balthazar, 20 Nebuchadnezzar.

Wineberry
See Edible fruits.

Winged bean
See Vegetables.

Witches' Sabbath
A midnight-to-dawn meeting of witches, demons and hangers-on led by the coven (12 witches and a devil) held on All Hallows' Eve, Candlemas, Lammas, and Roodmas.

Wonky trolley column
Wherein a journalist writes in humorous fashion at great length about day-to-day trivia.

Wireless

A word logically derived from 'wireless telegraphy' as opposed to telegraphy which needed wires, which emerged in the 1830s. Wireless telegraphy developed into wireless telephony, and the device that enabled receiving signals became a wireless (set). In the US, the word 'radio' (derived from the idea of radiating signals) entered the language quite early on; in Britain, it didn't become common currency until after WW2, particularly for domestic sets. The earliest equipment for domestic reception (in the 1920s) was the crystal set, in essence a tuning circuit of adjustable inductance and capacitance, a rectifier (the tip of a wire, or 'cat's whisker' adjusted against a crystal of galena (lead sulphate)), and a pair of headphones. The difficulty of finding and keeping a signal of often dismal quality was subsumed in the joy of getting the equipment to work at all. As the public became more interested in the entertainment possibilities, so wireless (or radio) sets developed until it was unusual for a family not to have at least one. Portability was a problem with early sets; an outdoor aerial was usually necessary to ensure adequate reception, and people that for one reason or another didn't have a mains-powered set had to maintain a wet (2-volt) accumulator to heat the valve filaments, a 9-volt grid-bias battery and a 120-volt HT battery. The development of the transistor enabled the production of truly portable sets with batteries of manageable size at the end of the 1950s, and radios have been getting smaller and smaller ever since.

Wood Family, The
(Theatrical slang) Empty seats.

Wood, Mr
Policeman's truncheon.

Woollen clothes
See Fashion.

Woollen tunic
A feature of Classical Greece's Fashion; see Fashion.

Woolly monkey
South American genus (*Lagothrix*) of three species, with strong jaws and teeth; eats fruit, nuts and leaves.

Woolly rhinoceros
Pleistocene extinct genus *Coelodonta*, with two horns, living in Eurasia and North Africa.

Woolly spider monkey
The rare arboreal vegetarian *Brachyteles arachnoides* found in SE Brazil.

Wonderful Parliament
See Merciless Parliament.

Work hardening
Technique of strengthening a metal workpiece by cold hammering, much used by manufacturers of armour and weapons.

Workhouse
A chiefly British institution wherein paupers might dwell, though the segregation of the sexes (separating husband and wife) and the conditions therein made them places of dread.

Worms, Diet of
Worms is a SW German city on the Rhine, C5 capital of Burgundy. The well-known Diet (assembly) of Worms was an ecclesiastical assembly held in 1521, at which Martin Luther refused to recant those views others saw as heretical.

Wormwood
Some 200 species of the aromatic herb genus *Artemesia* (Compositae) chiefly *A. absinthium*, principle of the drink absinthe.

Worsted
A woollen yarn spun by a method that gives a hard twist suitable for weaving higher-quality fabrics.

Wrenning Day
St Stephen's Day, 26 December, used to be so called, because it was a local custom among villagers to stone a wren to death on that day in commemoration of the stoning of St Stephen.

WTS
'Whale-tumour story', former name for an urban legend.

Wycombe chair
High Wycombe is well known for the Windsor chair dating back to 1750. The distinguishing feature of this chair is the way it is put together – the legs are fitted into the underside of the seat so as to form a stool, then the back is socketed in separately from the upper side of the seat. Typically made of beech wood.

X-height

A typographical measurement; in a given alphabet, the height of the lower-case x.

Xerography

A process for making photocopies, and printing computer output with a laser printer. An electrostatic image is formed as electrically charged areas on a selenium-coated plate or cylinder. The surface is then dusted with a resinous toner, which sticks selectively to the charged areas, the image then being transferred to a sheet of paper and fixed by heating. The uncommon element selenium was discovered by JJ Berzelius in 1817. Its peculiar property of varying electrical resistance according to the amount of light falling on it was discovered in 1873, but it took the genius of Chester Carlson to see that that property might be harnessed as a means of recording an image, a result he achieved in 1938. He approached a score of US industrial concerns for development support, but without success. At last, in 1944, the Battelle Memorial Institute agreed to finance development, and progress was such that the Haloid Company of Rochester, NY, became involved in manufacturing the Xerox Model A, first demonstrated in 1948. It weighed more than a quarter of a ton, and required a sequence of fourteen operations to produce a copy, making it no match for the wet copying processes then current. However, Haloid saw the potential of the process, and bought the patent rights in 1950. In 1956, the Rank Organisation in Great Britain took over marketing, forming Rank–Xerox and offering what by then had become the only slightly less cumbersome 1385 equipment, which was sold to enable printers who were experimenting with the small offset litho presses then becoming available (Gestelith, Multilith, Rotaprint), to produce cheap printing plates for these machines. See Rank–Xerox.

XXXX

'Four X', brand of Queensland beer (AS).

Yam; Yard-long bean

See Vegetables.

Yarn

Fibres twisted together so as to increase their length and strength in a process known as spinning (*qv*). The tighter the yarn is twisted, the stronger it will become, and thickness can be increased by plying. By varying the twist, size and effect along the length of the yarn; fancy and novelty yarns can be produced, such as bouclé, knop and slub.

Yarn

See **Fashion**.

Yellowberry

See **Edible fruits**.

Yewy, chuck a

Make a U-turn in traffic (AS).

Yonks

A long period of time, supposedly derived from components of Years, mONths, and weeKS.

Yorkshire Day

1 August, marking the Battle of Minden (*qv*) in 1759 when British and Prussian forces defeated the French. Soldiers including those of the 51st Foot, the King's Own Yorkshire Light Infantry (which became the 2nd Battalion the Light Infantry in 1968) picked white roses from the battlefield in memory of the fallen. Celebrations include the Yorkshire 'Declaration of Integrity' being read throughout the three Ridings.

Ysbyty

Welsh = hospital; watch out for news items stating that so-and-so was taken to the Ysbyty Hospital.

Yuppie

Young Upwardly-Mobile Professional; Young Urban Professional: a successful and ambitious young person, in a professional job with a high income and a fashionable lifestyle; by their red Porsches shalt thou know them. 'Yuppie' encouraged an endless list of such acronyms such as Dink (dual income, no kids) and Dinky (dual income, no kids – yet).

Yuquilla

See **Vegetables**.

Zack

Sixpence (5 cents) (AS).

Zodiacal characteristics

The following characteristics are claimed for those born under the associated zodiacal signs:

Aries aggressive, competitive, dominant, impatient, noisy
Taurus amicable, loyal, reliable, self-motivated
Gemini dilettante, loquacious, straightforward
Cancer caring, considerate, easy to get on with, reliable
Leo attention-seeking, creative, popular
Virgo helpful, organised, quiet, self-effacing
Libra charming, eloquent, equable, good teamworker, sociable
Scorpio considerate, disciplined, hard-working, intense, secretive, strong-willed
Sagittarius disorganised, forgetful, generous, good-humored, gregarious, messy
Capricorn ambitious, cynical, persevering
Aquarius ingenious, organising, stubborn, unpredictable
Pisces creative, imaginative, inspirational, thoughtful.

Zoëtrope

A hollow cylinder pivoted so that it can rotate on a stand, with slits parallel to its axis. A strip of paper with a series of images is placed inside the cylinder so that the pictures may be viewed through the slits. An appearance of the images in motion may thus be obtained when the cylinder is rotated.

Zouave

A French soldier.

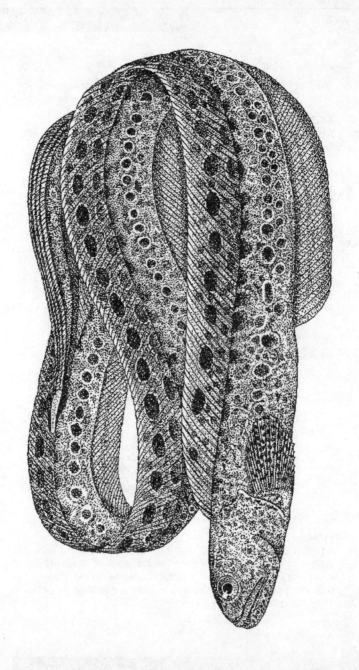

Part 2 The tables
Living things

Classification hierarchy

The taxonomies have been developed and refined since Carolus Linnaeus, or Carl von Linné (1707–78), the Swedish naturalist and physician published his *Systema Naturae* in 1737. Here is an exhaustive list, showing the standard suffixes at various levels.

Animals		Plants	
Kingdom		Kingdom	
Subkingdom			
Phylum		Division	*-phyta*
Subphylum		Subdivision	*-phytina*
Superclass			
Class		Class	*-opsida*
Subclass		Subclass	*-idea*
Infraclass			
Cohort			
Superorder			
Order		Order	*-ales*
Suborder		Suborder	*-ineae*
Superfamily	*-oidea*		
Family	*-idea*	Family	*-aceae*
Subfamily	*-inae*	Subfamily	*-oideae*
Tribe	*-ini*	Tribe	*-eae*
		Subtribe	*-inae*
Genus		Genus	
Subgenus		Subgenus	
Species		Section	
Subspecies		Subsection	
		Series	
		Subseries	
		Species	
		Subspecies	
		Variety	
		Subvariety	
		Form	
		Subform	

World fauna and flora

Key

Areas of the world

a Asia
b Africa
c Arctic
e Europe
i Indian sub-continent
n North America
o Australasia
s South America
t Antarctic

Flora

p plants
t trees
u useful plants

Fauna

b birds
d domestic animals
f fish, shellfish etc
m mammals
r reptiles and amphibians

The listings

em ape, Barbary
em badger
em bear, brown
em bison, European
em boar, European wild
em boar, north African wild
em chamois
em deer, fallow
em deer, red
em deer, roe
em dolphin
em elk
em ermine
em fox
em fox, Arctic
em gazelle, Mhorr
em genet
em glutton
em goat, Bezoar
em hamster
em hare, common
em hedgehog

em ibex, alpine
em ibex, Pyrennean
em jackal
em lemming
em lynx
em lynx, pardine
em marmot
em marten, pine
em mouflon
em narwhal
em otter
em polecat
em porcupine
em porpoise
em rabbit, wild
em reindeer
em seal
em seal, grey
em seal, harp
em squirrel
em squirrel, ground
em walrus

em wildcat
em wolf

ep agave
ep broom
ep cowberry
ep edelweiss
ep horseradish
ep oleander
ep pasqueflower
ep sunflower
ep thyme

et ash
et aspen
et beech
et birch
et chestnut
et chestnut, horse
et cypress
et elm
et fir
et hornbeam
et juniper
et larch
et lemon tree
et lilac
et oak, common
et oak, cork
et oak, durmast
et olive
et olive tree
et orange tree
et palm, date
et pine, Aleppo
et pine, Austrian
et pine, common
et pine, stone
et pine, Swiss
et spruce

et spruce, Serbian
et willow

am altai wapiti
am antelope, Beatrix
am argali
am badger, Amur
am bear, brown
am bear, Himalayan black
am bear, Japanese black
am beaver
am bison, European
am boar, European wild
am bobac
am caracal or Persian lynx
am cat, Indian civet
am cheetah
am deer sika
am deer, musk
am deer, Père David's
am deer, red
am deer, Siberian red
am deer, water
am elk
am fox, silver
am gazelle, goitered
am glutton
am goat, Bezoar
am goral
am hamster, golden
am hare, common
am horse, Przewalski's
am hyena, striped
am ibex, Siberian
am ichneumon
am jackal
am jerboa, big-eared
am kiang
am koulan
am lemming

am leopard, clouded
am leopard, Persian
am lynx
am lynx, Persian or caracul
am macaque, Japanese
am manul
am maral
am markhor
am narwhal
am nilgai
am onager
am otter
am ounce
am panda
am pika
am polecat, tiger
am reindeer
am rhinoceros, Indian
am sable
am saiga
am sea lion
am seal, Baikal hair
am seal, bearded
am seal, fur
am seal, grey
am sheep, red
am squirrel, flying
am squirrel, ground
am tahr
am takin
am tiger, Manchurian
am walrus
am wolf
am yak

ap bamboo
ap edelweiss
ap rhododendron
ap rose, dog
ap saxaul

ap tragacanth

at alder
at beech
at bilberry
at birch
at buckthorn, alder
at camphor
at cedar
at cedar of Lebanon
at cypress
at fig tree
at gingko
at larch
at maple
at mulberry
at oak
at olive tree
at palm, date
at pine, Scotch
at pine, Siberian stone
at spruce
at walnut

ad buffalo, cart
ad camel, Bactrian
ad camel, dromedary
ad cart-horse, west Russian
ad cattle, Buryat
ad cattle, Sind zebu
ad cattle, zebu
ad chicken
ad dog, sledge or husky
ad donkey, Muscat
ad elephant
ad goat, angora
ad goose
ad hog
ad horse, Arab
ad husky, or sledge dog

ad ox
ad pig, masked
ad reindeer
ad sheep, fat-tail
ad sheep, Karakul
ad sheep, pack
ad yak

au barley
au durra
au fig
au millet
au orange
au plum
au rice
au rose
au soya-bean
au sunflower
au tea
au wheat

im antelope, Beatrix
im ape, Celebes black
im argali
im babirusa
im badger, Amur
im bear, Himalayan black
im bear, Japanese black
im bobac
im buck, black
im buffalo, water
im caracal or Persian lynx
im cat, Hartwick's civet
im cat, Indian civet
im cheetah
im deer, Père David's
im deer, Prince Alfred's
im deer, Sika
im deer, water
im deer, musk

im elephant, Indian
im fox, flying
im gaur
im gazelle, goitred
im gibbon
im glutton
im goat, Bezoar
im goral
im hamster, golden
im horse, Przewalski's
im hyena, striped
im ibex, Siberian
im ichneumon
im jackal
im jerboa, big-eared
im jerboa, Egyptian
im kiang
im koulan
im kouprey
im leopard
im leopard, clouded
im leopard, Persian
im lion, Indian
im loris, slow
im lynx
im lynx, Persian or caracal
im macaque, Japanese
im manul
im maral
im markhor
im monkey, bonnet
im monkey, proboscis
im nilgai
im onager
im orang-utan
im ounce
im panda
im pangolin
im pika

im polecat, tiger
im porcupine, Malayan
im rhinoceros, Indian
im rhinoceros, Sumatran
im saiga
im sambar
im seal, Baikal hair
im sheep, red
im squirrel, Finlay's
im squirrel, flying
im tahr
im takin
im tapir, Malay
im tarsier
im thamin
im tiger, Bengal
im tiger, Manchurian
im yak

ip bamboo
ip camphor
ip cane, sugar
ip edelweiss
ip fern, palm
ip fern, tree
ip pandanus
ip pitcher plant
ip rafflesia

ap rattan
ap rhododendron
ap saxaul
ap tragacanth

at banyan
at beech
at cedar
at cedar of Lebanon
at cypress
at fig

at ginkgo
at maple
at mulberry
at oak
at olive
at palm, coconut
at palm, date
at palm, sago
at pine, scotch
at teak
at walnut

id buffalo, water
id camel, bactrian
id camel, dromedary
id cattle, Buryat
id cattle, zebu
id cattle, zebu nellore
id cattle, zebu, Sind
id donkey
id donkey, muscat
id elephant
id goat, angora
id horse, Arab
id pig, masked
id sheep, fat-tail
id sheep, karakul
id sheep, pack
id yak

it orange
it palm, coconut
it palm, date
it plum

iu barley
iu cane, sugar
iu cotton
iu durra
iu fig
iu jute

iu millet
iu palm, sago
iu poppy, opium
iu rice
iu rose
iu soya
iu tobacco
iu wheat

bm aardvark
bm addax
bm antelope, roan
bm antelope, sable
bm aoudad
bm ape, Barbary
bm ass, Somali wild
bm baboon, Gelada
bm baboon, Hamadryas
bm bongo
bm bontebok
bm buffalo, Cape
bm buffalo, Congo
bm bushbuck
bm cheetah
bm chimpanzee
bm dog, Cape hunting
bm dolphin, bottle-nosed
bm duiker, common
bm duiker, yellow-backed
bm eland, giant
bm elephant, bush
bm elephant, forest
bm fennec
bm fossa
bm gazelle, dama
bm gazelle, Loder's
bm gazelle, mhorr
bm gazelle, Soemmering's
bm gerenuk
bm giraffe, Masai

bm giraffe, Nubian
bm gnu, blue
bm gorilla
bm guereza
bm hartebeest
bm hippopotamus
bm hippopotamus, pygmy
bm hyena, spotted
bm jackal, yellow
bm klipspringer
bm kudu, greater
bm lechwe
bm lemur, ring-tailed
bm lemur, ruffed
bm leopard
bm lion
bm lion, Barbary
bm monkey, Brazza's
bm monkey, Diana
bm monkey, hussar
bm okapi
bm oryx, beisa
bm oryx, sabre-horned
bm pig, bush
bm porcupine, crested
bm porpoise
bm rhinoceros, black
bm rhinoceros, white
bm seal, Cape
bm springbok
bm whale, killer
bm zebra, Grevy
bm zebra, Hartmann

bf coelacanth
bf flying fish
bf shark, blue
bf sting-ray

bp aloe

bp aloe dichtoma
bp bamboo
bp cardamom
bp lobelia, giant
bp pachypodium
bp palm, dwarf fan
bp palm, oil
bp papyrus
bp shrub, coffee
bp spurge
bp weltwitschia

bt acacia
bt baobab
bt cedar
bt dragon tree
bt fig, Indian
bt mangrove
bt palm, date
bt traveller's tree

bd buffalo, water
bd cattle, Bechuana
bd cattle, Damara
bd cattle, gala
bd cattle, Masai
bd cattle, Watusi
bd dog
bd donkey
bd dromedary
bd goat, Cameroons dwarf
bd goat, Nubian
bd horse, Berber
bd sheep, Dinka
bd sheep, Karakul
bd sheep, Somali

bu palm, coconut
bu banana
bu cane, sugar
bu cassava

bu cotton
bu durra
bu maize
bu palm, date
bu palm, oil
bu palm, wine
bu peanut
bu wheat

nm badger
nm bear, black
nm bear, grizzly
nm bear, Kodiak
nm bear, polar
nm beaver
nm bison
nm cacomistle
nm coyote
nm deer, mule
nm deer, Virginia
nm dog, prairie
nm ferret, black-footed
nm fox, Arctic
nm fox, grey
nm fox, silver
nm goat, Rocky Mountain
nm hare, polar
nm hutia
nm lemming
nm lion, sea
nm lynx
nm moose
nm narwhal
nm ocelot
nm opossum
nm opossum, water or yapok
nm otter
nm ox, musk
nm paca
nm porpoise

nm pronghorn
nm puma
nm rabbit, jack
nm raccoon
nm reindeer
nm seal
nm seal, fur
nm seal, harp
nm seal, hooded
nm sheep, bighorn
nm sheep, Dall's
nm skunk, spotted
nm skunk, striped
nm solenodon
nm squirrel, grey
nm tamandua
nm tamarin, Geoffroy's
nm tapir, Baird's
nm walrus
nm wapiti
nm whale, Greenland
nm whale, sperm
nm wolf, timber
nm wolverine
nm yapok or water opossum

nf angelfish, blue
nf barracuda
nf cod
nf fish, flying
nf grunt, yellow
nf mackerel
nf marlin, blue
nf pigfish
nf salmon
nf sea-devil, black
nf shark, tiger

np agave
np bellflower

np cactus, cereus
np cactus, opuntia
np grass, cotton
np palmetto, cabbage
np pisang
np poppy, Iceland
np saguaro cactus

nt banana
nt birch
nt coconut
nt cypress, bald
nt fir, Douglas
nt fir, white
nt forest, mangrove
nt grapefruit
nt hickory
nt horn, tree
nt lemon
nt magnolia
nt maple, sugar
nt oak, red
nt orange
nt palm, Californian fan
nt palm, royal
nt sequoia
nt sequoia, giant
nt tree, Joshua
nt tree, tulip
nt willow, Arctic

nu barley
nu beet, sugar
nu cacao
nu cane, sugar
nu coffee
nu cotton
nu flax
nu maize
nu rice

nu rice, wild
nu sisal
nu sugar beet
nu sugar cane
nu tobacco
nu wheat, spring
nu wheat, winter

nd cattle
nd sheep
nd pigs
nd reindeer
nd fox
nd bear, polar
nd whale

sm ai or three-toed sloth
sm ant-eater, giant
sm armadillo, nine-banded
sm armadillo, three-banded
sm bear, spectacled
sm cavy, Patagonian
sm coati
sm deer, marsh
sm deer, pampas
sm deer, pudu
sm dog, Azara's
sm dog, round ears
sm dolphin, bottle nosed
sm guanaco
sm guemul
sm hog, water
sm jaguar
sm leopard, sea
sm manatee
sm marmoset
sm monkey, grey woolly
sm monkey, squirrel
sm monkey, uakari
sm monkey, red howling

sm nutria
sm opossum, Azara's
sm peccary, collared
sm peccary, white lipped
sm porcupine, woolly tree
sm puma
sm puma, Patagonian
sm sea lion, South American
sm sloth, three-toed or ai
sm sloth, two-toed or unau
sm solenodon
sm tapir, Baird's
sm tapir, mountain
sm tapir, South American,
northern type.
sm unau or two-toed sloth
sm vicuña
sm whale, humpback
sm whale, pygmy sperm
sm wolf, manned
sm yapok or water opossum

sp agave
sp bromelia, giant
sp cereus
sp opuntia
sp orchid, cattleya
sp orchid, Odontaglossum
sp palmetto, cabbage
sp philodendron

st fern, tree
st nut, brazil
st palm, assai
st palm, carnauba
st palm, coconut
st palm, royal
st palm, wax
st pine, araucaria
st tree, cacao

st tree, calabash
st tree, Hevea rubber

sd cattle, Creole
sd cimarrones
sd dog, Indian
sd llama
sd zebu

st banana
st palm, araucaria
st tomato tree
st tree, cacoa

su beans, lima
su cassava
su coffee
su cotton
su cotton, Peruvian
su leaves, coca
su maize
su mate
su peanuts
su pineapple
su potatoes
su seed, annatto
su tobacco

om bandicoot
om bat, fold-lipped
om cachalot
om dasyure
om devil, Tasmanian
om dingo
om dolphin, bottle nosed
om dolphin, Risso's
om dugong
om echidna
om fox, flying
om kangaroo, great grey
om kangaroo, red

om kangaroo, tree
om koala
om leopard, sea
om lion, sea
om mouse, honey
om phalanger, great flying
om phalanger, squirrel flying
om pig, papua wild
om platypus
om porpoise
om rabbit, wild
om wallaroo, black
om wolf, Tasmanian
om wombat

op acacia
op banana
op conifer
op eucalyptus
op kauri
op palm, coconut
op palm, fan
op palm, nipa
op palm, sago
op pandanus
op pine, araucaria
op spinifex
op tree, bottle
op tree, fern
op tree, grass

ou beans, soya
ou beet, sugar
ou cotton
ou oats
ou oranges
ou potatoes
ou rye
ou tobacco
ou wheat

cm bear, brown	**cm** whale
cm bear, polar	**cm** wolf
cm elk	
cm ermine	**tm** cachalot
cm fox, Arctic	**tm** dolphin, Risso's
cm fox, silver	**tm** elephant, sea
cm musk-ox hunt	**tm** leopard, sea
cm musk-ox reserve	**tm** seal, crab eater
cm sable	**tm** seal, ross
cm sea lion, Northern	**tm** seal, Weddell's
cm seal, bearded	**tm** whale, blue
cm seal, common	**tm** whale, finback
cm seal, fur	**tm** whale, humpback
cm seal, harp	**tm** whale, killer
cm seal, hooded	**tm** whale, pygmy sperm
cm walrus	

Outline of evolution

See table opposite.

The animal kingdom

Human evolutionary species (see table on pages 145–7)

Humans and our ancestral species are known as hominids, of the family *Hominidae*. Some time between 5 and 10 million years ago, the ancestors of humans and those of our closest relatives – chimpanzees – diverged. But the fossil record is scant, and the full picture of human evolution is not yet clear. This means that while distinct hominid species have been identified, often co-existing with others or overlapping in time, their exact relationship to each other and to the line which led to modern humans is not always known. The picture is complicated by the fact that while some species, such as Neanderthals, have been known for a long time, other species are being identified all the time, so that the state of knowledge of human evolution is constantly changing.

The time of the split between humans and living apes used to be thought to have occurred 15 to 20 million years ago, or even up to 30 or 40 million years ago. Some apes occurring within that time period, such

Outline of evolution

Dominant plants	Era	Period	Dominant animals	Estimated age in years
Very simple plants including bacteria	Archeozoic		Evolution of unicellular animals	Not less than 1,500 million
Blue-green algae	Proterozoic		Evolution of invertebrates	
Algae	Paleozoic	Cambrian Ordovician Silurian	Invertebrates – Sea Scorpions, Molluscs, Trilobites	320 million
Ancient spore plants		Devonian	Fishes	
Giant spore plants and seed ferns		Carboniferous Permian	Amphibians	
Gymnosperms	Mesozoic	Triassic Jurassic Cretaceous	Reptiles	120 million
Flowering plants	Cenozoic	Eocene Oligocene Miocene Pliocene	Mammals	60 million
		Pleistocene Recent	Man	

as *Ramapithecus*, used to be considered as hominids, and possible ancestors of humans. Later fossil finds indicated that *Ramapithecus* was more
closely related to the orang-utan, and new biochemical evidence indicated that the last common ancestor of hominids and apes occurred
between 5 and 10 million years ago, and probably in the lower end of that
range (Lewin 1987). *Ramapithecus* therefore is no longer considered a
hominid.

The field of science which studies the human fossil record is known as
paleoanthropology. It is the intersection of the disciplines of paleon-
tology (the study of ancient lifeforms) and anthropology (the study of
humans).

Hominid species

The species here are listed roughly in order of appearance in the fossil
record (note that this ordering is not meant to represent an evolutionary
sequence), except that the robust australopithecines are kept together.
Each name consists of a genus name (e.g. *Australopithecus*, *Homo*) which
is always capitalized, and a species name (e.g. *africanus*, *erectus*) which is
always in lower case. Within the text, genus names are often omitted for
brevity. Each species has a type specimen which was used to define it.

More recently, a number of fragmentary fossils discovered between
1997 and 2001, and dating from 5.2 to 5.8 million years old, have been
assigned first to a new subspecies, *Ardipithecus ramidus kadabba* (Haile-
Selassie 2001), and then later as a new species, *Ardipithecus kadabba*
(Haile-Selassie *et al*. 2004). One of these fossils is a toe bone belonging to
a bipedal creature, but is a few hundred thousand years younger than the
rest of the fossils and so its identification with *kadabba* is not as firm as
the other fossils.

Australopithecus afarensis

A. afarensis existed between 3.9 and 3.0 million years ago. *Afarensis* had
an apelike face with a low forehead, a bony ridge over the eyes, a flat
nose, and no chin. They had protruding jaws with large back teeth. Cranial
capacity varied from about 375 to 550 cc. The skull is similar to that of a
chimpanzee, except for the more humanlike teeth. The canine teeth are
much smaller than those of modern apes, but larger and more pointed
than those of humans, and shape of the jaw is between the rectangular
shape of apes and the parabolic shape of humans. However their pelvis
and leg bones far more closely resemble those of modern man, and leave
no doubt that they were bipedal (although adapted to walking rather
than running (Leakey 1994)). Their bones show that they were physically
very strong. Females were substantially smaller than males, a condition

Human evolutionary species

Species	Commonly called	Dated to	Fossils first discovered in	Identified as separate species in	Bipedal?	Average brain size in cubic centimetres	Comments
Sahelanthropus tchadensis	—	6–7 million years ago, not long after hominids and chimpanzees diverged	Chad, Central Africa	2002	?	Small, 350 cc	Some apelike features (small brain) but other hominid features (small canine teeth, brow ridges)
Orrorin tugenensis	—	c6 million years ago	Kenya	2001	Probably	?	Possibly adapted to both tree climbing and walking on 2 feet
Ardipithecus ramidus	—	5.8 million years ago	Ethiopia	1994	Probably	?	Height about 122 cm (4'0")
Australopithecus anamensis	—	4.2–3.9 million years ago	Kenya	1995	Probably	?	Primitive skull features but more modern body, especially arms
Australopithecus afarensis	Gracile australopithecines	3.9–3 million years ago	Ethiopia, Tanzania	1978	Yes, but probably not able to run	375–550 cc	Skull very like a chimpanzee's: apelike face with low forehead, eyebrow ridges, flat nose, no chin, protruding jaws. But, teeth and jaw shape half way between humans' and chimps'. About 107 cm (3'6") to 152 cm (5'0") tall. The specimen called Lucy and the footprints left in Laetoli belong to this probable human ancestor
Kenyanthropus platyops	—	3.5 million years ago	Kenya	2001	Yes	?	possible direct human ancestor

Species	Commonly called	Dated to	Fossils first discovered in	Identified as separate species in	Bipedal?	Average brain size in cubic centimetres	Comments
Australopithecus africanus	Gracile australopithecines	3–2 million years ago	Southern Africa	1925	Yes	420–500 cc (just bigger than chimpanzees)	Slightly bigger than *afarensis*. Teeth and jaws now more like modern humans than like apes
Australopithecus garhi	—	2.5 million years ago	Ethiopia	April 1999	Yes	?	Teeth bigger than previous australopithecines
Australopithecus aethiopicus	Robust australopithecines	2.6–2.3 million years ago	Ethiopia	1967	Yes	410 cc	Massive face, jaws and teeth. Mixture of older and newer features. Possibly ancestor of next 2 species. Robust australopithecines were probably not direct human ancestors
Australopithecus robustus	Robust australopithecines	2–1.5 million years ago	East Africa	1960s	Yes	about 530 cc	No forehead, large brow ridges, flat or dished face. Massive back teeth suggest its diet required a lot of chewing
Australopithecus boisei	Robust australopithecines	2.1–1.1 million years ago	East Africa	1960s	Yes	about 530 cc	Even bigger back teeth
Homo habilis	Handy man	2.4–1.5 million years ago	East Africa	1964	Yes	500–800 cc	Possibly had rudimentary speech. Made crude stone tools. About 127 cm (5'0") tall and weighed about 45 kg (100 lb)
Homo georgicus	—	c.1.8 million years ago	Georgia, E Europe	2002	Yes	600–680 cc	About 1.5 m (4'11") tall. Intermediate between H habilis and H erectus

Species	Common name	Period	Location	Discovered	Bipedal	Brain size	Description
Homo erectus	Upright man	1.8 million – 300,000 years ago	Africa, Asia, Europe	1894	yes	750–1225 cc.	Robust skeletons implying great strength. Protruding face with thick brow ridges and no chin. Made a limited range of stone tools, particularly hand-axes, and used fire. First hominid species to live in many areas of the planet
Homo antecessor	—	780,000 years ago	Western Europe	1977	yes	?	Possibly a type of *H erectus*
Homo sapiens (archaic) / Homo heidelbergensis	Wise man / Heidelberg man	500,000–200,000 years ago	Africa, Europe			1200	A range of skeletons with varied features of both *Homo erectus* and modern man
Homo sapiens neanderthalensis	Neanderthals	230,000–30,000 years ago	Europe, Middle East	1957	yes	Large, 1450 cc	Short, stocky, with heavy bones and strong muscles, adapted to living during the last Ice Age. Bump at the back of the skull, protruding faces. Made many, often sophisticated, tools. Carried out first known deliberate burials. Brain larger than modern man partly because of large skull size
Homo sapiens sapiens (modern man)	Modern man	From about 120,000 years ago			yes	Large, 1350 cc	Instead of adapting to the environment, adapts the environment to the point of destruction

known as sexual dimorphism. Height varied between about 107 cm (3'6")
and 152 cm (5'0"). The finger and toe bones are curved and proportionally
longer than in humans, but the hands are similar to humans in most other
details (Johanson and Edey 1981). Most scientists consider this evidence
that *afarensis* was still partially adapted to climbing in trees, others
consider it evolutionary baggage.

Kenyanthropus platyops

This species was named in 2001 from a partial skull found in Kenya with
an unusual mixture of features (Leakey *et al.* 2001). It is aged about 3.5
million years old. The size of the skull is similar to *A. afarensis* and *A.
africanus*, and has a large, flat face and small teeth.

Australopithecus africanus

A. africanus existed between 3 and 2 million years ago. It is similar to
afarensis, and was also bipedal, but body size was slightly greater. Brain
size may also have been slightly larger, ranging between 420 and 500 cc.
This is a little larger than chimp brains (despite a similar body size), but
still not advanced in the areas necessary for speech. The back teeth were a
little bigger than in *afarensis*. Although the teeth and jaws of *africanus* are
much larger than those of humans, they are far more similar to human
teeth than to those of apes (Johanson and Edey 1981). The shape of the
jaw is now fully parabolic, like that of humans, and the size of the canine
teeth is further reduced compared to *afarensis*.

Australopithecus garhi

This species was named in April 1999 (Asfaw *et al.* 1999). It is known from
a partial skull. The skull differs from previous *australopithecine* species in
the combination of its features, notably the extremely large size of its
teeth, especially the rear ones, and a primitive skull morphology. Some
nearby skeletal remains may belong to the same species. They show a
humanlike ratio of the humerus and femur, but an apelike ratio of the
lower and upper arm (Groves 1999; Culotta 1999).

Australopithecus afarensis and *africanus*, and the other species above,
are known as *gracile australopithecines*, because of their relatively lighter
build, especially in the skull and teeth. (Gracile means 'slender', and in
paleoanthropology is used as an antonym to 'robust'.) Despite this, they
were still more robust than modern humans.

Australopithecus aethiopicus

A. aethiopicus existed between 2.6 and 2.3 million years ago. This species
is known from one major specimen, the Black Skull discovered by Alan
Walker, and a few other minor specimens which may belong to the same

species. It may be an ancestor of *robustus* and *boisei*, but it has a baffling mixture of primitive and advanced traits. The brain size is very small, at 410 cc, and parts of the skull, particularly the hind portions, are very primitive, most resembling *afarensis*. Other characteristics, like the massiveness of the face, jaws and single tooth found, and the largest sagittal crest in any known hominid, are more reminiscent of *A. boisei* (Leakey and Lewin 1992). (A sagittal crest is a bony ridge on top of the skull to which chewing muscles attach.)

Australopithecus robustus

A. robustus had a body similar to that of *africanus*, but a larger and more robust skull and teeth. It existed between 2 and 1.5 million years ago.

The massive face is flat or dished, with no forehead and large brow ridges. It has relatively small front teeth, but massive grinding teeth in a large lower jaw. Most specimens have sagittal crests. Its diet would have been mostly coarse, tough food that needed a lot of chewing. The average brain size is about 530 cc. Bones excavated with *robustus* skeletons indicate that they may have been used as digging tools.

Animal names: male / female / young

Animal	Female	Male	Young
Alligator	cow	bull	hatchling
Ant	queen, princess, worker	prince, drone	antling
Antelope	cow	bull	calf, fawn, kid, yearling
Ass	jenny	jack, jackass	foal
Badger	sow	boar	cub
Bear	sow, she-bear	boar, he-bear	cub
Beasts of prey	—	—	whelp
Beaver	—	—	kit, kitten, pup
Bee	queen, queen-bee, worker	drone	larva
Bird	hen	cock	chick, fledgling, hatchling, nestling
Bison	cow	bull	calf
Boar (wild)	sow	boar	boarlet, farrow, piglet, shoat
Bobcat	—	—	kitten or cub
Camel	cow	bull	calf, colt

Animal	Female	Male	Young
Canary	hen	cock	chick
Caribou	cow, doe	bull, stag, hart	calf, fawn
Cat	tabby, queen	tom, gib	kit, kitling, kitten, pussy
Cattle	cow	bull	bullcalf (male), calf, heifer (female), stot, yearling
Chicken	hen, partlet	cock, stag	chick, chicken, cockerel (m), poult, pullet (f), rooster (m)
Cicada	—	—	nymph
Cod			codling, sprat
Cougar	lioness, she-cougar	lion, tom	cub, kitten
Coyote	bitch	dog	whelp, pup
Crocodile		bull	hatchling
Deer	doe, hind	buck, stag	fawn
Dog	bitch	dog	whelp or puppy
Dolphin	cow	bull	calf, pup
Donkey	jack	jenny	foal
Dove	hen	cock	pigeon, squab
Dragonfly	—	—	nymph
Duck	duck	drake	duckling, flapper
Eagle	—	—	eaglet, fledgling
Eel	—	—	elver, fry
Elephant	cow	bull	calf
Elephant seal	—	—	weaner
Elk	cow	bull	calf
Ferret	hob	jill	kit
Fish	—	—	fry, fingerling, minnow, spawn
Fly	—	—	grub, maggot
Fox	vixen	dog-fox, reynard, stag	cub
Frog	—	—	polliwog, froglet, tadpole
Giraffe	cow	bull	calf
Goat	nannie-goat, nanny, she-goat	billie-goat, billy, buck, he-goat	kid
Goose	dame, goose	gander, stag	gosling

Gorilla	—	—	infant
Grouse	—	—	cheeper, chick, poult, squealer
Guinea fowl	—	—	keet
Guinea pig	sow	boar	pup
Hare	jill	jack	leveret
Hawk	tiercel	hen	eyas
Hedgehog	sow	boar	pup, piglet
Hippopotamus	cow	bull	calf
Horse	dam, mare	rig, sire, stallion, stud	colt (m), filly (f), foal, hogget, hog-colt, stag, stat, yearling, youngster
Impala	ewe	ram	—
Kangaroo	doe	buck	joey
Leopard	leopardess	leopard	cub
Lion	lioness, she-lion	lion, tom	cub, lionet, whelp
Lobster	hen	cock	—
Louse	—	—	nit
Mackerel	—	—	blinker, spike, tinker
Manatee	cow	bull	calf
Mink	sow	boar	kit or cub
Monkey	—	—	infant, suckling, yearling
Moose	cow	bull	calf
Mosquito	—	—	flapper, larva, nymph, wiggler, wriggler
Mouse	doe	buck	kitten, pup
Mule	hinny, more, she-ass,	jack, jackass, stallion	foal
Muskrat	—	—	kit
Opossum	jack	jill	joey
Ostrich	hen	cock	chick
Otter	bitch	dog	cub, kitten, pup, whelp
Owl	jenny, howlet	—	howlet, owlet
Ox	beef, cow,	beef, bullock, ox, steer,	calf, stot,
Oyster	—	—	brood, set seed, spat
Partridge	hen	cock	cheeper
Peacock	hen, pea-hen	cock, peacock	chick, pea-chick
Pelican	—	—	chick, nestling

Animal	Female	Male	Young
Penguin	hen	cock	chick, fledgling
Pheasant	hen	cock	chick, poult
Pig	sow	boar	farrow, piglet, shoat, suckling
Pigeon	hen	cock	nestling, squab, squeaker
Platypus	—	—	puggle
Possum	jack	jill	joey
Quail	hen	cock	cheeper, chick, squealer
Rabbit	doe	buck	bunny, kit
Raccoon	sow	boar	cub, kit
Rat	doe	buck	kitten, pup
Reindeer	doe	buck	fawn
Rhinoceros	cow	bull	calf
Robin	hen	cock	—
Salmon	hen	jack	grilse, parr, smolt
Sea Lion	cow	bull	pup
Seal	cow	bull	bachelor, cub, pup, whelp
Shark	—	bull	pup
Sheep	dam, ewe	buck, ram, male-sheep, mutton	lamb, lambkin, shearling, yearling
Skunk	—	boar	kitten
Squirrel	doe	buck	pup
Swan	pen	cob	cygnet, flapper
Termite	queen	king	nymph
Tiger	tigeress	tiger	cub, whelp
Toad	—	—	tadpole
Trout	hen	jack	fry
Turkey	hen	gobbler, tom	chick, poult
Walrus	cow	bull	cub
Weasel	bitch, doe, jill	buck, dog, hob, jack	kit
Whale	cow	bull	calf
Wild fowl	—	—	flapper
Wolf	bitch	dog	cub, pup
Woodchuck	she-chuck	he-chuck	cub, kit
Zebra	mare	stallion	colt, foal

Animal homes

Animal	Home
Ant	hill / formicary
Badger	sett
Bat	roost / cave
Bear	den
Beaver	lodge
Bee	hive
Bird	nest
Bird of prey	eyrie
Cat	cattery / lair / den
Fox	earth / den / hole / lair
Hare	form
Lion	den
Mole	burrow / fortress / tunnel
Otter	holt / ledge
Rabbit	warren / burrow
Snake	nest
Spider	web
Squirrel	drey
Termite	mound
Tiger	lair
Wasp	nest / vespiary
Wolf	lair / den

Collective nouns for animals

The English language contains a huge number of collective nouns for animals. Many are colourful and unusual, often deriving from the tradition of giving poetic titles to beasts and birds which were hunted for food – a sounder of boar. Some are fanciful plays upon the characteristics of the animal – a prickle of porcupines. Others describe the animals' behaviour – an ambush of tigers. Yet others are lyrical – an exultation of larks. But despite the number and variety of collective nouns, few are compulsory, and many of the old-fashioned ones are seldom used nowadays. It is quite acceptable to use words such as 'herd' to describe groups of many animals, 'flock' for most birds, and 'school' for any species of fish or aquatic fishlike mammal.

Animals	Collective name
Antelopes	herd
Ants	colony
Apes	shrewdness
Asses/donkeys	herd / pace
Baboons	troop
Bacteria	culture
Badgers	cete
Bass	shoal
Bats	colony
Bears	sleuth / sloth
Beavers	colony / family
Bees	flight / grist / hive / swarm
Birds	dissimulation / flight / flock / volery
Bitterns	sedge / sege / siege
Boars	singular / sounder
Bucks	brace / clash / leash
Budgerigars	chatter
Buffalo	herd / obstinacy
Bullocks	drove
Butterflies	rabble / swarm
Buzzards	wake
Camels	flock
Caterpillars	army
Cats	clouder / clowder / clutter / glaring
Cats (house cats)	dout
Cats (kittens)	kindle / kendle / litter
Cats (wild cats)	destruction
Cattle	drove / herd
Chamois	herd
Chickens	brood / peep
Chicks	chattering / clutch
Chimpanzees	cartload
Chinchillas	herd
Choughs	chattering
Clams	bed
Cobras	quiver
Cockroaches	intrusion
Colts	rag / rake

Conies	bury
Coots	cover / covert
Cormorants	flight
Cows	kine
Coyotes	band
Cranes	sedge / siege
Crocodiles	congregation / float
Crows	murder
Cubs	litter
Curs	cowardice
Curlew	herd
Deer	herd
Dogs	pack / show
Dolphins	pod
Donkeys / asses	herd / pace
Doves	dule / flight
Dragons	flight / weyr
Ducks (on water)	paddling / badelyng
Ducks (in flight)	brace / team
Dunlins	flight
Eagles	aerie / convocation
Eels	swarm
Elephants	herd
Elk	gang
Emus	mob
Ferrets	business / fesnying
Finches	charm
Fish	draft / run / school / shoal
Flamingoes	stand
Flies	swarm
Foxes	leash / skulk
Frogs	army / colony
Geese	gaggle
Geese (in flight)	skein
Giraffes	tower
Gnats	cloud / horde / swarm
Goats	flock / herd / tribe / trip
Goldfinches	charm
Goldfish	troubling

Gorillas	band
Goslings	skein
Greyhounds	leash
Grouse	covey / pack
Gulls	colony
Guinea pigs	group
Hamsters	horde
Hares	down / husk
Hawks	cast / kettle
Hedgehogs	array
Hens	brood
Herons	hedge / sedge / sege
Herrings	army / shoal
Hippopotami	bloat
Hogs	drift / parcel
Hornets	nest
Horses	harras / herd / show / stable / stud / team
Hounds	cry / kennel / leash / mute / pack
Hummingbirds	charm
Hyenas	clan
Jays	band / party / scold
Jellyfish	smack
Kangaroos	mob / troop
Kittens	kindle
Lapwings	deceit / desert
Larks	ascension / exaltation / bevy
Leopards	leap / lepe
Lions	pride / troop
Llamas	herd
Locusts	cloud / plague / swarm
Magpies	tiding
Mallards	sord
Mares	stud
Martens	richesse / richness
Mice	mischief / nest
Minnows	steam
Moles	labour
Monkeys	troop
Moose	herd

Mules	barren / span
Nightingales	watch
Otters	romp
Owls	parliament
Oxen	drove / herd / team
Oxen (two)	yoke
Oysters	bed
Parrots	company
Partridges	covey
Peacocks	muster / ostentation / pride
Penguins	colony / huddle / parcel
Pheasants	nest
Pheasants (on the ground)	nide / nye
Pheasants (when flushed)	bouquet
Pigeons	flight / flock / kit
Pigs	litter
Piglets	farrow
Pilchards	shoal
Plovers	congregation / wing
Pochards	bunch / flight / knob / rush
Polecats	chine
Ponies	string
Porcupines	prickle
Porpoises	pod / school
Possum	passel
Poultry	run
Prairie dogs	coterie
Puppies	litter
Quails	bevy / covey
Rabbits	bury / colony
Rabbits (young)	nest / wrack
Racoons	gaze / nursery
Racehorses	string / stud
Rats	pack / swarm
Rattlesnakes	rhumba
Ravens	storytelling / unkindness
Reindeer	herd

Rhinoceri	crash
Roebucks	bevy
Rooks	building / clamour
Ruffs	hill
Salmon	run / school / shoal
Sardines	family
Seals	herd / pod
Sharks	school / shiver
Sheep	drove / flock / fold
Sheldrakes	dopping
Snakes	nest
Snipe	walk / wisp
Sparrows	host
Squirrels	dray / scurry
Starlings	murmuration
Storks	mustering
Swallows	flight
Swans	bevy / herd / lamentation
Swans (flying in a 'V')	wedge
Swifts	flock
Swine	doylt / drift / dryft / sounder
Teals	knob / spring
Tigers	ambush / streak
Toads	knob / knot
Trout	hover
Turkeys	flock / rafter
Turkeys (young)	brood
Turtles	bale
Turtledoves	pitying / dule
Vipers	nest
Vultures	colony
Wallabies	mob
Walruses	pod
Wasps	nest
Weasels	pack / sneak
Whales	gam / pod / school
Whelps	litter
Whiting	pod
Wigeon	company / flight / knob

Wildfowl	plump / sord / sute
Wolves	herd / pack / rout
Wombats	warren
Woodcock	fall
Woodpeckers	descent
Wrens	herd
Yaks	herd
Zebras	herd / zeal

The plant kingdom

Food

Vitamins and minerals

Vitamins are organic substances that are essential in the human diet. They are often called micronutrients because they are needed in very small quantities, as opposed to the macronutrient components which are needed in larger amounts in a healthy diet – carbohydrate, protein and fat. Each vitamin has its own special biochemical function in maintaining a healthy body, so if one is missing from the diet for a long time, a deficiency disease or illness inevitably occurs. If a vitamin is not totally missing, but is not being absorbed in sufficient amounts, there will also be signs of ill health. The word vitamin comes from a combination of 'vital' (to do with life) and 'amine', one of the building blocks of proteins, which is what they were originally thought to be. It is now known that they have a separate organic structure from proteins.

With a few exceptions – Vitamin D, which can be synthesised by the skin in sunlight, Vitamin K and Biotin, which can be made by bacteria in the colon, and Niacin (Vitamin B3), which can be made from the amino acid tryptophan – they have to be absorbed through food because most are not made in the body in sufficient quantities. Water-soluble vitamins are constantly being lost from the body through sweat, urination, etc. so must be regularly replaced. Fat-soluble vitamins are stored to some extent in the fatty parts of the liver, but there must be some fat present in the diet for them to be absorbed.

There are 13 accepted vitamins, some are still referred to by a letter of the alphabet, whereas others are known by the chemical name they were given when their structures were fully discovered. Synthetic – and expensive – vitamins are now available, though doctors continue to urge us to

Vitamins

Vitamin name	Other names	Soluble in	Essential jobs	Good for	Specific deficiency diseases	Discovered in / by	Good sources	RDA (US) Male	RDA (US) Female	RDA (UK / EU)	Toxic in excess?
Vitamin A	Retinol, Carotene	fat	protecting linings of many organs	skin, sight, growth	night-blindness	1912–15, Elmer V. McCollum and M. Davis	liver fish dairy products	900 mcg	700 mcg	800 mcg or 2664 iu	yes
Thiamin(e)	B1	water	processing proteins, fats and carbohydrates	nervous system, digestion	beri-beri	1912, Casimir Funk	wheatgerm bran bread nuts	1.2 mg	1.1 mg	1.4 mg	
Riboflavin	B2	water	processing amino acids and fats, metabolism of carbohydrates to energy	skin, sight	retarded growth	1926, D. T. Smith, E. G. Hendrick	many fruits, spinach, liver	1.3 mg	1.1 mg	1.6 mg	
Niacin	B3, Niacinamide, Nicotinic acid	water	metabolism of carbohydrates, processing alcohol		pellagra	1937, Conrad Elvehjem	bean peas nuts	16 mg	14 mg	18 mg	yes
Pantothenic acid	B5, Calcium pantothenate	water	metabolism of fats		—	1938	legumes soy	—	—	6 mg	possibly
Pyridozine	B6	water	creating essential compounds	skin	—	1934, Paul Gyorgy	fish bananas	1.3 mg	1.3 mg	2 mg	possibly
Biotin	B7	water	metabolism of protein, fats, and carbohydrates		—	1935	oatmeal yeast	—	—	150 mcg	

Folic acid	B9, Folacin, Folate	water	cell replication, DNA synthesis	pregnancy, growth	foetal deformities	1933, Lucy Wills	liver wheatgerm bran green leafy vegetables	200 mcg	200 mcg	200 mcg	
B12	Cynocobalam in, Cobalamin	water	helps nerve cell activity		—	1948–9, Karl Folkers and T. Alexander Todd	fish liver yeast	2.4 mcg	2.4 mcg	1 mcg	
Vitamin C	Ascorbic acid	water	anti-oxidant, formation of collagen	resisting infection, healthy blood	scurvy	1912, A. Holst and T. Froelich (1747, James Lind identified citrus fruits as preventing scurvy)	citrus fruits green vegetables tomatoes	90 mg	75 mg	60 mg	yes
Vitamin D	Calciforol	fat	absorption of calcium	healthy bones and teeth	rickets	1922, Edward Mellanby	dairy foods fish liver, sunlight	—	—	5 mcg	yes
E	Tocopherol	fat	antioxidant, protects cell membranes	skin, heart	—	1922, Herbert Evans and Katherine Bishop	wheatgerm vegetable oils wholegrains nuts leafy green vegetables	15 mg	15 mg	10 mg	possibly
K	Menadione	fat	blood coagulation	growth	—	1929, Henrik Dam	green, leafy vegetagbles	—	—	—	yes

Dietary minerals

Mineral	Essential for	Specific deficiency diseases	Food sources	RDA (US) Male	RDA (US) Female	RDA (EU PRI)	Toxic?	Comments
Calcium	healthy bones and teeth, nerve transmission, blood clotting	rickets, osteoporosis	green leafy vegetables, citrus fruits, sardines, soy, nuts, dairy products	1000 mg	1000 mg	700 mg	possibly	needs vitamin D for absorption
Chloride	fluid balance, formation of gastric juice	—	salt	—	—	—	mildly	
Chromium	regulates insulin and maintains normal blood sugar levels	adult diabetes	yeast, liver, meat, wholemeal breads, spices and herbs	—	—	—	yes	
Cobalt	Constituent of B12		milk, seafood, meat	—	—	—		
Copper	heart, arteries, blood vessels and blood, nerve transmission, metabolism	anaemia	fish, liver, oysters, green vegetables, meat	900 mcg	900 mcg	1.1 mg	unlikely	
Fluoride	teeth	tooth decay	seafood, tea	—	—	—	disputed	added to drinking water in the developed world, also added to toothpaste
Iodine	thyroid gland, metabolism	goitre, growth and mental growth retardation	fish, shellfish, yeast	150 mcg	150 mcg	130 mcg	yes, at 25 times RDA	World Health Organization makes prevention of iodine deficiency a priority. It is the greatest cause of preventable mental retardation. Most common in inland mountainous areas
Iron	healthy, functioning blood	anaemia	meat, liver, leafy green vegetables, legumes, nuts, seeds	8 mg	18 mg	9 mg	yes	only micronutrient which women require more of than men do. Most common micronutrient deficiency

Mineral	Function		Food sources				Toxic?	Notes
Magnesium	metabolism, bones, muscles, nervous system	—	avocados, bananas, beans and peas, nuts, seeds, whole grains	420 mg	320 mg	150–500 mg	possibly	
Manganese	formation of bones, blood clotting factors, connective tissues	—	blueberries, pineapple, raisins, spinach, tea	—	—	1–10 mg	unlikely	
Molybdenum	important for several enzymes	—	liver, kidney, milk, legumes, cereals	45 mcg	45 mcg	—	mildly	
Phosphorus	bones and teeth, growth, nerves, muscles, cellular repair	—	meat, fish, chicken, dairy products, wheatgerm	700 mg	700 mg	550 mg	possibly	
Potassium	body fluids, nerve transmission	—	avocados, bananas, potatoes, oranges	—	—	—	unlikely	helpful in correcting high blood pressure caused by too much sodium
Selenium	foetal development, antioxidant, protects against cancer and heart disease	—	all plant foods grown in selenium-rich soil, meat, eggs	55 mcg	55 mcg	55 mcg	in amounts greater than 600mcg to 750 mcg	known to be toxic before its nutritional benefits were discovered. Needed very much as a trace in the diet
Sodium	fluid balance, nerve function, muscles	—	salt	500 mg	500 mg	575–3500 mg	yes	excessive intake through processed foods very common in developed world, often contributing to high blood pressure
Zinc	enzyme function, metabolism of carbohydrates, protein and fats, functioning of insulin, genetic code, prostate gland	—	meat, fish, wholegrains, eggs	11 mg	8 mg	9.5 mg	yes	

Other minerals that are believed to have a biological function include: boron, cobalt, tin, vanadium, silicon and nickel absorb our vitamins through a balanced and healthy diet. The RDA (Recommended Dietary Allowance in the USA, Recommended Daily Amount in the UK / EU) of a vitamin is the minimum required by a healthy adult every day to prevent a serious deficiency disease. Children, pregnant women and elderly people would probably have different RDAs. An RDA is measured in International Units (iu), micrograms (mcg or μg) or milligrams (mg).

Dietary minerals are the inorganic micronutrients which are essential in small amounts in the human diet. Some are needed in such small quantities that they are often called trace elements. Often, very little is known about the specific function and purpose of minerals within the body, and in many cases there is no formal RDA. The European Union has issued some guidelines for RDAs in the form of Population Reference Intake for adult males.

Most important edible fruits
In technical botanical terms, a fruit is the mature or ripened ovary, containing a seed or seeds, of a flowering plant. This means that nuts, nutmeg, grains such as corn and wheat, peppers, cucumbers, tomatoes, gourds such as pumpkin, and many other foods are all technically fruits, although for purposes of cooking, none of these would normally be considered as such. In culinary terms, fruit is usually held to be any sweet and fleshy part of a plant. An example of this wider application of the word is rhubarb, whose only edible part is the leaf stem, but is generally thought to be a fruit when considered as food.

Temperate fruits
Most fruits which grow in temperate climate zones actually need a period of cold weather (chill) during the year in order for the flower buds to set. For this reason, they will not properly grow in countries with a warm winter. Some temperate fruits thrive in the wetter areas, others require dryer temperate zones and may also thrive in subtropical or Mediterranean conditions. The vast majority of temperate fruits come from trees or woody shrubs, with by far the greatest variety coming from the *Rosaceae* (plants of the Rose family). They are divided into groups, depending on how the fruit develops.

Rosaceae pome fruits
The pome is an enlarged, fleshy floral cup which acts as a container holding the ovary and seeds as a core in its centre:

Apple (*Malus pumila*)
Chokeberry (*Aronia melanocarpa*)

Haw, from hawthorn (*Crataegus laevigata*)
Medlar (*Mespilus germanica*)
Pear (*Pyrus communis*)
Quince (*Cydonia oblonga*)
Saskatoon or juneberry (*Amelanchier alnifolia*)
Sorb apple, from the service tree (*Sorbus domestica*)

Rosaceae stone fruits
There is a single, stony-seeming seed. The fruit is botanically called a drupe. All are of the genus *Prunus*:

Apricot (*P. armeniaca*)
Cherry, sweet, sour, and wild species (*P. avium, P. cerasus*)
Damson (*P. damascena*)
Greengage (*P. italica*)
Nectarine (*P. persica nectarina*)
Peach (*P. persica*)
Plum (*P. domestica*); when dried called prunes

Rosaceae 'false fruits'
Strawberry is a 'false fruit' because what we consider to be the fruit is actually just a container for the seeds. Apart from strawberries, the other *Rosaceae* 'false fruits' are aggregates of several ovaries within a single flower. They are all bramble fruits of the genus *Rubus* apart from the strawberry, and are known as false berries:

Blackberry or bramble (*R. fruticosus*)
Boysenberry (*R. ursinus*)
Cloudberry or salmonberry or yellowberry (*R. chamaemorus*)
Dewberry (*R. caesius*)
Loganberry (*R. loganobaccus*)
Raspberry (*R. idaeus*)
Wineberry (*R. phoenicolasius*)
Strawberry (*Fragaria ananassa*)

True berries
Small soft-seeded fruits which can be eaten whole. They are all members of the *Ericaceae* family, and are often hardy in the subarctic:

Bearberry (*Arctostaphylos uva-ursi*)
Bilberry or whortleberry (*Vaccinium myrtillus*)
Blueberry (*Vaccinium corymbosum*)
Cranberry (*Vaccinium oxycoccus*)
Crowberry (*Empetrum nigrum*)

Huckleberry (*Vaccinium membranaceum*)
Lingonberry (*Vaccinium vitis-idaea*)

Currants and gooseberries
The fruit is similar to a berry but contains extra plant material:

Barberry (*Berberis vulgaris*)
Blackcurrant (*Ribes nigrum*)
Elderberry (*Sambucus canadensis*)
Gooseberry (*Ribes grossularia*)
Nannyberry or sheepberry (*Viburnum lentago*)
Redcurrant (*Ribes rubrum*)
Sea-buckthorn or seaberry (*Hippophae rhamnoides*)
Whitecurrant (*Ribes rubrum cv*)

Other temperate fruits
American persimmon (*Diospyros virginiana*)
Buffaloberry (*Shepherdia argenta*)
Kiwi fruit or Chinese gooseberry (*Actinidia chinensis*), which also
   grows in semi-tropical areas
Pawpaw (*Asimina triloba*), not papaya (*Carica papaya*) also known as
   pawpaw
Persimmon or date-plum (*Diospyros kaki*)
Rhubarb (*Rheum rhaponticum*)

Mediterranean and subtropical fruits
Fruits of the genus Citrus

All have a hard outer skin or peel

Citron *(C. medica)*
Grapefruit *(C. paradisi)*
Shaddock *(C. maxima* or *C. decumana)*
Lime *(C. aurantifolia)*
Lemon *(C. limon)*
Mandarin or tangerine *(C. reticulata)*
Clementine *(C. reticulata)*
Satsuma *(C. reticulata)*
Orange *(C. sinensis)*
*Ugli fruit or minneola or tangelo *(C. tangelo)*
Pomelo *(C. maxima)*

* Discovered by Henry Q Levy on the Trout Hall Estate, Manchester,
Jamaica in the 1920s; alternative name for Ugli = Queensborough.

Other Mediterranean fruits

Cornelian cherry (*Cornus mas*)
Date (*Phoenix dactylifera*)
Fig (*Ficus carica*)
Grape (*Vitis vinifera*); currant, raisin or sultana when dried
Jujube (*Ziziphus zizyphus*)
Mulberry (*Morus nigra*)
Pomegranate (*Punica granatum*)

Other subtropical fruits

Cape gooseberry or physalis (*Physalis peruviana*)
Chinese jujube (*Ziziphus chinensis*)
Feijoa (*Feijoa sellowiana*)
Guava (*Psidium guajava*)
Indian jujube (*Ziziphus mauritiana*)
Kumquat (*Fortunella margarita*)
Longan (*Euphoria longan*)
Loquat or Japanese medlar (*Eriobotrya japonica*)
Lychee (*Litchi chinensis*)
Melon (*Cucumis melo*) – cantaloupe, honeydew and other muskmelons
Passion fruit (*Passiflora edulis*)
Pear melon (*Solanum muricatum*)
Watermelon (*Citrullus vulgaris*)

Fruits from cacti

These can also grow in dry temperate areas

Dragonfruit or pitaya (*Hylecereus guatemalensis*)
Prickly pear (*Opuntia ficus-indica*)
Saguaro (*Carnegiea gigantea*)

Tropical fruits

Tropical fruits grow on all types of plants.

Acerola (*Malpighia glabra*)
Akee (*Blighia sapida*)
Avocado (*Persea americana*)
Bael (*Aegle marmelos*)
Banana (*Musa acuminita*)
Breadfruit (*Artocarpus altilis*)
CamuCamu (*Myrciaria dubia*)

Carambola or star fruit (*Averrhoa carambola*)
Chempedak (*Artocarpus champeden*)
Coconut (*Cocos nucifera*)
Custard apple or cherimoya (*Annona cherimola*)
Duku (*Lansium domesticum*)
Durian (*Durio zibethinus*)
Galo (*Anacolosa frutescens*)
Guarana (*Paullinia cupana*)
Jackfruit or nangka (*Artocarpus heterophyllus*)
Langsat or longkong or duku (*Lansium domesticum*)
Mamoncillo or quenepa or genip (*Melicoccus bijugatus*)
Mango (*Mangifera indica*)
Mangosteen (*Garcinia mangostana*)
Monkey bread, from the baobab tree (*Adansonia digitata*)
Papaya or pawpaw (*Carica papaya*) – see other temperate fruits
Pineapple (*Ananas comosus*)
Poha (*Physalis peruviana*)
Rambutan (*Nephelium lappaceum*)
Rose apple or Malay apple (*Syzygium aquem*)
Salak or snakefruit (*Salacca edulis*)
Sapodilla or chiku (*Manilkara zapota*)
Soursop (*Annona muricata*)
Tamarind (*Tamarindus indica*)

Edible grasses

Edible grasses, or cereals, were the first plants to be cultivated by humans. It was a milestone in prehistory. Until then, people had been nomadic, following animals and plant growth in an annual round. But by cultivating and planting crops – and domesticating animals – our ancestors were able to settle down in one place. Instead of moving to where the food was, they brought the food sources near their homes. Farming village settlements grew into towns, which grew into cities, and into nation states. Staying all the time in one place enabled a phenomenal growth in consumerism. Now people didn't have to carry their worldly goods around with them all the time; arts, crafts and conspicuous consumption flourished – all because of humble little grasses. And, because the human body evolved before grains and dairy products were part of our diet, allergies to gluten (a protein found in cereals, especially in wheat), or to dairy foods, are extremely common.

The main grass crops are:

Corn or maize (*Zea mays*)
Sugar cane (*Saccharum officinarum*)
Sorghum (*Sorghun bicolor*)
Millet, common (*Panicum miliaceum*)
Millet, finger (*Eleusine coracana*)
Millet, pearl or bulrush (*Pennisetum glaucum*)
Rice (*Oryza sativa*)
Barley (*Hordeum distichum* and others)
Wheats (*Triticum aestivum* and others)
Rye (*Secale cereale*)

Grapes for wine

White wine grapes

Albariño
Aligoté
Arinto
Blanc Fumé
Bual
Chardonnay (Chard)
Chasselas
Chenin Blanc (Chenin Bl)
Clairette
Colombard
Fendant
Folle Blanche
Fumé Blanc (Fumé Bl)
Furmint
Gewürztraminer *alias* Traminer (Gewürz)
Grauburgunder
Grechetto or Greco
Grüner Veltliner
Italian Riesling
Kéknyelü
Kerner
Loureiro
Macabeo
Malvasia
Marsanna
Müller-Thurgau (Müller-T)
Muscadelle
Muscadet, *alias* Melon de Bourgogne
Muscat
Palomino *alias* Listan
Pedro Ximénez *alias* PX
Pinot Blanc (Pinot Bl)
Pinot Gris (Pinot Gr)
Pinot Noir (Pinot N)
Riesling (Ries)
Rülander
Sauvignon Blanc (Sauv Bl)
Scheurebe
Sémillon (Sém)
Sercial
Seyval Blanc (Seyval Bl)
Steen
Silvaner *alias* Sylvaner
Tokay
Traminer
Trebbiano
Ugni Blanc (Ugni Bl)
Verdejo
Verdelho
Verdicchio

Vermentino
Vernaccia
Viognier

Viura
Weissburgunder
Welschriesling

Red wine grapes

Aleatico
Baga
Barbera
Brunello
Cabernet Franc *alias* Bouchet
   (Cab F)
Cabernet Sauvignon (Cab S)
Cannonau
Carignan
Cinsaut
Dolcetto
Gamay
Gamay Beaujolais
Grenache *alias* Garnacha,
   Alicante, Cannonau
Grignolino
Kadarka *alias* Gamza
Kékfrankos
Lambrusco
Malbec *alias* Cot

Merlot
Montepulciano
Mourvèdre *alias* Mataro
Nebbiolo *alias* Spanna and
   Chiavennasca
Periquita
Petit Verdot
Pinot Noir (Pinot N)
Pinotage
Saint-Laurent
Sangiovese (or Sangioveto)
Saperavi
Spätburgunder
Syrah or Petite Sirah *alias*
   Shiraz
Tannat
Tempranillo
Touriga nacional
Zinfandel (Zin)

Vegetables

'Vegetable' is a vague and all-encompassing term. It includes all edible plants which do not obviously fit into any of the other, more clearly defined, food categories such as fruits, grains, herbs, nuts or spices. In general, we consider that any plant which we eat as part of a main course, not desert, is a vegetable. Unlike fruit, which has a specific botanical meaning (the ripened ovary of a plant), our veggies might be roots, leaves, stalks or even plants which technically belong in one of the other categories. The most obvious of these are fruits which are not sweet, and so are not usually thought of as 'fruit', such as tomatoes, cucumbers and pumpkins. Then common vegetables such as beans and peas are actually seeds, although when thinking about cooking and food categories, few people would lump them in with sunflower and sesame seeds.

In times of necessity people will eat practically every plant on the planet apart from those that are poisonous or indigestible. Unless there is need, however, people throughout the world mainly eat vegetables that are easy to grow and therefore cheap, highly nutritious and tasty, or those easy to pick. This list considers only the most common vegetables. Plants such as stinging nettles are not included; even though they grow profusely in the British countryside and their leaves are nutritious and – apparently – very tasty, the pain most of us would suffer in gathering the leaves means that hardly any of us consider them to be common veggies.

Vegetables can be grouped in several different ways. Colour may be one grouping, since vegetables of the same colour often contain similar vitamins and minerals. Perhaps one of the most obvious groupings is whether the part of the plant we eat is a tuber (potato, taro, yam), a leaf (cabbage, lettuce), a root (carrot, parsnip), a stem or shoot (asparagus, kohlrabi), a fruit (avocado, beans, cucumber, green pepper, pumpkin, tomato), etc. Another way, chosen here, is to group the plants by their botanical family. While this is straightforward in the case of vegetables such as cabbages, which have a wide variety all belonging to the same species, it can throw up some surprising and illuminating groupings such as turnip and cabbage being in the same family, or the pairings of potato and pepper, asparagus and onion.

Some temperate/Mediterranean vegetables

The Cabbage family (*Brassicaceae*)

Mostly temperate in origin
Cabbage (*Brassica oleracea*).
    Varieties: broccoflower, broccoli, Brussels sprouts, calabrese, cauli-flower, collard greens, kale, kohlrabi, savoy
Chinese leaf or Chinese cabbage or pe tsai (*Brassica pekinensis*)
Cress (*Lepidium sativum*)
Mustard greens (*Brassica juncea*)
Pak choi or bok choi (*Brassica chinensis*)
Rocket or arugula or rucola or roquette (*Eruca sativa*)
Sea kale (*Crambe maritima*)
Watercress (*Nasturtium officinale*)

and some usually thought of as root vegetables:
Swede or rutabaga (*Brassica napus*)
Turnip (*Brassica rapa*)
Radish (*Raphanus sativa*)

The Carrot family (*Apiacerae* [*Umbelliferae*])

Originally found in temperate regions – Europe and northern Asia
Carrot (*Daucus carota*)
Celery and celeriac (*Apium graveolens*)
Fennel (*Foeniculum vulgare*)
Parsnip (*Pastinaca sativa*)

The Daisy family (*Asteraceae*)

The largest family of flowering plants, with over 20,000 species, almost totally temperate so originally found in Europe and northern Asia
Cardoon (*Cynara cardunculus*)
Chicory and radicchio (*Cichorium intybus*)
Endive (*Cichorium endivia*)
   Varieties: curly endive or frisee
Globe artichoke or artichoke (*Cynara scolymus*)
Jerusalem artichoke (*Helianthus tuberosus*)
Lettuce (*Lactuca sativa*)
   Varieties: cos, leaf, iceberg
Salsify or purple salsify or oyster plant (*Tragopogon porrifolius*)
Scorzonera (*Scorzonera hispanica*)

The Goosefoot family (*Chenopodiaceae*)

Found worldwide
Beetroot (*Beta vulgaris*)
   Varieties: chard or swiss chard, mangel-wurzel, sugar beet
Spinach (*Spinacea oleracea*)

The Lily family (*Liliaceae*)

Mainly temperate and Mediterranean plants
Asparagus (*Asparagus officinalis*)
Garlic (*Allium sativum*)
Leek (*Allium ampeloprasum*)
Onion (*Allium cepa*)
   Varieties: shallot (when immature, spring or green onion)
Scallion (*Allium fistulosum*)

The Marrow family (*Cucurbitaceae*)

Originally tropical or subtropical plants
Buttersquash (*Cucurbita moschata*)
Chow-chow or christophine or chayote (*Sechium edule*)

Cucumber (*Cucumis sativus*)
Marrow (*Cucurbita pepo*)
   Varieties: courgette or zucchini, gourds, pumpkin, summer squashes
Squashes, winter (*Cucurbita maxima*)

The Nightshade family (*Solanaceae*)

Found worldwide but especially in the tropics
Aubergine or eggplant (*Solanum melongena* or *S. esculentum*)
Bird chili pepper or chili leaves and cayenne (*Capsicum frutescens*)
Habanero pepper (*Capsicum chinense*)
Pepper (*Capsicum annuum*)
   Varieties: chili, jalapeño, paprika, pimento, sweet pepper or bell pepper
         or capsicum or green pepper and red pepper and yellow pepper
Potato (*Solanum tuberosum*)
Tomatillo (*Physalis ixocarpa*)
Tomato (*Lycopersicon esculentum*)

The Pea family (*Leguminosae*)

*Pods or legumes are the fruits of these plants, and peas, beans or pulses are
actually their seeds*

*Usually tropical in origin, many of this large family of plants have adapted
to temperate regions*
Azuki or adzuki or red bean (*Vigna angularis*)
Bean, common (*Phaseolus vulgaris*)
   Varieties: berlotti, canellini, chilli, flageolot, French, green, haricot,
         kidney, navy, pinto, snap, string
Bean sprouts, commonly mung or soy
Black Eye Bean (*Vigna unguiculata*)
Black gram (*Phaseolus mungo*)
Broad bean or fava bean or horse bean or field bean (*Vicia faba*)
Butter or Lima bean (*Phaseolus lunatus*)
Chickpea or ceci beans or garbanzos (*Cicer arietinum*)
Fenugreek (*Trigonella foenum-graecum*)
Green gram (*Phaseolus aureus*)
Lentil (*Lens culinari* or */esculenta*)
Liquorice (*Glycyrrhiza glabra*)
Mung bean or golden gram (*Vigna radiata*)
Pea (*Pisum sativum*)
   Varieties: Mangetout or snow pea, sugar snap pea, Chinese pea
Runner bean (*Phaseolus coccineus*)

Soybean (*Glycine max*)
Yard-long bean (*Vigna sinensis or sesquipedalis*)

Miscellaneous
Alfalfa (*Medicago arabica* and others)
Olive (*Olea europa*)
Lamb's lettuce or corn salad or lamb's tongue (*Valerianella locusta*)

Some tropical vegetables
Akee (*Blighia sapida*)
Alligator pepper (*Afromomum melegueta*)
Amaranth (*Amaranthus tricolor*)
Anato (*Bixa orellana*)
Arrowroot or yuquilla (*Maranta arundinacea*)
Basket Vine (*Trichostigma octandrum*)
Belembe (*Xanthosoma brasiliense*)
Bitter greens (*Cestrum latifolium*)
Breadfruit (*Artocarpus altilis*)
Bull nettle (*Solanum oleraceum*)
Calabash or bottle gourd (*Lagenaria siceraria*)
Calabaza (*Cucurbita moschata*)
Cassava or manioc or tapioca (*Manihot esculenta*)
Ceylon spinach (*Basella alba*)
Chaya (*Nidoscolus chayamansa*)
Cranberry hibiscus or false roselle (*Hibiscus acetosella*)
Creeping peperomia (*Peperomia rotundifolia*)
Daikon or white radish (*Raphinus sativus*)
    Variety: black radish
Daun salam (*Eugenia polyantha*)
Dudi gourd (*Laganeria siceraria*)
Fitweed (*Eryngium foetidum*)
Jackfruit or jakfruit (*Artocarpus heterophyllus*)
Jicama (*Pachyrhizus tuberosum*)
Karella or karela or bittermelon or bittergourd or alligator pear (*Momordica charantia*)
Katuk (*Sauropus androgynu*)
Kembang turi (*Sesbania grandiflora poir*)
Lemongrass (*Cymbopogon citratus*)
Loofah gourd or cee gwa (*Luffa cyclindrica*)
Masusa (*Renealmia exaltata*)
Mooli (*Raphanus sativus*)
Moringa or drumstick fruit (*Moringa oleifera*)

Okinawa spinach (*Gynura crepioides*)
Okra or bhindi or lady's finger (*Hibiscus esculentus*)
Plantain (*Musa acuminata* and others)
Purslane (*Portulaca oleracea*)
Ridged luffa (*Luffa acutangula*)
Roselle (*Hibiscus sabdariffa*)
Samba lettuce or sissoo spinach (*Alternanthera sissoo*)
Sesame (*Sesamum indicum*)
Shiny bush (*Peperomia pellucida*)
Skirret (*Sium sisarum*)
Sponge luffa (*Luffa cylindrica*)
Sweet potato (*Ipomoea batatas*)
Taro or cocoyam or colocassi or dasheen or eddoe (*Colocasia esculenta*)
Water Chestnut (*Eleocharis dulcis*)
Winged bean (*Psophocarpus tetragonolobus*)
Yam (*Dioscorea alata*)

Some non-vegetable vegetables
Bamboo shoots (*Phyllostachys pubescens* and others); actually a grass
Fiddleheads or ostrich fern (*Matteuccia struthiopteris*); actually young
 fern leaves
Sweetcorn or corn on the cob (*Zea mays*); actually a grass grain

Mushrooms fungi, not vegetative plants
Non-poisonous mushroom varieties include:
Cep (*Boletus edulis*)
Chanterelle or girole (*Cantharellus cibarius*)
Cultivated mushroom (*Psalliota bisporus*)
Field mushroom (*Psalliota campestris*)
Horn of plenty (*Craterellus cornucopiodes*)
Horse mushroom (*Psalliota arvensis*)
Oyster mushroom (*Pleurotus ostreatus*)
Saffron milk cap (*Lactarius deliciosus*)
Shiitake (*Lentinus edodes*)
Truffle, Italian white (*Tuber magnatum*)
Truffle, Perigord (*Tuber melanosporum*)

Some trees of the Northern Hemisphere

Family etc	Latin name	Common name	Height (m)	NB
Coniferæ	*Abies pectinata*	Silver Fir		
Sapindaceæ	*Acer campestre*	Field maple	10–15 +	
Sapindaceæ	*Acer campestre* Elsrijk	Field maple – cultivar	15–20	
Sapindaceæ	*Acer campestre* Louisa Red Shine	Field maple – cultivar	15–20	
Sapindaceæ	*Acer campestre* Queen Elizabeth	Field maple – cultivar	15–20	SC
Sapindaceæ	*Acer cappadocium Aureum*	Cappadoci Maple, cultivar	15–20	
Sapindaceæ	*Acer cappadocium Rubrum*		15–20	
Sapindaceæ	*Acer cissifolium*	Vineleaf Maple	10–15	
Sapindaceæ	*Acer ginnala*	Amur Maple	10–15	
Sapindaceæ	*Acer griseum*	Paperbark Maple	10–15	
Sapindaceæ	*Acer negundo*	Box Elder	15–20	W
Sapindaceæ	*Acer platanoides*	Norway Maple	20+	
Sapindaceæ	*Acer platanoides* Cleveland		15–20	
Sapindaceæ	*Acer platanoides* Columnare		15–20	SC
Sapindaceæ	*Acer platanoides* Crimson King		20+	
Sapindaceæ	*Acer platanoides* Deborah		20+	
Sapindaceæ	*Acer platanoides Drummondii*		15–20+	
Sapindaceæ	*Acer platanoides* Emerald Queen		20+	
Sapindaceæ	*Acer platanoides* Olmstead		15–20	
Sapindaceæ	*Acer platanoides* Royal Red		20+	
Sapindaceæ	*Acer pseudoplantanus Atropurpureum*		20+	
Sapindaceæ	*Acer pseudoplatanus*	Sycamore	20+	
Sapindaceæ	*Acer pseudoplatanus Brilliantissimum*		10–15	
Sapindaceæ	*Acer pseudoplatanus Leopoldii*		15–20	P
Sapindaceæ	*Acer pseudoplatanus Negena*		20+	P
Sapindaceæ	*Acer pseudoplatanus* Simon Louis Frère		15–20	D
Sapindaceæ	*Acer pseudoplatanus Spaethii*		20+	Cos

Sapindaceæ	Acer pseudoplatanus Worleei	Golden Sycamore	15–20+	
Sapindaceæ	Acer rubrum	Canadian Maple	20+	
Sapindaceæ	Acer rubrum Armstrong		10–15	
Sapindaceæ	Acer rubrum Scanlon		15–20+	
Sapindaceæ	Acer saccharinum	Silver Maple	20+	
Sapindaceæ	Acer saccharinum Laciniata Wierii		20+	
Sapindaceæ	Acer saccharinum Pyramidale		20+	
Sapindaceæ	Acer saccharum Louisa Lad	Sugar Maple	15–20+	
Sapindaceæ	Aesculus flava	Yellow Buckeye	15–20	
Sapindaceæ	Aesculus hippocastanum	Horse Chestnut	20+	
Sapindaceæ	Aesculus hippocastanum Baumanii	Sterile Horse Chestnut	20+	
Sapindaceæ	Aesculus hippocastanum Digitata	Dwarf form	10	
Sapindaceæ	Aesculus X Carnea briotto	Red Horse Chestnut	15–20	
Sapindaceæ	Aesculus X Carnea plantierensis		20+	
Simaroubaceae	Ailanthus altissima	Tree of Heaven	20+	
Cupuliferæ	Alnus cordata	Italian Alder	15–20	W
Cupuliferæ	Alnus glutinosa	Common Alder	15–20	W
Cupuliferæ	Alnus glutinosa laciniata		15–20	
Cupuliferæ	Alnus incana	Grey Alder	10–15	
Cupuliferæ	Alnus incana aurea		10–15	
Cupuliferæ	Alnus incana laciniata		15–20	
Cupuliferæ	Alnus rotundifolia	Alder		
Cupuliferæ	Alnus spaethii		15–20	W
Orchidaceae	Amelanchier arborea Robin Hill		10–15	SC
Coniferæ	Araucaria imbicata	Chili Pine		
Ericaceæ	Arbutus unedo	Killarney Strawberry Tree	10–15	
Cupuliferæ	Betula alba	Birch		
Cupuliferæ	Betula albonsinensis Fascination		15–20	
Cupuliferæ	Betula ermanii		15–20	
Cupuliferæ	Betula ermanii Holland		15–20	
Cupuliferæ	Betula jacquemontii		15–20	SC
Cupuliferæ	Betula nigra	River Birch	10–15	W
Cupuliferæ	Betula papyrifera	Paper Birch	15–20	

Family etc	Latin name	Common name	Height (m)	NB
Cupuliferæ	Betula pendula	Silver Birch	15–20	
Cupuliferæ	Betula pendula dalecarlica	Swedish Birch	15–20	
Cupuliferæ	Betula pendula fastigiata		15–20	
Cupuliferæ	Betula pendula tristis		15–20	
Cupuliferæ	Betula pendula youngii	Young's Weeping Birch	10–15	
Cupuliferæ	Betula pubescens	Common White Birch	15–20	
Moraceae	Broussonetia papyrifera	Paper Mulberry	10–15	
Euphorbiaceæ	Buxus sempervirens	The Box		
Cupressaceae	Calocedrus decurrens	Incense Cedar	20+	
Cupuliferæ	Carpinus betulus	Hornbeam	20+	
Cupuliferæ	Carpinus betulus fastigiata		15–20	P
Cupuliferæ	Carpinus betulus fastigiata Frans Fountaine		15–20	
Cupuliferæ	Carpinus betulus quercifolia		15–20	
Cupuliferæ	Carpinus japonica	Japanese Hornbeam	10–15	
Cupuliferæ	Castanea sativa	Sweet Chestnut	20+	Pk
Cupuliferæ	Castanea sativa variegata		20+	
Bignoniaceae	Catalpa bignonioides	Indian Bean Tree	15–20	
Bignoniaceae	Catalpa bignonioides aurea		15–20	
Bignoniaceae	Catalpa speciosa	Western Catalpa	15–20	
Coniferæ	Cedrus atlantica	Atlas Cedar	20+	
Coniferæ	Cedrus atlantica glauca	Blue Cedar	20+	
Coniferæ	Cedrus deodara	Deodar Cedar	20+	
Coniferæ	Cedrus libani	Cedar of Lebanon	20+	
Ulmaceae	Celtis australis	Nettle Tree	10–15	
Cercidiphyllaceae	Cercidiphyllum japonicum	Katsura	10–15	
Leguminosae	Cercis siliquastrum	Judas Tree	15–20	D
Arecaceae	Chamaerops humilis			
Cornaceæ	Cornus kousa chinensis		5–10	
Cornaceæ	Cornus mas	Cornelian Cherry	10–15	
Cornaceæ	Cornus sanguinea	Dogwood		
Cupuliferæ	Corylus avellana	Hazel		
Cupuliferæ	Corylus colurna	Turkish hazel	20+	SC
Rosaceae	Cotoneaster cornubia		10–15	
Rosaceae	Cotoneaster hybridus pendulus		5	
Rosaceæ	Crataegus laevigata Paul's Scarlet		10–15	P

Rosaceæ	*Crataegus lavellei plena*		10–15	
Rosaceæ	*Crataegus monogyna*	Common Hawthorn	10–15	
Rosaceæ	*Crataegus monogyna stricta*		10–15	
Rosaceæ	*Crataegus prunifolia*	Broad leafed Cockspur Thorn	10–15	SC Pk
Rosaceæ	*Crataegus prunifolia splendens*		10–15	
Rosaceæ	*Crataegus X lavallei*	Hybrid Cockspur Thorn	10–15	
Rosaceæ	*Crataegus X lavallei carrierei*		10–15	
Rosaceæ	*Cratœgus oxyacantha*	Hawthorn		
Cupressaceae	*Cupressocyparis leylandii* Castlewellen	Golden Leyland Cypress	10–15	
Coniferæ	*Cupressus arizonica glauca*		15–20	
Coniferæ	*Cupressus lawsoniana*	Lawson's Cypress	15–40	
Coniferæ	*Cupressus macrocarpa* Goldcrest		15–20	
Coniferæ	*Cupressus sempervirens*	Italian Cypress	15–20	
Cornaceae	*Davidia involucrata vilmoriniana*	Handkerchief Tree	15–20	
Ebenaceae	*Dispyros lotus*	Date Plum	10–15	
Celastraceae	*Euonymous europœus*	Spindle-tree		
Cupuliferæ	*Fagus sylvatica asplenifolia*	Cut leaf Beech	20+	
Cupuliferæ	*Fagus sylvatica*	Common Beech	20+	
Cupuliferæ	*Fagus sylvatica* Dawyck	Fastigiate Beech	15–20	
Cupuliferæ	*Fagus sylvatica* Dawyck Aurea		15–20	
Cupuliferæ	*Fagus sylvatica* Dawyck Purpurea		15–20	
Cupuliferæ	*Fagus sylvatica pendula*	Weeping Beech	15–20	
Cupuliferæ	*Fagus sylvatica purpurea*	Purple Beech	20+	Pk
Cupuliferæ	*Fagus sylvatica purpurea pendula*		10–15	
Cupuliferæ	*Fagus sylvatica roseomarginata*		10–15	
Cupuliferæ	*Fagus sylvatica* Zlatis		15–20	
Oleaceæ	*Fraxinus angustifolia* Raywood		15–20	
Oleaceæ	*Fraxinus excelsior*	Ash		
Oleaceæ	*Fraxinus excelsior altena*		15–20	
Oleaceæ	*Fraxinus excelsior diversifolia*	One-Leafed Ash	20+	P

Family etc	Latin name	Common name	Height (m)	NB
Oleaceæ	Fraxinus excelsior jaspidea	Golden Ash	20+	
Oleaceæ	Fraxinus excelsior pendula	Weeping Ash	15–20	
Oleaceæ	Fraxinus excelsior Westhof's Glory		20+	
Oleaceæ	Fraxinus ornus	Manna or Flowering Ash	15–20	
Oleaceæ	Fraxinus ornus Arie Peters		15–20	
Oleaceæ	Fraxinus ornus Louisa Lady		15–20	
Oleaceæ	Fraxinus ornus Obelisk		15–20	
Oleaceæ	Fraxinus pennsylvanica Summit	Red Ash	15–20	
Ginkoaceae	Gingko biloba	Maidenhair Tree	20+	
Caesalpiniaceae	Gleditsia triacanthos Skyline		15–20	SC
Caesalpiniaceae	Gleditsia triacanthos Sunburst		15–20	D
Caesalpiniaceae	Gymnocladus dioica	Kentucky Coffee Tree		
Eleaginaceae	Hippophae salicifolia Robert		10–15	Cos
Ilicineæ	Ilex aquifolium	Holly		
Juglandaceæ	Juglans nigra	Black Walnut	20	
Juglandaceæ	Juglans regia	Common Walnut	15–20	Pk
Coniferæ	Juniperus communis	Juniper		
Coniferæ	Juniperus virginiana	Virginian Juniper		
Sapindaceae	Koelreuteria paniculata fastigiata		10–15	Pk
Leguminosæ	Laburnum vulgare	Laburnum		
Leguminosæ	Laburnum X watereri vossii	Golden rain	10–15	
Coniferæ	Larix decidua	European Larch	20+	
Coniferæ	Larix europœa	Larch		
Lauraceæ	Laurus nobilis	Bay Tree		
Oleaceae	Ligustrum lucidum	Chinese Privet	10–15	
Oleaceae	Ligustrum lucidum variegata		10–15	
Hamamelidaceae	Liquidambar styraciflua	Sweet Gum	20+	
Hamamelidaceae	Liquidambar styraciflua Moraine		20	
Hamamelidaceae	Liquidambar styraciflua Worplesdon		20	
Magnoliaceae	Liriodendron tulipifera	Tulip Tree	20	Pk

Magnoliaceae	*Liriodendron tulipifera fastigiata*		15–20	
Magnoliaceae	*Magnolia acuminata*	Cucumber Tree	20	
Magnoliaceae	*Magnolia grandiflora*	Southern Magnolia	15–20	
Magnoliaceae	*Magnolia kobus*	Northern Japanese Magnolia	15–20	
Rosaceae	*Malus floribuna*	Japanese Crab	15–20	
Rosaceae	*Malus baccata* Street parade		15–20	
Rosaceae	*Malus evereste*		15–20	
Rosaceae	*Malus* Golden Hornet		10–15	
Rosaceae	*Malus* John Downie		10–15	
Rosaceae	*Malus* Red Sentinel		10–15	
Rosaceae	*Malus* Rudolph		10–15	
Rosaceae	*Malus* Toringo		10–15	
Rosaceae	*Malus trilobata*		15–20	
Rosaceae	*Malus tschonoskii*	Pillar Crab	15–20	P
Rosaceae	*Mespilus germanica*	Medlar	10–15	
Taxodiaceae	*Metasequoia glyptostroboides*	Dawn Redwood	20+	W
Moraceae	*Morus alba*	White Mulberry	15–20	
Moraceae	*Morus nigra*	Black Mulberry	10–15	Pk
Fagaceae	*Nothofagus antarctica*	Antarctic Beech	15–20	
Fagaceae	*Nothofagus obliqua*	Roble Beech	20+	
Oleaceae	*Olea europeaus*	Olive	10–15	
Oleaceae	*Osmanthus heterophyllus purpurea*		10–15	
Betulaceae	*Ostrya carpinifolia*	Hop Hornbeam	15–20	
Hamamelidaceae	*Parrotia persica*	Persian Ironwood	5–10	
Hamamelidaceae	*Parrotia persica* Vanessa		10–15	
Scrophulariaceae	*Paulownia tomentosa*		15–20	Pk
Agavaceae	*Phormium tenax*	New Zealand Flax		
Agavaceae	*Phormium tenax purpureum*			
Agavaceae	*Phormium tenax variegata*			
Rosaceae	*Photinia X fraseri* Red Robin		10–15	
Gramineae	*Phyllostachys aurea*	Bamboo		
Gramineae	*Phyllostachys aureasulcata spectabilis*			
Gramineae	*Phyllostachys nigra*	The Black Bamboo		
Coniferæ	*Picea excelsa*	Spruce Fir		
Coniferæ	*Picea omorika*	Serbian Spruce	15–20	

Family etc	Latin name	Common name	Height (m)	NB
Coniferæ	*Pinus nigra austriaca*	Austrian Pine	20+	Cos
Coniferæ	*Pinus pinea*	Stone Pine	10–15	
Coniferæ	*Pinus sylvestris*	Scot's Pine	20+	
Platancaceæ	*Platanus acerifolia*	Plane Tree		
Platancaceæ	*Platanus orientalis digitata*		20+	
Platancaceæ	*Platanus X hispanica*	London Plane	20+	P
Salicineæ	*Populus alba*	White Poplar	20+	Cos
Salicineæ	*Populus alba* Racket	White Poplar	20+	
Salicineæ	*Populus nigra*	Black Poplar	20+	
Salicineæ	*Populus nigra italica*	Lombardy or Italian Poplar	20+	
Salicineæ	*Populus robusta*		20+	
Salicineæ	*Populus tremula*	Aspen	15–20	
Salicineæ	*Populus X Candicans aurora*	Variegated Ontario Poplar	20+	P
Rosaceæ	*Prunus accolade*		10–15	
Rosaceæ	*Prunus amanogawa*		10–15	
Rosaceæ	*Prunus avium*	Gean		
Rosaceæ	*Prunus avium*	Wild Cherry	15–20	
Rosaceæ	*Prunus avium plena*		15–20	
Rosaceæ	*Prunus cerasifera nigra*	Purple Leaf Plum	10–15	
Rosaceæ	*Prunus kanzan*		15–20	
Rosaceæ	*Prunus maackii* Amber Beauty	Manchurian Cherry	15–20	
Rosaceæ	*Prunus padus*	Bird Cherry	15–20	
Rosaceæ	*Prunus padus albertii*		15–20	P
Rosaceæ	*Prunus padus watereri*		15–20	Pk
Rosaceæ	*Prunus* Pink Perfection		15–20	
Rosaceæ	*Prunus rotundifolia*			
Rosaceæ	*Prunus* Rudolph Billeter			
Rosaceæ	*Prunus schimidsu Sakura*		10–15	
Rosaceæ	*Prunus shirotae*		10–15	
Rosaceæ	*Prunus spinosa*	Wild Plums		
Rosaceæ	*Prunus subhirtella autumnalis*		10–15	
Rosaceæ	*Prunus subhirtella autumnalis rosea*		10–15	
Rosaceæ	*Prunus ukon*		15–20	
Rosaceæ	*Prunus umineko*		15–20	
Rosaceæ	*Prunus virginiana Schubert*		15–20	
Rosaceæ	*Prunus X hillieri Spire*		10–15	
Rosaceæ	*Prunus X scmittii*		15–20	

Coniferæ	*Pseudotsuga douglasii*	Douglas Fir		
Juglandaceae	*Pterocarya fraxinifolia*		20+	Pk
Rosaceæ	*Pyrus aria*	White Beam		
Rosaceæ	*Pyrus aucuparia*	Mountain Ash or Rowan		
Rosaceæ	*Pyrus calleryana* Chanticleer		15–20	
Rosaceæ	*Pyrus calleryana* Redspire		15–20	
Rosaceæ	*Pyrus communis*	Wild Pear		
Rosaceæ	*Pyrus communis* Beech Hill		15–20	W
Rosaceæ	*Pyrus germanica*	Medlar		
Rosaceæ	*Pyrus malus*	Wild Apple		
Rosaceæ	*Pyrus salicifolia pendula*	Willow-leafed Pear	15–20	
Cupuliferæ	*Quercus cerris*	Turkey Oak	20+	
Cupuliferæ	*Quercus coccinea*	Scarlet Oak	20+	
Cupuliferæ	*Quercus frainetto*	Hungarian Oak	20+	
Cupuliferæ	*Quercus ilex*	Evergreen/Holm Oak	20+	Cos
Cupuliferæ	*Quercus nigra*	Water Oak	15–20	
Cupuliferæ	*Quercus palustris*	Pin Oak	20+	
Cupuliferæ	*Quercus robur*	English Oak	20+	Cos
Cupuliferæ	*Quercus robur fastigiata koster*	Cypress Oak	20+	SC
Cupuliferæ	*Quercus rubra*	Red Oak	20+	Pk
Rhamneæ	*Rhamnus*	Buckthorn		
Rhamneæ	*Rhamnus frangula*	Breaking Buckthorn		
Anacardiaceae	*Rhus typhina*	Stag's-horn Sumach	10–15	
Leguminosæ	*Robinia pseudoacacia*	False Acacia or Locust Tree	20+	
Leguminosæ	*Robinia pseudoacacia bessoniana*		15–20	D
Leguminosæ	*Robinia pseudoacacia* Casque Rouge		15–20	D
Leguminosæ	*Robinia pseudoacacia frisia*		10–15	
Leguminosæ	*Robinia pseudoacacia umbraculifera*		10–15	D
Leguminosæ	*Robinia pseudoacacia unifolia*		15–20	
Salicineæ	*Salix alba*	White Willow	20+	
Salicineæ	*Salix alba chermesina*	Scarlet Willow	20+	Cos
Salicineæ	*Salix alba liempde*		20+	
Salicineæ	*Salix alba tristis*	Golden Weeping Willow	20+	W

Family etc	Latin name	Common name	Height (m)	NB
Salicineæ	Salix caprea	Goat Willow/Pussy Willow	5–10	
Salicineæ	Salix caprea pendula	Kilmarnock Willow	2–3	
Salicineæ	Salix coerulea	Cricket bat Willow	25–30	
Salicineæ	Salix daphnoides	Violet Willow	10–15	W
Salicineæ	Salix matsudana tortuosa	Corkscrew Willow	15–20	
Salicineæ	Salix pentandra	Bay Willow	10–15	
Salicineæ	Salix sepulcralis chrysocoma	Golden Weeping Willow	20+	
Caprifoliaceæ	Sambucus nigra	Elder	6	
Taxodiaceae	Sequoia sempervirens	Coast Redwood	20+	
Taxodiaceae	Sequoidendron giganteum	Giant Redwood	20+	
Taxodiaceae	Sequoidendron giganteum glauca	Blue Clone	20+	
Leguminosae	Sophora japonica	Japanese Pagoda Tree	15–20	D
Rosaceae	Sorbus aria lutescens	Whitebeam	10–15	
Rosaceae	Sorbus aria magnifica		15–20	
Rosaceae	Sorbus aria majestica		15–20	
Rosaceae	Sorbus arnoldiana schouten		10–15	
Rosaceae	Sorbus aucuparia asplenifolia		15–20	
Rosaceae	Sorbus aucuparia Cardinal Royal		15–20	
Rosaceae	Sorbus aucuparia edulis		15–20	
Rosaceae	Sorbusa ucuparia Golden Wonder		15–20	
Rosaceae	Sorbus aucuparia Rossica Major		15–20	
Rosaceae	Sorbus aucuparia Sheerwater Seedling		15–20	
Rosaceae	Sorbus commixta	Chinese Scarlet Rowan	10–15	
Rosaceae	Sorbus huphehensis	Hupeh Rowan	10–15	
Rosaceae	Sorbus intermedia	Swedish Whitebeam	15–20	Cos
Rosaceae	Sorbus intermedia Brouwers		15–20	
Rosaceae	Sorbus torminalis	Wild Service Tree	15–20	
Rosaceae	Sorbus X Thuringiaca fastigiata	Bastard Service Trees	10–15	D
Rosaceae	Taxodium distichum	Swamp Cypress	20+	W
Taxaceæ	Taxus baccata	English Yew	10–15	
Taxaceæ	Taxus baccata fastigiata	Irish Yew	10–15	

Taxaceæ	*Taxus baccata fastigiata aurea*		10–15	
Taxaceæ	*Thuya plicata atrovirens*	Western Red Cedar	20+	
Tiliacaæ	*Tilia cordata*	Small-leafed Lime	20+	P
Tiliacaæ	*Tilia cordata* Greenspire		15–20	
Tiliacaæ	*Tilia cordata* Rancho		10–15	
Tiliacaæ	*Tilia euchlora*	Caucasian Lime	15–20	
Tiliacaæ	*Tilia mongolica*	Mongolian Lime	10–15	
Tiliacaæ	*Tilia petiolaris*	Weeping Silver Lime	20+	
Tiliacaæ	*Tilia platyphyllos*	Broad-leafed Lime	20+	
Tiliacaæ	*Tilia platypyllos rubra*	Red twigged Lime	15–20	
Tiliacaæ	*Tilia tomentosa*	Silver Lime	20+	
Tiliacaæ	*Tilia tomentosa* Brabant		20+	
Tiliacaæ	*Tilia tomentosa* Doornik		20+	
Tiliacaæ	*Tilia X europaea*	Common Lime	20+	
Tiliacaæ	*Tilia X europaea Pallida*		20+	
Arecaceae	*Trachycarpus fortunei*	Chusan Palm	10–15	
Urticaceæ	*Ulmus*	Wych Elm		
Urticaceæ	*Ulmus camperdownii*	Camperdown Elm	10–15+	
Urticaceæ	*Ulmus carpinifolia Wredii Aurea*		15–20	
Urticaceæ	*Ulmus clusius*		20+	
Urticaceæ	*Ulmus dodoens*		20+	
Urticaceæ	*Ulmus lobel*		20+	
Caprifoliaceæ	*Viburnum lantana*	Wayfaring-tree		
Caprifoliaceæ	*Viburnum opulus*	Guelder Rose		
Ulmaceae	*Zelkova serrata* Green Vase		15–20	

Suitable for ...

C Car park planting
Cos Coastal sites
D Dry soils
P Polluted areas
Pk Parkland areas
S Street planting
W Wet soils

The human world

Business and commerce

Forms of money

M0 Narrow money – notes and coins in public circulation together with cash in banks' tills and their operational balances with the Bank of England. Term in current use.

M1 Notes and coins in circulation and deposited in current bank accounts. Term no longer used in UK.

M2 M1 plus private sector holdings of building societies and national savings; ordinary accounts and bank deposit accounts. Term no longer used in UK.

M3 M2 plus interest-bearing, non-sterling deposit accounts held by UK residents and other certificates of deposit. Term no longer used in UK.

M4 M0 plus all deposits in UK banks and building societies. Designed to measure spending power. Term in current use.

Communication

Language

Some native Australian languages
This list of some of the native Australian languages should surely cause us to stop and reflect on the rich variety of culture that has been, and is liable to be, lost if no steps are taken to preserve it.

East coast of Queensland – from Cape York in the north to Brisbane in the south

1	Kala Lagaw Ya	7	Dyirbal
2	Yadhaykenu	8	Warrgamay
3	Wik-Mungkan	9	Nyawaygi
4	Guugu Yimidhirr	10	Warungu
5	Kuku-YAlandji	11	Gureng-gureng
6	Yidiny	12	Gabi-gabi

13 Waga-waga
14 Gowar
15 Yagara

South border of Queensland
16 Bigambil
17 Gunya

East coast of New South
Wales from north to south
18 Band jalang
19 Djangati
20 Kattang
21 Awabakal
22 Dharuk
23 Dharawal
24 Dhurga
25 Thawa

SE NSW
26 Ngarigo
27 Wiradhuri

Central NSW
28 Ngiyambaa
29 Kamilaroi

N NSW
30 Yuwaalaraay

SW NSW
31 Yitha-yitha

Victoria
32 Ganay
33 Wuywurung
34 Wathawurung
35 Wemba-wemba
36 Kuurn Kopan Noot

South coast South Australia
37 Yaralde
38 Gaurna

39 Banggala
40 Nhangka

Western border NSW
41 Baagandji
42 Malyangaba

NE South Australia
43 Adnyamathanha
44 Diyari
45 Yandruwnadha
46 Arabana
47 Wangganguru
48 Ngamini

W border Queensland
49 Midhaga
50 Wangka-Yutjuru
51 Pitta-pitta
52 Kalkatungu
53 Mayi-Kutuna
54 Mayi-Yapi
55 Mayi-Kulan
56 Lardil

Northern Territory (S–N)
57 Aranda
58 Warlpiri
59 Warumungu
60 Djingulu
61 Yolngu
62 Gunwinygu
63 Margu
64 Wuna
65 Waray
66 Tiwi
67 Pajamal

E Western Australia
68 Djaru
69 Walmatjari

70 Western Desert language	77 Ngarluma
71 Kalaaku	78 Yindjibarndi
	79 Panyjima
West coast Western Australia	80 Nyangumarda
72 Nyungar	81 Karadjeri
73 Nhanta	82 Yawor
74 Watjari	83 Bardi
75 Yingkarta	84 Ungarinjin
76 Martuthunira	85 Wunambal

The language of flowers

Plants, and especially flowers, have held symbolic meanings throughout history. The idea of using flowers as a complete symbolic language was probably introduced to Britain from Turkey in the early C18. The Victorians adopted this concept enthusiastically, developing the language and creating large and complicated bouquets. Much of the language of flowers is to do with love matters, and the Victorians used flowers as symbols to express their feelings. Sometimes a flower can have two contradictory meanings; in such cases, the experienced Victorian would know how to read the flower in its context with the other blooms in the bouquet.

The language of flowers requires several things that today make us wonder about its practicability.

It needs the sender – and the receiver – to be versed, not only in the language itself, but in the identification of the flowers that constitute its 'words'. Even more difficult perhaps is the task of finding the appropriate materials when needed, for most of them are seasonal and some, such as the night-flowering cereus, have botanists keeping watch night after night to catch their evanescent beauty. Or was the message better expressed through the medium of art? Perhaps this explains the prevalence of floral watercolour paintings.

A	
Acacia – Secret love	Allspice – Compassion
Agrimony – Thankfulness	Ambrosia – Love returned
Almond blossom – Hope	Amaryllis – Pride; Timidity
Aloe – Grief	Anemone – Unfading love
	Angelica – Inspiration

Aniseed – Restoration of youth

Arbutis – Only love

Apple – Preference

Aster – Love; Daintiness

Azalea – Take care of yourself for me; Fragile passion (Chinese symbol of womanhood)

B

Bachelor's buttons – Celibacy

Baby's breath – Everlasting love

Basil – Best wishes, Love

Bay leaf – Strength

Begonia – Beware

Bird of paradise – Magnificence

Bittersweet – Truth

Bluebell – Humility; Constancy

Borage – Courage

Bryony – Be my support

Burnet – A merry heart

Buttercup – Cheerfulness

C

Cactus – Endurance; Warmth

Calendula – Joy

Camellia – Admiration; Perfection; Good luck gift to a man

Candytuft – Indifference

Canterbury bell – Acknowledgement

Carnation (in general) Bonds of affection; Health and energy; Fascination

Carnation (pink) – I'll never forget you

Carnation (purple) – Capriciousness; Whimsical; Changeable

Carnation (red) – My heart aches for you; Admiration

Carnation (solid colour) – Yes

Carnation (striped) – No; Refusal

Carnation (white) – Sweet and lovely; Innocence; Pure love; Woman's good luck gift

Carnation (yellow) – Rejection; Disdain

Cattail – Peace; Prosperity

Chamomile – Patience; Attracts wealth

Chicory – Frugality

Chrysanthemum (in general) – Cheerfulness; You're a wonderful friend

Chrysanthemum (red) – I love

Chrysanthemum (white) – Truth

Chrysanthemum (yellow) – Slighted love

Columbine – Folly

Coreopsis – Always cheerful

Coriander – Lust

Cornflower – Delicacy

Cowslip – Pensiveness; Winning grace

Crocus – Cheerfulness; Abuse not

Cyclamen – Resignation and goodbye

Clover – Good luck

D

Daffodil – Respect

Daisy – Innocence
Dandelion – Wishes come true
Dog-violet – Faithfulness

E
Eucalyptus – Protection

F
Fennel – Worthy of all praise
Fern – Sincerity
Fern (magic) – Fascination; Confidence and shelter
Fern (maidenhair) – Secret bond of love
Feverfew – Protection
Flax – Domestic symbol
Forget-me-not – True love; Memories
Forsythia – Anticipation
Foxglove – Insincerity

G
Gardenia – You're lovely; Secret love
Garland of roses – Reward of virtue
Garlic – Courage; Strength
Geranium (scented) – Preference
Gladiolus – Love at first sight
Grass – Submission
Guelder rose – Winter; Age

H
Harebell – Submission; Grief
Hawthorn – Hope
Heather (lavender) – Admiration; Solitude
Heather (white) – Protection; Wishes will come true
Heliotrope – Devotion; Faithfulness

Hibiscus – Delicate beauty
Holly – Good will; Defence; Domestic happiness; Foresight
Honeysuckle – Generous and devoted affection
Hyacinth (general) – Games and sports; Rashness
Hyacinth (blue) – Constancy
Hyacinth (purple) – I'm sorry; Please forgive me; Sorrow
Hyacinth (red or pink) – Play
Hyacinth (white) – Loveliness; I'll pray for you
Hyacinth (yellow) – Jealousy
Hydrangea – Thank you for understanding; Frigidity; Heartlessness
Hyssop – Wards away evil spirits

I
Iris – Faith; Hope; A message
Ivy – Fidelity and friendship
Ivy – Anxious to please; Affection

K
Kingcup – I wish I were rich
Kennedia – Intellectual beauty

J
Jasmine – Amiability
Jonquil – Love me; Affection returned; Desire; Sympathy
Juniper – Protection

L
Larkspur – Fickleness
Lavender – Devotion
Lemon – Zest
Lemon balm – Brings love

Lilac – Humility
Lily (calia) – Beauty
Lily (day) – Coquetry
Lily (eucharis) – Maiden
  charms
Lily (orange) – Hatred
Lily (tiger) – Wealth; Pride
Lily (white) – Virginity; Purity;
  Majesty; It's heavenly to be
  with you
Lily (yellow) – I'm walking on
  air; False and gay
Lily of the valley – Sweetness;
  Return to happiness

M

Magnolia – Sweetness; Beauty;
  Love of nature
Mallow – Mildness
Marigold – Comforts the heart
Michaelmas daisy –
  Afterthought
Mint – Protection from illness;
  Warmth of feeling
Marjoram (sweet) – Joy and
  happiness
Mistletoe – Kiss me; Affection
Monkshood – Beware, a
  deadly foe is near; Chivalry
Moss – Maternal love; Charity
Mulberry (black) – I shall not
  survive you
Mulberry (white) – Wisdom
Myrtle – Love

N

Narcissus – Egotism; Formality
Nasturtium – Conquest;
  Victory in battle; Maternal
  love; Charity
Nightshade – Truth

O

Old Man's Beard – Artifice
Oleander – Caution; Beware
Orange – Generosity
Orange (mock) – Deceit
Orchid – Love; Beauty;
  Refinement; Beautiful lady

P

Pansy – Thoughts; Love
Peach – Longevity
Peony – Aphrodisiac
Periwinkle – Pleasure of
  memory
Petunia – Resentment; Anger
Pine – Hope; Pity
Pinks – Boldness; Tears
Poppy (red) – Pleasure;
  Consolation
Poppy (white) – Consolation;
  Sleep
Poppy (yellow) – Wealth;
  Success
Prickly pear – Satire
Primrose – I can't live without
  you; Early youth
Primrose (evening) –
  Inconstancy

R

Ragwort – Early youth
Red clover – Industry
Rose (general) – Love; Beauty
Rose (black) – Death
Rose (dark crimson) –
  Mourning
Rose (pink) – Perfect
  happiness; Please believe
  me
Rose (red) – Love; I love you;
  Beauty

Rose (red and white) –
   Together; Unity
Rose (white) – Eternal Love;
   Innocence; Heavenly;
   Secrecy and silence
Rose (yellow) – Friendship; Try
   to care
Rose bud – Beauty and youth;
   A heart innocent of love
Rose bud (red) – Pure and
   lovely
Rose bud (white) – Girlhood
Rose (garland or crown of) –
   Reward of merit; Crown
Rose (musk cluster) –
   Charming
Rose (single, full bloom) – I
   love you; I still love you
Rose (thornless) – Love at first
   sight
Rose (cabbage) – Ambassador
   of love
Rose (Christmas) – Ease my
   anxiety; Anxiety
Rose (damask) – Brilliant
   complexion
Rose (tea) – I'll always
   remember
Rosemary – Remembrance

S
Sage – Wisdom; Long life
Salvia (blue) – I think of you
Scarlet pimpernel – Change;
   Lover's secret meeting
Shepherd's purse – I offer you
   my all
Smilax – Loveliness
Snapdragon – Deception;
   Gracious lady

Snowdrop – Hope;
   Consolation
Spiderflower – Elope with me
Stephanotis – Happiness in
   marriage; Desire to travel
Stock – Lasting beauty
Strawberry – Perfect goodness
Sunflower – Loyalty; Wishes
Sweetpea – Goodbye;
   Departure; Blissful pleasure

T
Tansy – I declare war against
   you
Thyme – Strength and courage
Traveller's joy – Safety to
   travellers
Tulip (general) – Fame; Perfect
   lover
Tulip (red) – Believe me;
   Declaration of love
Tulip (variegated) – Beautiful
   eyes
Tulip (yellow) – Hopeless love

V
Violet – Modesty
Violet (blue) – Watchfulness;
   Faithfulness; I'll always be
   true
Violet (white) – Let's take a
   chance on happiness
Viscaria – Will you dance with
   me?

W
Wallflower – Faithfulness in
   adversity; Misfortune
White clover – Think of me
Windflower – Sickness;
   Expectation

Withered flowers – Rejected love
Wormwood – Absence
Woodruff – Sweet humility

Y
Yarrow – War

Z
Zinnia (general) – Thoughts of friends

Zinnia (magenta) – Lasting affection
Zinnia (mixed) – Thinking of an absent friend
Zinnia (scarlet) – Constancy
Zinnia (white) – Goodness
Zinnia (yellow) – Daily remembrance

The names of the days of the week

Sunday The sun's day. Once known as Sonday or Sounday, it took its modern form in late C18.

Monday The moon's day. Once Munenday, it took its modern form in late C16.

Tuesday Named after the Norse/Anglo-Saxon god of war Tiw or Tew. In the Middle Ages it was known as Tisdei or Tewisday; it took its modern form by the end of C17.

Wednesday Named after the chief Norse/Anglo-Saxon god, Woden. Once known as Wodnesday or Weddinsday, it took its modern form mid C18.

Thursday Named after the Norse/Anglo-Saxon thunder god, Thor. Once known as Thoresday or Thurisday, it took its modern form in late C18.

Friday Named after the Norse/Anglo-Saxon goddess Frigga or Freya. Spelt as Fridaei in the Middle Ages, and later Frydaye, it took its modern form early C17.

Saturday Named after the Roman god of seeds and crops, Saturnus. Originally Saturnesday, it took its modern form in late C18.

Phonetic alphabets
Ever since there has been a need to spell words – especially via some means of remote communication – there has been a need for a standard phonetic alphabet; a set of words which unambiguously convey their initial letters. There have been changes over the years, as shown below; we also include a comic alphabet for light relief.

Current	WW1 RN [1]	WW1 slang [2]	WW2 RAF [3]	Old mil [4]	Comic [5]
Apple	Apples	Ack	Apple	Able	A for orses
Bravo	Butter	Beer	Beer	Baker	B for mutton
Charlie	Charlie	Charlie	Charlie	Charlie	C for thighlanders
Delta	Duff	Don	Dog	Dog	D for mation
Echo	Edward	Edward	Edward	Easy	E for lution
Foxtrot	Freddy	Fredie	Freddy	Fox	F for vescence
Golf	George	Gee	George	George	G for fstaff
Hotel	Harry	Harry	Harry	How	H for voting
India	Ink	Ink	Ink	Item	I for lootin
Juliet	Johnny	Johnnie	Jug/Johnny	Jig	J for oranges
Kilo	King	King	King	King	K for restaurant
Lima	London	London	Love	Love	L for leather
Mike	Monkey	Emma	Moth	Mike	M for sis
November	Nuts	Nuts	Nuts	Nan	N for mation
Oscar	Orange	Oranges	Orange	Oboe	O for the open road
Papa	Pudding	Pip	Peter	Peter	P for comfort
Quebec	Queenie	Queen	Queen	Queen	Q for fish
Romeo	Robert	Robert	Roger	Roger	R for mo
Sierra	Sugar	Esses	Sugar	Sugar	S for you
Tango	Tommy	Toc	Tommy	Tare	T for two
Uniform	Uncle	Uncle	Uncle	Uncle	U for mism
Victor	Vinegar	Vic	Vic	Victor	V for la France
Whiskey	Willie	William	William	William	W for quits
X-ray	Xerxes	X-ray	X-ray	X-ray	X for breakfast
Yankee	Yellow	Yorker	Yoke/Yorker	Yoke	Y for runts
Zulu	Zebra	Zebra	Zebra	Zebra	Z (Zee) for yourself

[1] First World War Royal Navy version

[2] First World War slang. The Tommies, who devised such terms as 'SanFairyAnn' and 'Wipers' also gave us the time descriptors AckEmma and PipEmma, and TocH for Talbot House, in memory of Gilbert Talbot, son of the Bishop of Winchester and popularised by Revd 'Tubby' Clayton.

[3] Second World War RAF version.

[4] Used in the 50s by both British and US military.

[5] Comic alphabet popularised by the pre-1940 music hall double act Clapham and Dwyer, and explored exhaustively by Eric Partridge. There are many variations, but we have chosen one that embodies the best. Read G as 'chief', H as 'age', K as 'cafe' (to rhyme with safe) and S as a somewhat twisted 'just'. The perfection of 'L for leather' is to be savoured.

Polari

Polari was once an in slang used by groups which might have become as 'lost' as Cornish, were it not for the 'Julian and Sandy' sketches on the BBC radio programme *Round the Horne* (presently enjoying a London stage revival), and a growing interest in language and its use.

The following list comprises words which have converged from a variety of sources which Polari-users have absorbed into the vocabulary. Some may have become common currency but are included on the 'you saw it here first' principle.

ajax nearby
basket codpiece
batts shoes
bijou small
bona good
butch behaving as a masculine lesbian
camp effeminate. The idea is that the word is derived from KAMP =
    Known As Male Prostitute is probably a back-formation
capello hat
carts/cartso penis
carsey toilet
chicken young boy
charper search
charpering omi policeman
cod deeply unpleasant. Not the same as cod = conscious self-parody
cottage public loo (particularly with reference to cottaging)
cottaging having or looking for sex in a cottage
crimper hairdresser
dish an attractive male; buttocks
dolly pretty, nice, pleasant
drag clothes, especially women's clothes worn by a man
ecaf face. A backslang word, shortened to eek
ends hair
esong nose (backslang)
fantabulosa wonderful
feele child
fruit queen in the gay sense
glossies magazines
handbag money
hoofer dancer
jarry food see **mangarie**
kaffies trousers
khazi see **carsey**
lallies legs
latty room, house or flat
lills hands
luppers fingers
mangarie food, also jarry
measures money
meese plain, ugly (from Yiddish)
meshigener nutty, crazy, mental

metzas money

mince walk affectedly

naff bad, drab. The idea that the word is derived from Not Available For F***ing may be a back-formation; it began as a Northern England dialect word and was made known by Princess Anne's dealings with the press before being popularised by Ronnie Barker as Norman Stanley Fletcher, the old lag in the BBC sitcom *Porridge*.

nanti not, no

national handbag dole

nishta nothing, no

oglefakes glasses

ogles eyes

omi man

omi-polone effeminate man (see polone)

onk nose

orbs eyes

park give

polari chat, talk

polari pipe telephone

polone woman

pots teeth

riah/riha hair (backslang)

riah shusher crimper

sharpy policeman

shush bag holdall. Perhaps to hold shush = ill-gotten gains

shyker/shyckle wig

slap makeup

strillers piano

thews thighs

trade sex

troll to walk about (esp. looking for trade)

willets breasts

Rhyming slang

Rhyming slang was originally developed by London Cockneys, a word which from C17 has denoted East Enders; traditionally those born within the sound of the Bow bells. The idea is simple enough: to replace a word with another word or phrase that rhymes with it. Thus 'Davy Crockett' for pocket, or 'Spanish guitar' for cigar. The next stage is to suppress the rhyme, which gives rise to a more impenetrable language: in fact, some slang words so generated have entered everyday speech, their rhyming origins forgotten – thus 'use your loaf' (loaf of bread = head) and 'need some bread' (bread and honey = money). The following list gives some of the words that have lost their rhymes and passed into everyday speech.

Phrase	1st RS word	2nd RS word	Meaning
I was on me tod	Tod	Sloane	Alone
Got 'im right up the khyber	Khyber	Pass	Arse
'E bin cyril e'since I known im	Cyril	Lord	Bald*
S'load ole cobblers	cobblers'	awls	Balls
I gave up me ain't she on the train	Ain't she	sweet	seat
I need some airs for me trousers	airs and	graces	braces
There's some dodgy looking airs in 'ere tonight	airs and	graces	faces
I got an Alan in me finger	Alan	Minter	splinter
Hang your Alans on the line	Alan	Whickers	knickers
The money's in the J Arthur	J Arthur	Rank	bank
The radishes made me Raquel	Raquel	Welch	belch
'E kicked 'im in the Darby	Darby	Kelly	belly
'E's a stupid Charlie	Charlie	Smirke	berk †
He needs laces for his daisies	daisy	roots	Boots
Put it in the nervo	Nervo	and Knox	Box
He needs to tighten his Epsoms	Epsom	races	Braces
Go and get yer Wilkies	Wilkie	Bards	Cards
The Gregory's in the post	Gregory	Peck	Cheque
They got married in chicken	chicken	perch	Church
She played some lovely Norfolks	Norfolk	Broads	Chords
I'll be wearing my weasel ...	weasel	and stoat	Coat ‡
... as it's a bit Naughton	Naughton	and Gold	Cold
It's all a load of pony	pony	and trap	Crap
Close the montagus ...	Montagu	Burtons	Curtains
... it's getting Finsbury	Finsbury	Park	Dark
Shut that Rory	Rory	O'Moore	Door
He's a bit elephant's	elephant's	trunk	Drunk
A loud raspberry	raspberry	tart	fart
Went to the disco in me Grosvenors	Grosvenor	Squares	Flares
alternatively in me Lionels	Lionel	Blairs	Flares
Fell down on the Rory	Rory	O'Moore	Floor
They sent the Sweeney	Sweeney	Todd	Flying Squad
I can't see without me hackneys	Hackney	Marshes	Glasses
I told 'im to scarper	Scapa	Flow	Go §
She's got tiny germans	German	bands	hands

She's combing her barnet	Barnet	Fair	Hair
I'm wearing my titfer	tit for	tat	Hat
Use your loaf	loaf	of bread	Head
'E spent six years in jug	Jug	and pail	Jail
'E was a good barnaby	Barnaby	Rudge	Judge
I need a zorba	Zorba	the Greek	Leak (wee)
'E's been telling porkies	Pork	Pies	Lies
Let's have a butchers	Butcher's	Hook	Look
Give it 'ere me ole china	China	Plate	Mate
Give us the bread	Bread	and honey	Money
I must have a jimmy	Jimmy	Riddle	Piddle (wee)
Got me in the barnacles	Barnacle	Bill(s)	Pills (testicles)
'E's a right Hampton	Hampton	Wick	Prick
It's really Irish	Irish	Stew	True
He was wearing an Irish	Irish	Jig	Wig
Got to send 'im an elephant	Elephant	and Castle	Parcel
Get 'im on the dog	Dog	and Bone	Phone
There's merlins all over the lolly	Merlin	the Magician	Pigeon
	Lolly	pop	shop
Get me 'alf a pint of frankies	Frankie	Vaughan	Prawn
Just poppin' u the frog	frog	and toad	road
'ere, don't I get a geoffrey?	Geoffrey	Chaucer	saucer
Get yourself a clean dicky	Dicky	Dirt	shirt
I need a good eiffel	Eiffel	Tower	shower
Me trouble's up the apples	trouble	and strife	wife
	apples	and pears	stairs
Where'd yer get that whistle	whistle	and flute	suit‡
Time for a nice cuppa rosie	Rosie	Lea	tea
'e's doing bird	bird	lime	time
Lovely bristols	Bristol	City	titty
Straight up irish?	Irish	stew	true
See you in a bubble	bubble	and squeak	week
'alf a dollar on the nose	nose	and chin	win

* Cockney pronunciation, with the untransliterable 'nasal w' sound for 'l'.
† Itself rhyming slang for a vulgar – if not taboo – word for part of the female anatomy.
‡ May be related to 'Pop [ie to pawn] Goes the Weasel' or 'Whistle'.
§ There is some debate as to whether 'scarper' comes from the Italian *scappare* = escape or from Scapa Flow, the Orkney Islands anchorage, where the German fleet scuttled itself in 1919.

Yiddish already

Yiddish is a Jewish language born in Poland from elements of Hebrew characters, and spoken by the widely-dispersed Jews of the world. Sometimes Yiddish words are interspersed with everyday English and we give a selection here. Some such as bagel, boo-boo, chutzpah, glitch and so on have entered the English language.

Ahntoishung disappointment
Alevay I wish it were so
Alter kocker (lecherous) old fuddy-duddy; has-been
Amorets peasant; ignoramus
Apikoros hedonist; unbeliever
Aroysgevorfeneh wasted; discarded
Arumgeflikt fleeced
Arumloifer street urchin
Bagel hard ring-shaped roll
Baitsim eggs; vulgar: testicles
Balagoleh a vulgar person
Balbatim boss, leader
Balebatish honourable
Baleboss male owner, boss or head of household
Baleboste woman who keeps a fastidious household; a bossy, over-bearing woman
Balebosteven to bustle like a meticulous housewife
Balmalocha a connoisseur (often sarcastic)
Balmechule a bad worker
Bar mitzvah ceremony in which a boy of thirteen is accepted as a member of the adult religious community
Batlan an idler; a mediocre thinker pretending to be intellectual
Behayma a farm animal (particularly a cow); a dummy
Bestitt shit (literal and figurative)
Bialy a soft flat-baked roll
Billik cheap
Blintz a pancake wrapped round a cheese or fruit filling
Bobbe-myseh an old wives' tale
Bonditt a beguiler; a sharpie
Boo-boo a minor gaffe
Borax low quality merchandise (attractive but shoddy)
Borax-house a store (furniture)
Borsht belt Jewish resorts in the Catskill Mountains in New York State
Boychick a little boy
Bren a real go-getter; someone who thinks fast on his feet
Briss the circumcision rite
Broche a blessing
Brust a breast

B'suleh virgin, young lady

B'sulim hymen

Bubehleh grandmother

Bubkes nothing

Bulbe a potato; a mistake, a goof

Bulbenik someone who frequently screws up, a bumbler

Bulvan bruiser, lout, dolt

Bummerkeh a woman bum

Burtshen to mutter, grumble

Chaim life

Chatchka a knick-knack or trinket; a minor cut or bruise
darling, dear, sweetie; a dishy woman

Chazzer a pig, literal and figurative

Chazzerei pig food; junk

Chazerishe unpalatable

Cheder Hebrew school

Chelm a mythical city inhabited by lovable morons

Chevra a gang

Chloppeh to rain cats and dogs

Chmallyeh a karate chop

Choleria cholera, plague; a fishwife

Chutzpah gall, nerve

Daven to pray

Donstairsikeh the downstairs neighbour

Dopes a bystander who offers help with words not action

Draidkoff a sophist; someone who turns facts to his own advantage;
someone whose head is turned round; a confused person

Dreck shit! (lit and fig); shit (exclamation); shitty

Dreydel a four-sided top (toy)

Dyebuk the ghost of a dead person possessing a living person who has
wronged him/her when alive; an evil spirit, incubus

Echt genuine

Einredenish a self-induced delusion

Eizel a fool

Emes Honest! truly!

Eppis something

Essen to eat

Faigeleh a little bird; a homosexual

Farantvortlech responsible, accountable

Farbisseneh a bitter woman (male *farbissener*)

Farblondjhet wandering about aimlessly; confused

Farmatert utterly tired
Farmisht mixed up, emotionally confused
Farpotshket messed up
Farputzt decked out
Farshtinkener stinking
Farshvitst sweaty
Fartootst mixed up
Fartumelt disoriented, confused
Feh Ugh! Phooey! Baloney! (exclamation)
Feinschmecker someone who has a discerning palate, a gourmand
Fonfeven to nasalise; to double-talk; a double-talker; a swindler
Fressen to gobble, to eat like an animal
Frim devout
Frosk to smack hard
Futz to copulate; to screw around; behaving as in having consumed too
     many illegal, mind-expanding substances; vagina (vulgar)
Gaon a genius
Geferlech terrible
Gehakteh tsores total misery
Gehenna hell
Gelibteh a beloved woman (male *gelibter*)
Gelt money
Genug enough
Gesheft business
Geshmak delicious, yummy
Geshrei a scream, clamour, yell
Geshtank foul-smelling
Geshvollen swollen pride
Gevalt Help! Oh my God!
Glitch a sudden surge of power or other technological irregularity that
     interferes with the smooth operation of a computer; a systemic defect,
     a fly in the ointment; to do something inadvertently that cuts short
     the execution of a computer program; an unexpected irregularity in a
     data run (particle-physics patois)
Glitz glitter; showy, ostentatious
Golem a robot
Gonif a crook; someone who is clever, perhaps to the point of being
     diabolical; a swindler; a precocious child
Gornisht nothing
Gott God

Goy a non-Jew; a non-religious Jew someone who is unfeeling and insensitive; a Gentile

Graub brutish, vulgar; a brute or lout

Greps to belch; a belch or burp

Haimish homely, cosy

Handlen to do business, to engage in commerce; to haggle over prices

Heldish brave

Hinten buttocks

Hitskop hothead; someone who is easily excitable

Hok to strike, bang or chop

Holdupnick a mugger

Hotcha! Great! A cry of approval, uttered especially at lively theatrical events. Sometimes the cry is sarcastic

Hubba-hubba! Bravo!

Kabsten a pauper; a good-for-nothing

Kaddish a prayer for the dead

Kadoches convulsions, malaria, fever; less than nothing; good for nothing

Kakapitshi an inedible concoction; a conglomeration

Kalamutneh gloomy

Kalikeh a crippled woman; a misfit; an inept craftsperson or performer (male *kalycher*)

Kamtsan a tightwad, a stingy person

Kaneh an enema

Kapore forgiveness, atonement, sacrifice; a good-for-nothing

Kashe mush, cereal; a mess, a mix up; a question

Kasnik a hothead, an angry person

Kasokeh cross-eyed

Kayn aynhoreh! spare us the evil eye! Knock on Wood!

Kemfer a fighter, a militant supporter of a cause

Kibbitz to comment while others are playing a game, to offer gratuitous advice; a meddlesome onlooker

Kibosh Nonsense! Bosh!; To make into nonsense, to jinx, to frustrate

Kike a jew (vulgar)

Kishka intestine; stuffed derma

Klaperkeh a female chatterbox

Klipeh a hag, a shrew; a demonic woman

Klogmuter a complainer, whiner

Klots-kashe a simply worded but difficult question artfully interjected into a discussion or presentation that is proceeding smoothly; the purpose is to derail the discussion or to throw off the speaker.

Kloymersht pretended

Klug smart

Klupper an incompetent worker

Klutz a dullard; someone who's always tripping over his own feet; adjective: klutsy; noun: klutziness

K'nacker a big shot; an old fogey

Knippel a button; money tied in a knot in the corner of a handkerchief; any money stashed away; a nest egg; hymen; virginity (vulgar)

Knish a dumpling filled with chopped liver, cheese, potatoes, onion or buckwheat groats; vagina (slang)

Kochleffel someone who stirs up trouble; a busybody

Kop head

Kopvaitik headache

Kosher fit to eat according to Jewish dietary laws; pious; proper

Krank ill

Krechts sigh!; to groan; to protest

Kreplach triangular dumplings filled with meat or cheese; Jewish ravioli; nothing

Kush a kiss

Kushvokh a honeymoon

Kuzina a female cousin

Kvell to be proud; to gloat, especially about the accomplishments of a child

Kvetch to complain; to whine; *Kvetchy*: crotchety

Leiden to suffer

Letz a cynic; a comic, prankster or wit

Ligner a liar

Litvak a Lithuanian Jew; a clever but insensitive person

Loch a hole; vagina (vulgar)

Loksh a noodle; a thin person, someone who is as thin as a noodle; Italian

Loz im gayn! Let him go! What do you need him for? Forget it!

Luftmensh a 'man of air'; someone who has his head in the clouds; a dreamer; someone who doesn't have a job who wanders aimlessly

Lump a scoundrel

Macher someone who is going places; a wheeler-dealer; someone who has gone places; a big shot; the boss

Maidel a young girl; a virgin

Make plague; nothing; *bubkes*

Malach an angel

Malach-hamoves the male angel of death; a bad wife

Maven an expert; a connoisseur; a customer who thinks he knows more than the tailor does about clothes

Mazel (Maazl) luck; *Mazel tov!* Congratulations! literally = Good Luck!

Mechuleh failed; spoiled; aborted; out of order, bankrupt

Meeskeit an ugly person or thing

Megillah a long story; a rigmarole

Melamed a teacher of religion or Hebrew; a wise man; a parochial bore; someone who is too 'bookish' to notice what's going on around him.

Mensh an admirable human being; a person of great dignity; the finest specimen of our species

Meshugge crazy, mad; (*messhuggener* or *meshugginer* for a man; *meshuggeneh* or *meshugina* for a woman) a madman

Meshumed a Jew who has converted to Christianity

Metsieh a find; a bargain; a great discovery; (sarcastic) a real prize; (idiomatic) deal as in 'So what's the big metsieh?'

Mezuma money

Mezuze a scroll containg the ancient credo 'Hear O Israel, the Lord our God, the Lord is One' that Jews attach to the right-hand post of every door of the house as an affirmation of faith

Mies ugly

Miesse meshina an ugly death

Mikvah a ritual bath; used by converts to Judaism, by married women seven days after each menstrual period, and by women who have just given birth

Milchik describing foods that contain milk and therefore cannot be eaten with meat in accordance with Jewish dietary laws; weak; Caspar Milquetoast (a cartoon character devised by H T Webster (1885–1952))

Minyan the ten men needed to have a religious service; a quorum

Mishegoss Insanity

Mish-mosh a hotchpotch; confusion; crossed signals; a mess

Mishpocheh an extended family; all one's relatives

Mittelmessiker the average person; the common man; John Doe; Joe Shmo; hoi polloi

Moishe kapoyr Mr Upside Down; someone who always puts the cart before the horse, swims against the tide, and marches to a different drummer

Monzer an illegitimate child. In Judaism this includes a child born of a religiously mixed marriage or of an incestuous marriage; a despicable individual; a 'bastard'; a shrewd conman; someone who spends a lot of time in one shoestore but buys a pair of shoes in a neighbouring store

Moyl one who performs circumcisions

Mutek brave

Muttelmessig someone who makes a mess in the middle; a *kibbitzer*

Nadan a dowry

Nafkeh a prostitute

Nar a fool; foolish; foolishness

Nayfish someone who is pathetic or inconsequential; someone you always forget to introduce at a party

Neb a nobody; a sad sap

Nebbish a nobody; a loser; a drip; ineffectual; hapless; (Interjection) Unfortunately!

Nechtiger tog an impossibility

Nekaiveh a woman; a woman of low morals; a prostitute

Neshomeleh sweetheart

Nextdoorsikeh the female neighbour next door

Nishtgutnikff a good for nothing

Nishtikeit a nobody

Nochshlepper someone who follows after; a hanger-on

Nogoodnik a person to be avoided, for whatever reason; someone who is 'no good'; a bum

Noodge a nagger; a badgerer; to nag; to pester; nagged to death; nauseous

Nosh to snack; to nibble; to eat a small bit of; a snack; a tit bit; a little something; someone who nibbles

Nu Well! So!

Nudnik a colossal, talkative bore

Ongeblozzen puffed up; conceited; peevish; an arrogant person

Ogeshtopt overstuffed; super-rich

Ongetrunken drunk; soused

Ostairsikeh a female upstairs neighbour; *upstairsiker* = male upstairs neighbour

Oy! (Exclamation) Oi!

Oysgamitched totally worn out

Oysgematert fatigued

Oysgemutshet tormented to distraction; tortured

Oysgeputzt overdressed

Oysvorf an outcast; an outsider; a nasty *kibitzer*

Oyster a treasure; (Sarcastic) a real treasure

Parech a wretched disease in which one sprouts scales on the head; someone suffering from this disease; a shady, disgusting character

Parnosseh livelihood

Paskudne revolting; unmentionably ugly; an odious person

Patsh a slap; to slap

Patshken to work in a half-assed way. Often used as in 'patshkied around'; an idler; a lazy worker

Petsel penis

Petseleh little penis

PhG acronym for 'Papa has gelt' (money)

Phudnik an overly studious doctoral candidate

Pishen to piss; (*pisher* for males, *pisherkeh* for females) a little squirt; a term of endearment for an infant; a very little squirt; (*pisher* for males, *pisherkeh* for females) a nobody, someone of no consequence; urine

Pisk a big mouth

Plagen to work; to suffer

Plaplen chatter

Platke-macher a gossip maker

Plusher a gossip

Plotz to burst; to explode

Prinsesen a prima donna; a pampered woman

Prost vulgar; low class

Punim a face

Pupik a belly button

Pushke a small box, especially for collecting money for charity; a nest egg

Pustunpashnik a loafer

Putz penis; a jerk; a prick; to fool around

Rachmones leniency; mercy

Rebbe Rabbi

Rebbitzin the wife of a rabbi

Rov an ordained rabbi

Sachel commonsense

Schlag a poor sale

Shlahger someone who looks like he can be pushed around; a sucker

Schlemiel a fool; a blunderbuss; a social misfit who fails because of his own inadequacy; as distinguished from the *schlimazel* who fails through no fault of his own – just bad luck

Schlep to drag; to drag one's feet or body around; to walk as if one is dragging heavy packages; a slob, a bum; to steal; (underworld patois) to steal things that have been left in a car; (underworld patois) the act of stealing things from a car; (underworld patois) schlepper: a car-package thief; (shoestore slang) *schlepper* a salesman who tries to lure passersby into the store; someone who is on the lookout for a bargain or freebie; (furniture store jargon) to rearrange the furniture in the store window or on the display floor

Schlimazel a born loser; someone who's always unlucky; a confusion; a complication; a mess; to run away from a mess

Schlock something shoddy; poorly crafted; a peeve; a complainer; a wretch; (furniture store slang) an overcharge; (*schlock house/joint*) a store that sells inferior merchandise; (furniture store slang); (*schlock joint*) a store without fixed prices; (*schlock meister*) someone who specialises in selling cheap merchandise; a preacher who solicits contributions over the radio

Schmaltz melted fat, especially chicken fat; mawkishness; over-sentimentality; pathos; to make maudlin; hair tonic; (army and navy slang) *schmaltz artist* a sycophant; too sentimental, mushy, corny or gaudy

Schmate a rag; a cheap dress; a shoddy garment; anything that is cheap or worthless; a slut

Schmuck (vulgar) penis; an idiot; a fool; (vulgar) a bastard; a son of a bitch

Schneck affectation; sexual advances; particularly ones not backed up by feeling

Schnecken little fruitcakes or nut cakes

Schneider a tailor (garment worker slang); anyone connected with the garment industry; to win a game, especially gin rummy, before the opponent is able to score even a single point; a shutout, as in baseball or gin rummy

Schnorrer a beggar, a panhandler; to beg; a cheapskate; a miser; (shoestore slang) a customer who haggles in a store where the prices are fixed

Schreien to complain or talk loudly

Schvartz black; (*schvartze* or *schvartzeh* for a female; *schvartzer* for a man) a black person. Usually refers to domestics.

Shabbes the Sabbath

Shabbes goy a non-Jew hired by Orthodox Jews to turn lights on and off and to perform other physical tasks that Jews are forbidden to do on the Sabbath; a disparaging term for a Jew who strays from the faith

Shadchen a marriage broker; a matchmaker

Shah! Hush! Shut up!

Shainkeit beauty

Shalom peace; salutation: Hello or goodbye. Yiddish has the greeting *shalom aleichem* 'peace be with you' and the obligatory response *aleichem shalom* 'and peace to you'

Shamus a guard, detective or policeman; a police informer; anyone who sucks up to a politician

Shanda shame; an embarrassment; a scandal

Shanhoiz a house of prostitution

Shaygetz (vulgar) a non Jewish male; (vulgar) a Jew who adopts the attitudes of gentiles; a man of any religious persuasion who charms the pants off women

Sheeny (vulgar) a Jew

Shekel a coin, especially a silver dollar (Today the shekel is also a unit of currency in Israel); weight

Shihi-pihi a mere bagatelle; nothing

Shikker a drunkard; a drunk; 'on the shicker' drinking (Australian slang); to get drunk (Australian slang)

Shiksa a non-Jewish woman, especially one who is young and attractive; a Jewish woman who strays from the faith

Shlect bad

Shlogen to beat up

Shlong penis; a troublesome wife

Shlosser meccanic

Shlump a slob; a drip; to droop; to do something in a half-assed and unenthusiastic way

Shlumper a slut

Shlumperdik sloppy; unkempt

Shmeck smell; (underworld patois) narcotics, especially powdered drugs (underworld patois) heroin, smack; (underworld patois) drug user

Shmeer to smear; (delicatessen slang) a glob of cream cheese; to grease the palm of; to bribe; a bribe; everything; the whole deal; the shebang; (sports) to wipe out an opponent; (furniture store slang) to flatter a customer

Shmegegge a buffoon; an idiot

Shmeikle to talk someone into something

Shmeis a bang; (furniture store slang) to break off a sale, especially because the store offers such bad terms that the customer walks out.

Shemdrik a weak, ineffectual person; a little penis

Shmo mistake; error

Shmohawk (vulgar) penis

Shmooz a heart-to heart talk; idle talk; to chitchat; (garment worker slang) to talk shop

Shmuts filth, dirt, garbage, smut

Shnaps liquor

Shnell quick

Shnook a pathetic but lovable fool; (salesman slang) easy mark, sucker; (English public school slang) to gesture derisively by putting the thumb to the nose and extending, or wiggling the fingers; (English public school slang) to complete an exam; to outargue an opponent

Shnoz a nose, a huge proboscis; a long-nosed person; (underworld patois) an addict who takes drugs only through the nose.

Shpigel a mirror

Shpilkes jitters; anxiety; the condition of having ants in one's pants

Shtark strong; strong one; a strong-arm man; a violent criminal

Shtetl a peasant village of Eastern European Jews; characteristic of a peasant village

Shtik a bit; a piece; a characteristic mannerism, routine, or gesture, especially of a performer

Shtikle a little bit; a piece of; a bit of, somewhat of

Shtinken to stink

Shtrahmel velvet hat worn by Orthodox Jews on special occasions; a run-of-the-mill hat

Shtunk something that smells gross; an ungrateful jerk

Shtup to push; to force something on someone; to bribe; to tip excessively in a way that is almost like offering a bribe; (vulgar) to fuck; (vulgar) a female fornicator; (vulgar) *schtupper* or *shtupper* a male fornicator; (vulgar) the act of sexual intercourse

Shtuss nonsense; an uproar; a fuss

Shul a synagogue

Shvebeleh a very excitable person

Shvengern pregnant

Shvindle swindle; to swindle

Shvindeldik dizzy; unsteady

Shvitzer someone who sweats a lot, especially a nervous seducer; a braggart

Shvontz penis; an ungallant fool

Simcha a joy; a great pleasure; a celebration

Szhlok a nincompoop

Tam taste; appropriateness; a simpleton

Tamavateh dopey

Tareram hubbub; commotion; uproar

Tata Dad

Teival a devil, or the Devil

Toches rear; bum

Trayf non kosher; a despicable individual

Tripper gonorrhea

Trombenik a boaster; someone who blows his own trumpet; a mooch; a freeloader a fraud

Tsedrait twisted; kooky; (*tsedrateh*) a female kook; (*tsedrayter*) a male kook

Tsimmes fuss; a sweet carrot or turnip compote

Tsitser someone who says 'ts! ts!' a lot; a bystander who commiserates but offers no real help

Tsores trouble; woes; afflictions; problems

Tsutumelt disoriented; dizzy

Tummel a commotion

Tush an affectionate word for rear end

Tushie kids' talk for rear end

Tzadik a pious person; (sarcastic) wicked old man, especially one who is miserly as well

Umgeduldik petulant

Ummeglick extremely unlikely

Ungepachkit cluttered

Untershmeichlen to butter up

Utz to needle; to nag

Vai (exclamation) pain; a pain

Vantz a bedbug; an inconsequential person; a nobody

Veib a wife

Verlierlen (garment worker slang) to lose a customer to a fellow salesman

Vitz a joke

Vitzel a philosophical witticism

Vonneh a bath; a bathtub

Vund a wound

Vyzoso an idiot; a dolt; (vulgar) penis

Yachneh a shrew; a loud woman

Yehudi a Jew

Yenta a blabbermouth; a nag; to badger

Yentzen to whore; to 'screw'; to swindle; someone who sleeps around a lot; a slut; a con man (underworld patois) a cheater

Yid (vulgar) a Jew

Yold a dope; a half-wit

Zaftig juicy, plump and sexy

Zhlub someone who is insensitive and uncouth; (*zhlubby*) boorish

Zitsflaish patience; endurance; buttocks

Lifestyle

Boxing

There were practically no rules in the bare-knuckle prize fights which continued into the C20. Grabbing, wrestling and even biting were allowed. The fighters shaved head and face so their opponent could not find an easy grip, and brutal blows to the testicles or to the Adam's Apple were popular incapacitating attacks. Neither blow forms part of the modern sport: in the former case hitting 'below the belt' is banned; in the latter case the use of gloves means that a boxer can no longer directly hit the Adam's Apple. A round ended when one of the fighters fell or was forced to the ground, so if either fighter needed a breather, he would promptly fall to the ground. In the late C18 there were two trends encouraging the development of rules. First, there was a growing 'scientific' approach to sport. Second, the supporters and spectators of prize fights wanted better entertainment than watching two hulks grabbing and slugging at each other with no controls. There were several attempts to introduce rules. In 1867 John Graham Chambers of the London Amateur Athletic Club drew up a comprehensive set of rules and persuaded John Sholto Douglas, the 9th Marquess of Queensberry (1844–1900), who was a well-known patron of sport, particularly of boxing, to support their introduction and lend his name to the system. His rules included compulsory gloves, 3-minute rounds with a 1-minute break, no wrestling, and 3 weight divisions – lightweight (up to 140 lbs), middleweight (up to 154 lbs), and heavyweight (over 154 lbs). Later the rule giving a downed boxer 10 seconds to rise was introduced. By 1891 the so-called Queensberry Rules were adopted by boxing associations around the world, forming the basis of the modern sport, and the age of the bare-knuckle fighter began to draw to an end. By 1920 the major national federations had agreed on 8 weight divisions, known as the 'Classic' weights: fly, bantam, feather, light, welter, middle, light-heavy, and heavy. As boxers' physiques and bodyweights changed in the C20, new grades were introduced by various of the international federations, and gradually were accepted throughout the sport.

Major International Boxing Federations:

World Boxing Association (WBA) created 1962
World Boxing Council (WBC) created 1963
International Boxing Federation (IBF) created 1982
World Boxing Organization (WBO) created 1988

(There is a shifting number of smaller, more obscure federations, many of which are never recognised outside a particular city or small geographical area, or do not last longer than a year or two.) The last undisputed world champion at any weight was Mike Tyson, who claimed the world heavyweight title by beating Frank Bruno in 1989. Since then, a 'World Champion' is only the champion of the particular international federation which agreed the fight, and no boxer has claimed the title of all 4 of the leading international boxing federations.

Boxing divisions and weights

On the day of the pre-fight weigh-in the boxer can weigh no more than:

	UK	US	Metric (kilos)	Date initiated	Initiated by
Strawweight (Mini Flyweight)	7 st 7 lb	105 lb	47.627	1987	IBF
Light-flyweight (Junior Flyweight)	7 st 10 lb	108 lb	48.988	1975	WBC
Flyweight	8 st	112 lb	50.802	Classic	—
Super Flyweight (Junior Bantamweight)	8 st 3 lb	115 lb	52.163	1979	WBC
Bantamweight	8 st 6 lb	118 lb	53.524	Classic	—
Super Bantamweight (Junior Featherweight)	8 st 10 lb	122 lb	55.338	1976	WBC
Featherweight	9 st	126 lb	57.153	Classic	—
Super Featherweight (Junior Lightweight)	9 st 4 lb	130 lb	58.967	1921	New York Commission of Boxing
Lightweight	9 st 9 lb	135 lb	61.235	Classic	—
Light-welterweight (Junior Welterweight)	10 st	140 lb	63.503	1926	National Boxing Association of the USA
Welterweight	10 st 7 lb	147 lb	66.678	Classic	—
Light-middleweight (Junior Middleweight)	11 st	154 lb	69.853	1962	WBA
Middleweight	11 st 6 lb	160 lb	72.575	Classic	—
Super Middleweight	12 st	168 lb	76.203	1984	IBF
Light-heavyweight	12 st 7 lb	175 lb	79.379	Classic	—
Cruiserweight (Junior Heavyweight)	13 st 8 lb	190 lb	86.183	1979	WBC
Heavyweight	no upper limit	no upper limit	no upper limit	Classic	—

Oriental Martial arts

Unlike boxing or other western fighting systems, Oriental martial arts include teachings on meditation, philosophy, strengthening the internal organs, and self-discipline. They also emphasise defence rather than aggression. Many of the oldest systems are Chinese, and according to tradition, were developed about 3000 years ago. Originally teaching was oral, so no firm dates are provided until the Shaolin Temple, which kept written records, began teaching its techniques about 1400 years ago. Chinese martial arts are usually lumped together under the name 'kung fu', a term which really means nothing more than long, disciplined study. From China kung fu spread throughout Asia, and although eventually new, different systems were developed and adapted, all the well-known ones derive from the original Chinese techniques. The Japanese schools became known in the west in the late C19, but the Chinese systems were not widely known until the 1960s. For this reason, many Chinese schools in the west copied well-known Japanese features such as coloured belts and grades. There are a great many separate schools which only teach fighting with weapons, *eg* the Japanese kempo or kendo, and weapons training is part of most martial arts schools, but this list looks at the most common Oriental unarmed combat systems. Note that spellings of Chinese and Japanese words can often vary widely!

Kung Fu

Chinese. The origin of all Asian martial arts. Mainly punches, kicks and blocks rather than 'grabbing' techniques. Huge number of different schools, often regional, such as wing chun, tiger-crane, monkey style, or jeet kune do, developed by Bruce Lee (1940–1973), the actor and probably the most famous Chinese martial artist. The northern Chinese styles are often acrobatic and emphasise kicks and long-range techniques. Southern styles are mostly close-range, emphasising hand techniques. Has generated a booming film industry.

Tai Chi Ch'uan

Chinese, meaning 'great ultimate'. Practised as an extremely slow, almost dance-like series of movements, often by large groups of older people in the park. About 1000 years old, with an emphasis on relaxation, developing internal strength and well-being, rather than beating people up.

Ju-jitsu

Japanese, meaning 'the gentle art' or 'art of subtleness'. The traditional martial art of the samurai warrior class, founded by Shirobei Akiyama in

C16, after techniques he had learnt in China. It includes holds, locks and throwing techniques as well as methods of striking an opponent.

Judo

Japanese, meaning 'the way'. A system of holding, locking and throwing. No punches or real kicks. Founded in 1882 by Jigoro Kano (1860–1938), a Japanese professor, who developed this particular unarmed combat out of ju-jitsu. He created a uniform of loose trousers, wrap-around tunic, and belt, and organised formal grades of achievement, denoted by the colour of the belt. The black belt is the final colour to be gained, and at that stage practitioners are given the rank of Dan, which simply means 'step' or 'degree'. Most judo schools will have more than 1 Dan rank, usually 3 but as many as 10. Judo soon became popular in Japan and was taught in many schools. Judo belt colours are:

Rank	Belt colour
Beginner	Red or White
6th Grade	White
5th Grade	Yellow
4th Grade	Orange
3rd Grade	Green
2nd Grade	Blue
1st Grade	Brown
1st Dan	Black

Karate

Japanese/Okinawan, meaning 'empty hands'. Developed in C16 in Okinawa, an island in the Ryukyu group south of the main Japanese islands. Mainly striking and blocking techniques rather than 'grabbing'. It was introduced to the Japanese public in 1922 by Gichin Funakoshi, the 'Father of Modern Karate' (1868–1957), who created systems for the exercises and teaching. He based the grades and belt colours upon the already established system of judo. The belts listed are for Funakoshi's style, Shotokan karate, the most widely practised system, although there are now some other karate schools, such as Goju-Ryu, Kyokushinkai, Shito-Ryu, and Wado-Ryu. Shotokan karate belt colours are:

Novice	Grades
Beginner	White
9th	Red
8th	Orange
7th	Yellow

Middle	Grades
6th	Green
5th	Purple
4th	Purple and white

Advanced	Grades
3rd	Brown
2nd	Brown and white
1st	Brown and red

Master	Grades
1st Dan	Black
2nd Dan	Black
3rd Dan	Black

Ninjitsu

Japanese, meaning 'the art of stealthy movement'. The black-clad Ninja assassins, with weapons such as the shuriken throwing stars, are the popular conception of this school. Dates back to the C7, when communities of Buddhist priests, threatened by warlords, used their knowledge of Chinese military spying and subterfuge techniques to survive. Secretive, clan-like groups of spies, saboteurs and assassins developed.

Aikido

Japanese, meaning the 'way of harmony'. Founded by Morihei Ueshiba (1883–1969) as a method of self-defence which brings the least harm to the attacker. Both striking and holding techniques are included, but is an extremely non-aggressive style.

Tae Kwon Do

Korean, means 'the way of the hand and foot'. Founded in 1955 by General Choi Hong Hi (1918–2002) to be Korea's own martial art. Heavily based on karate, emphasises kicks but includes powerful punches.

Muy Thai

From Thailand, meaning Thai boxing. Believed to be about 2,000 years old. Probably developed as a close combat battlefield skill, but all early records were lost when Burmese invaders burnt the royal city of Ayuddhaya in 1767. Practised by many Siamese kings. Employs a barrage of fast, powerful kicks and uses heads, knees and elbows more than many styles. In America has been altered into kickboxing, the martial art used by Buffy the Vampire Slayer.

Collectors and their collectables

Arranged by collector

Collector	Objects collected
Aerophilatelist	Airmail stamps
Arctophilist / Arctophile	Teddy bears
Audiophile	Music
Bestiarist	Medieval books on animals
Bibliophile	Books
Brandophilist	Cigar bands
Cactophile	Cactus and Succulent plants
Cameist	Cameos
Conchologist	Shells
Copoclephilist	Keyrings
Deltiologist	Postcards
Discophile	Records or CDs
Ephemologist	Ephemera
Errinophilist	Revenue or tax stamps
Ex-librist	Book plates
Exonumist	Numismatic material other than coins or notes
Fusilatelist	Phone cards
Helixophile	Corkscrews
Heortologist	Religious calendars
Iconophile	Prints and engravings
Labeorphilist	Beer bottles
Lepidopterist	Butterflies
Notaphilist	Paper money
Numismatist	Money and medals
Oologist	Birds' eggs
Philatelist	Postage stamps
Phillumenist	Matchbook covers
Philographist	Autographs
Phonophile	Phonograph records
Plangonologist	Dolls
Receptarist	Recipes
Sinistrophilist	Left-handed objects
Sucrologist	Sugar packets
Tegestologist	Beer mats
Telegerist	Telephone calling cards
Vecturist	Transport tokens

| Vexillologist | Flags |
| Xylographer | Woodcuts / engraving |

Arranged by object

Objects collected	*Collector*
Airmail stamps	Aerophilatelist
Autographs	Philographist
Beer bottles	Labeorphilist
Beer mats	Tegestologist
Birds' eggs	Oologist
Book plates	Ex-librist
Books	Bibliophile
Butterflies	Lepidopterist
Cactus	Cactophile
Cameos	Cameist
Cigar bands	Brandophilist
Corkscrews	Helixophile
Dolls	Plangonologist
Flags	Vexillologist
Keyrings	Copoclephilist
Left handed objects	Sinistrophilist
Matchbook covers	Phillumenist
Medieval books on animals	Bestiarist
Money and medals	Numismatist
Music	Audiophile
Numismatic material other than coins or notes	Exonumist
Paper money	Notaphilist
Phone cards	Fusilatelist
Phonograph records	Phonophile
Postage stamps	Philatelist
Postcards	Deltiologist
Prints and engravings	Iconophile
Recipes	Receptarist
Records or CDs	Discophile
Religious calendars	Heortologist
Revenue or tax stamps	Errinophilist
Shells	Conchologist
Sugar packets	Sucrologist
Teddy bears	Arctophilist / Arctophile
Telephone calling cards	Telegery

| Transport tokens | Vecturist |
| Woodcuts / engraving | Xylographer |

Fashion in the Western world

Clothing has several functions, keeping us warm in cold climates, protecting us from a harsh environment, meeting religious requirements, identifying us through a uniform, or providing decoration and body adornment.

Costume is a term applied to distinctive forms of clothing, especially when used for ceremonial or official functions. Examples include coronation robes, religious vestments, academic or legal gowns. The term also includes accessories such as belts, gloves, hats, shoes or jewellery.

Fashion, however, relates to the clothes we choose to put on. Fashion is embodied in styles of clothing. It reflects ideas of aesthetics and beauty. It allows us to be individuals, but at the same time our style of clothing marks us as belonging to certain social groups, for example: goths, punks, Marks & Spencer women. It is a language, and it carries messages about us that we wish the world to know – or, conversely, that we cannot hide. We can be slaves to fashion, or we can determinedly ignore it – all part of the luxury of choosing for ourselves.

This is a brief overview of the costume and fashions of wealthy people at different periods of history in the western world, followed by an alphabetical list of various items of clothing. Note that most people in most periods of history would have worn simple, rough, cheap clothes whose basic styles barely changed through the centuries: nothing like the high fashion of the court. Moreover, styles from one period would merge into another, and no doubt old fogies in the Renaissance period were still wearing Medieval costume – and probably experiencing the ridicule of the younger, fashionable generation.

Stone Age We assume a fine line in furs during the Ice Age, but apart from that we can only guess. Stone scrapers, probably for scraping animal skins, have been found from the Middle Stone Age onwards, along with bone needles from the late Stone Age. Non-industrial hunter–gatherer societies today use a variety of plant fibres for clothing, often simply for body decoration, although in colder climates, fur and leather are common.

Bronze Age Introduced the spindle for hand-spinning yarn and looms for weaving cloth from the yarn. So, woollen clothes became common. Cotton and flax fibres were also used.

Ancient Assyria Draped, patterned skirts and tunics, held by pins. Fringes were very common.

Ancient Egypt Women wore a tight, sheath-like dress, which developed into a tunic worn by men, who originally wore only a loincloth or a kilt. In later years Egyptian costume was elaborate and highly decorative, and included wigs. The female pharaoh, Hatshepsut, was depicted on occasion wearing a false beard.

Classical Greece Generally loosely-draped and flowing, held by pins. Both men and women wore a loose woollen tunic, the chiton, tied with a girdle, knee-length for men, longer for women. From C6 BCE, women wore a peplos or peplum, a large piece of fabric wrapped around the body, pinned at the shoulders with excess material draping like a cape.

Classical Rome Heavily influenced by the Greeks. A tunic and toga, a large cloth draped around the body in a complicated and restrictive way. Underwear, very similar to bikinis, worn by women dancers or for exercise.

Byzantine dress Byzantium became Constantinople when Roman Emperor Constantine chose it as his capital city in 330 CE. As centre of the Eastern Roman Empire, it set the standard for courtly continental European clothes for centuries. Elaborate, colourful and with an increasingly Oriental bent, clothes were loose, layered, highly decorated and grand. Silkworms were smuggled from China.

European Middle Ages; Dark Ages Northern Europe adopted the clothes of 'barbarian' invaders: instead of flowing, draped clothes, T-shaped tunics were cut 'to shape'. Both men and women wore a loose over-tunic (later a robe or gown) and a tighter, sleeved under-tunic (chemise). Indoor cloaks, or mantles, were often needed. Introduction of the spinning wheel enabled much faster production of yarn, but most people had only one or two outfits. About 1000 CE, in the early Gothic period, sleeves and hemlines become more flared: sometimes women's dresses were so long they had a trailing train. Men tended to wear stockings or hose, wrapped leg-bandages, or long braies (trousers or breeches), which over time shrank to become drawers.

European Middle Ages (Late Medieval period from c1200); fashion or style began in feudal Europe, when Crusaders brought back from the Middle East a great variety of fine fabrics (often originally from even further afield in Asia) such as damask, silk, and woven gold, as well as a variety of ways or styles of cutting basic clothes. One of the most significant imports was the use of buttons to alter the fitting of clothes, instead of just for ornament. Buttons allowed the overtunic, then called the cote or cotte, to be shaped. By 1300, women's cotes had become gowns, with a tight waist created by buttons. Men's cotes developed into high-collared robes. Sometimes a surcote (sleeveless and with wide armholes) was worn on top, often displaying the new trend for family crests or coats of arms. From about 1300 a houppelande, which later became known as a gown, belted, fitted at the shoulders and loose below, was common for both genders.

Experimental styles appeared in the late Middle Ages: parti-coloured clothes made out of pieces of different colours, dagged or scalloped edges, extremely pointed shoes, hats with huge veils, elaborate head-dresses, very short tunics with padded codpieces, long liripipe hoods, and tippets – long strips of cloth attached at the elbows.

Renaissance c1450 Corsets and longer hose appeared, chemises began to give way to shorter shirts. The bulky 'square look' seen in portraits of the time soon begain to dominate, instead of the straight, vertical lines of the late Middle Ages. Men wore bombasted or padded doublets, which were tightly fitting jackets with or without sleeves, puffed trunk hose, balloon-sleeved shirts, square-toed shoes, large ruff collars, jerkins. Codpieces became elaborate. Women wore a square- or V-necked gown with an attached bodice laced up the front. The wide, pleated skirt was held up by hoops or wire or wicker, often revealing petticoats at the front. Swiss and German mercenaries, becoming rich through booty, began to wear layers of expensive, looted cloth, slashing those on top to allow those underneath to show through. The fashion for lined and slashed clothes soon spread through Europe.

Elizabethan England late 1500s Sumptuary Laws became more frequent, defining which materials and styles could be worn by different social classes. More than ever before, clothing defined wealth and social status. For nobles, dress became even more elaborate and stiffened, using heavy, ornamented materials. Farthingales or hoop-skirts became massive by c1600, with V-shaped waists. Both men and women wore a pointed stomacher: a stiffened piece of cloth at the front. The ruff expanded into high, starched or wire-supported collars, and sleeves became even more puffed. Headdresses and elaborate hairstyles were common amongst nobles.

C17 'Cavalier' costume was much softer, using silks and satins, with elaborate trimmings much reduced. Women's dresses had lower, square necklines and higher waists and, for the first time in centuries, sleeves revealed the lower arm. Collars fell from the ruff until they were wide and round. Separate sections at the waist, and aprons, were often added to dresses. Men's doublets shortened, and instead of tight, stiff hose they wore full trunk hose, which were long, full, trimmed pantaloon breeches with softer hose below. Collars were broad and lacy. Cloaks were short and worn over one shoulder.

'Puritan' costume did away with the trimmings, revealed less flesh, and was usually confined to sober grey or black. Presumably by accident, these Protestants were copying the current restrained, black, Catholic Spanish style.

After the Restoration of the monarchy in England in 1660, dress became more elaborate and frilly. Occasionally ribbons at the waist held men's short doublets and breeches together, and at one time lacy breeches became full-skirted wide petticoat breeches, worn low on the hips. In 1666 King Charles II announced a new fashion – the vest. Modelled after Persian coats, it was the forerunner of the waistcoat, but originally was longer, reaching the knees, and had sleeves. It was worn over a shirt and breeches, and under a coat. Cravats of lace or muslin were introduced and, in the 1660s, the perriwig or peruke for men. The cravat neck-cloth was the forerunner of the modern tie or necktie.

C18 By the beginning of the century France had established itself as the source of European fashion: 'Fashion is a mirror' said the Sun King, Louis XIV of France. Brocade, embroidery, feathers and frippery were the order of the day. A variety of powdered wigs – including some massive ones – were worn, and women's dresses showed variety too: shapeless 'sacks'; open to show a petticoat; closed; or hooped. Often a dress was finished with a triangular scarf, or fichu, at the neck. Some paniers or side-hoops were so wide women had to turn sideways to go through a doorway. Wigs also rose in height, and some extremely fashionable women found that there was insufficient headroom inside a coach, and had to stick their heads out of the coach windows when going to a ball. In the 1770s the hoop gave way to the forerunner of the bustle, and with the introduction of fashion plates in 1770 in *The Lady's Magazine*, more and more styles of all types of clothes spread quickly around Europe.

For the first three-quarters of the century men's dress remained variations on shirt, waistcoat, coat and cravat. The main introductions were knee-breeches, buttoned or buckled below the knee, and the tricorne (three-cornered) hat, with three points at 120° on the circular brim pushed up to the crown.

In 1789 the French Revolution shattered the modish world. The extravagance of the aristos was no longer fashionable. In Britain the upper classes adopted the plainer materials and cuts of their 'country' clothes. Jackets and boots and hats – the forerunner of the top hat – modelled on riding and fox-hunting clothes became fashionable. It was perhaps the first appearance of sporting clothes setting the trend.

Early C19 At the beginning of the century women wore very little. The Empire gown, associated in early 19th-century France with Empress Josephine, was a thin muslin dress with a high waist, a low round neck, and puffed short sleeves. Often transparent, the material was so flimsy that small bags, reticules or ridicules, were needed as pockets were not possible. Later, women tried wetting dresses to shape them; death from pneumonia sounded its warning. After 1815 the hourglass shape became fashionable – usually achieved only by means of an extremely tight corset – and flounces appeared on dresses. Because clothes were so light, shawls became fashionable, either cashmere or Paisley. Men's clothes became military in style: tail coats with a cutaway short waist, high collars and large lapels or the fitted frock coat which had a knee-length skirt. Dandies took their appearances deadly seriously; at first wearing well-fitting and well-cut clothes, then soon branched out into extremes of fashion. Trousers were slowly introduced.

Victorian C19 Victoria became queen of Britain in 1837, and what we think of as typically 'Victorian' styles soon appeared. For men, bright colours and flamboyant clothing disappeared, and did not return until the 1960s. The growth of sporting pursuits such as tennis and golf from the 1860s affected men's clothing, re-introducing knee-breeches as knickerbockers or knickers and introducing sweaters. Coats, waistcoats and trousers became looser and the visible parents of C20 clothing. Women's clothing, however, became complex, layered, accessorised, and modestly hid all sight of the natural female body. Layers of petticoats progressed to crinoline skirts (hooped petticoats) in the 1850s and '60s, partly because the weight of the petticoats was becoming ridiculous. Underneath, women wore frilly, ankle-length pantaloons, and to make absolutely sure that no man could see a woman's ankle in case the wind blew her dress up, a new fashion for women's boots began. At its height, (or perhaps its width) around 1860, the crinoline was so large all round the body that it was quite impossible for a woman to get close enough to another person to share a kiss.

Crinolines gradually gave way to bustles, with the reinforcement of the skirt at the back only. Throughout all these styles, women were tightly corseted. The tea gown was the only chance to 'get into something loose'. In the 1850s, Amelia Bloomer attempted to introduce 'rational dress' for women in the form of loose trousers under a loose skirt, but her 'bloomers' were not successful until the turn of the century, and were adopted first for bicycling. From the 1880s there was also the Aesthetic Movement (lampooned by Gilbert and Sullivan in *Patience*) to introduce looser, corset-free dresses and floppier clothes – the sort of clothes Oscar Wilde is often depicted wearing.

In the latter part of the century, women wore first tailored jackets with lapels and collar and, in the 1890s, the shirtwaist dress was introduced, with a tight wasp waist and balloon sleeves.

Victorian men were supposed to wear frock coats during the day, or perhaps the new morning coat, cut away in a curve over the hips. Otherwise, the cutaway coat was now only for evening dress, and was embellished with black silk lapel facings. Norfolk jackets – with breast pockets and a box pleat down the back – became the norm for shooting, and lounge suits with a patterned waistcoat appeared. The Bowler hat (1849) became respectable.

1900–1914 Edwardian Britain (*La belle époque* in France, from mid 1890s); a period of extravagance and luxury. The new, so-called 'health corsets', now gave women an S-shape, throwing bust forward and hips back over bell-shaped skirts. Frothy blouses developed. In 1910 a craze for Orientalism hit Britain, inspired by the Ballets Russes' *Scheherazade,* and new, looser drapes became fashionable. Dresses often tapered towards the feet (hobble skirts), hampering movement. Some women wore hobble-garters or fetters to prevent them accidentally taking a long step and splitting the garment. As feet and legs began to be put on show, women's shoes became important as fashion accessories. The V-neck appeared, and more sensible, tailor-made clothes boomed.

1914–18 WW1 Women in the USA were asked to stop buying corsets in 1917 so that the steel bones could be used for war industries; corsets never reclaimed their top spot in women's fashion.

1918–39 Between the Wars Tubular or barrel-shaped dresses, and flat busts were fashionable. Waist-lines dropped and hems rose, and in 1925 old-fashioned moralists were scandalised to see short skirts introduced and 'flappers' looking like boys with short, short haircuts. At the end of the '20s skirts dropped again to form slim straight lines, for the first time in history hugging the bottom, and with shoulders wider than hips. But, sportswomen were sticking to shorter and shorter skirts and some even wore shorts.

Before WW2, fashion was beginning to show the huge variety characterising later periods. Nylon was introduced in 1939 and new fabrics were beginning to offer huge possibilities. Paris confirmed itself as the centre of haute couture or high fashion with female designers such as Coco Chanel and Elsa Schiaparelli. Men's clothes continued to become informal. Wide Oxford bags and the hugely baggy plus-fours, usually associated with golf, appeared in the 1920s.

1939–45 WW2 Rationing of fabric and clothing in Britain led to simple but stylish mass-produced Utility clothes. Box-jackets had padded shoulders, and skirts reached below the knee. Women workers adopted trousers, and with stockings in short supply, so did other women.

1946 – Post-War The New Look, a return to soft, feminine shapes with corseted waists and long, billowing skirts hence the 'A-line'. Chanel's two-piece suits had a higher skirt. As a result of the levelling effect of the War, people from all social classes began to wear the same styles, differing only in price and designer. Although the ubiquitous trilby hat for men was part of the 'demob outfit', the idea that a man without a hat was not properly dressed soon faded away.

End-1950s A revolution in fashion and social culture. Young people had their own disposable money and chose their own styles, distinctive from those of their parents. Youth fashion and popular music became linked. Teddy Boys and Mods fought over their styles. Hollywood made jeans, leather jackets and T-shirts universally popular. Fashionable young women wore 'barrel' skirts and coats, along with the hair style known in Liverpool as 'dockers' 'ooks'.

1960s Revolutionary changes appeared in the 'swinging sixties' with the miniskirt, the introduction of ethnic and hippie fashions, purely casual clothing, space-age designs, and 'anything goes'. For the first time in about a century men were encouraged to wear bright colours and flamboyant clothes. Unisex clothes appeared. New materials included polyester and acrylic and wet-look PVC. The '60s laid the ground for today's wide variety of fashion styles.

1970s Flared trousers gave way to the anarchic Punk look made up of ripped clothes, studded leather, random safety pins and brightly dyed hair. More than any other style, it was designed to shock the older generation. Sports clothes as ordinary day or night wear appeared, and retro-dressing, or re-introducing past styles, began.

End C20 Padded shoulders for both men and women created the power-dressing look. The baggy-trousered, baseball cap-on-backwards hip hop or rap look appeared. The grunge look became a popular youth style. Fleece jumpers left the mountainside and appeared throughout the world. Urban sportswear – overalls, heavy boots *etc* – continued the trend of making sports or work clothes into fashion gear. New styles came and went within months. A new wave of army-surplus-style clothes, including combat and cargo pants hit the streets. More than anything else, the new millennium solidified the recent trends towards having a multiplicity of fashionable styles. Although high-street shops and fashion designers try hard, no one single look can dominate or dictate how we all must dress. Not until we have the benefit of hindsight will the characteristics of the period come into perspective.

Anaxaridian trousers See harem pants.

Anorak An Alaskan Inuit word for jacket. First became popular in the western world in the 1920s as padded or quilted water-resistant jackets for outdoor activities and skiing. The word became – not altogether fairly – associated with train-spotters, and now signifies anyone (usually male) who takes a deep interest in some subject that most people who think themselves normal regard as weird.

Armani suit In 1974 Giorgio Armani launched a loosely cut, comfortable, relaxed but formal business suit for men, freeing them forever from constricting clothes.

Bandana Brightly patterned or coloured neckcloths first imported from India around 1700.

Batty riders Tiny shorts, riding up the buttocks, worn mostly in night-clubs by young girls from the 1990s onwards.

Bell-bottoms Flared trousers traditionally worn in the British Royal Navy, a style that spilled into the high street as loons around 1970, sometimes with Vee-knees.

Bib and brace Trousers with a bib at the front and shoulder straps, long worn by painters, engine drivers and the like, the former in white; the latter in faded blue with jacket to match, and oil-hat. Land girls wore the serviceable garment in brown during WW2. Wrongly called dungarees, unless made of that material.

Bikini A two-piece swimming costume, named after the Bikini Atoll in the Marshall Islands where atomic bombs were tested in 1946 (and later in 1954). A two-piece costume was first launched in France in 1946, and later renamed the Bikini. The pants then were large shorts, though wall paintings show that much smaller bikinis were worn by women for exercise or dance in Roman times.

Blouson A short jacket with bat's-wing sleeves.

Bombast The stuffing for the padded clothes of the Renaissance and Elizabethan eras. Any handy material would be used: often as a last resort, the stuffing was sawdust. This caused an unfortunate trickle out of the clothes if the material was ripped.

Boot cut or **kick flare** 1990s trousers similar to 1970s loons but with a much more restrained flare. Tight from hip to knee; then flaring.

Bowler hat Named after Thomas and William Bowler, who designed and manufactured it for hatters Lock & Co of St James's (London), whence it had been ordered by William Coke (pronounced Cook) of Holkham (pronounced Hokum) in Norfolk. Coke took delivery on 17 December 1849 after stamping on it twice and pronouncing it acceptable; it cost him 12/–.

Brassière or **bra** In 1913 the only available women's underwear was a whalebone corset. But New York socialite Mary Phelps Jacob wanted to wear a new, low-cut, sheer evening dress, under which her corsets could not be seen. With some ribbon and two silk handkerchiefs she arranged a new type of breast support, and after enquiries from friends, patented her brassière – after a French word for upper arm – in 1914. In 1928 American Ida Rosenthal devised the system of cup sizes for bras.

Breechclout A loincloth.

Caftan or **kaftan** A Persian robe.

Capri pants or **pedal pushers** Tight trousers cut off at mid-calf. Introduced in Italy in the 1950s for the new generation of young women who rode motor-scooters and needed clothes that wouldn't get caught in the machinery or fly up in the wind.

Cheongsam Chinese woman's sheath dress with side slits and short, stiff mandarin collar. Elaborately embroidered.

Chinos or khakis Casual, cotton twill trousers.

Corset In the 1550s Catherine de Médici, wife of King Henri II of France, decreed that no one attending the French court could have a thick waist. Thus was born the corset, designed to squeeze a woman's waist to a fashionably narrow size. Stiffened originally with whalebone and later with steel, corsets were only successfully laced by an assistant, sometimes pushing against the unfortunate wearer with his or her foot. In Victorian England it was recommended that the wearer lie on the ground and the maid or assistant put one foot on her back to help with the pressure. The Vapours, a very common illness among C19 women, was nothing but a faint due to the tightness of the corset. Some vain men have been known also to attempt to reshape themselves by the use of corsets.

Cowboy hat Originally called 'ten-gallon hats', the tall, wide-brimmed hats invented by John B Stetson in 1865 were later renamed Stetsons in his honour. His hats not only kept sun and rain off the cowboy; they were used also for carrying water (though hardly ten gallons, which would weigh nearly one hundredweight).

Denim A tough material originally made in France and called serge de Nîmes, Jeans or overalls, made of the material are loosely referred to as 'denims'.

Derby (Rhymes with herby); American name for the Bowler hat or Coke.

Dhoti Long loincloth worn by men in India.

Doc(tor) Martens Heavy, steel-reinforced work boots originally associated with thugs and 'bovver boys'; the company re-branded them in the 1980s and they became a fashion icon with brightly coloured and patterned styles.

Dungarees Trousers with a bib and shoulder straps made from a material, known since C17, whose name is derived from the Hindi word for sailcloth, since sailors would cut up torn sails to make clothes. The word is wrongly applied to bib-and-brace overalls made of other materials.

Fedora hat Hat made out of felt or other soft material, medium-rimmed, usually with a band; said to have taken its name from *Fédora*, a play by Victorien Sardou (1831–1908).

Grass skirt Worn on many Polynesian islands. Woven grasses and reeds in strips strung from a belt.

G-string See thong.

Harem pants Loose, baggy trousers of a light material, gathered at the ankle. Created in 1906 as a copy of Turkish clothing, although the similar 'anaxaridian trousers' had been exhibited at the Great Exhibition (London, 1851).

Haute couture French for high fashion. The styles decided by the authoritative designers, buyers and magazines of the fashion world. Its catwalk shows bear little resemblance to what people actually wear.

Hipsters Trousers whose 'waist' begins at the hip.

Hot pants Very short shorts launched by the designer Mary Quant (1934–) in the 1960s.

Jeans In 1873 Levi Strauss and his partner Jacob Davis began to make tough, durable trousers out of denim, with rivets to strengthen the pockets and the bottom of the fly, and sell them to Gold Rush miners in California.

Kerchief Originally, in the Middle Ages, a piece of cloth worn tied over the head. When used for different purposes the bit of cloth became a neck-kerchief, worn around the neck, and the hand-kerchief.

Kirtle Old-fashioned word for a woman's dress or skirt, or a man's coat.

Little black dress (LBD) In 1926 the French couturier Gabrielle, known as Coco, Chanel (1883–1970) took the black dress, the symbol of mourning, and made it into a practical (black doesn't show dirt), adaptable (can be worn during the day or in the evening), and hence indispensable item for women.

Loons Flared trousers tight from hip to knee. Often with a patterned inset in the flare. Popular in the late 1960s and 1970s.

Mao suit Dark trousers suits worn by both men and women in Communist China.

Nehru jacket Slim-cut jacket, buttoned to the round neck with no collar or a short, stand-up collar. Named by Pierre Cardin, who introduced the garment to Europe in the early 1960s, after Indian prime minister Jawaharlal Nehru (1889–1964), who often wore one. The Beatles adopted the style in 1962.

Parka A Greenland Inuit word for long coat. Fur-lined, long parkas were adopted by the US army and then worn in the 1950s by the clothes-conscious Mods – see **Rocker**.

Pashmina Cashmere shawl made in Kashmir. Indispensable fashion item for women in the late 1990s.

Peasant dress A supposedly rustic costume of full skirt, a full blouse (sometimes with smocking) with puffed sleeves, and a laced bodice, together with apron and headdress. A variation on the theme is usually adapted for a national costume in European countries.

Pelisse Long-sleeved jacket cut three-quarters down the length of the skirt, worn by women in the early part of C19.

Penis hat The only clothing worn by men on many Micronesian islands is a phallocrypt, or wrapping round the penis. Men vie with each other in creating elaborate and giant 'hats'.

Platform shoes Shoes with a high platform and heel, often with a wedge running between them. Actually created in the 1930s, they became a high-street fashion in the 1970s for both men and women.

Ray-bans The first branded sunglasses, developed for aviators in the 1920s and launched to the public in 1937. Frequently spotted in Hollywood films.

Rocker 1960s leather-clad, motorcycling youth, opposed to the Mods.

Sack or **saque coat** Worn in the daytime by Victorian men for travel or business. A loose-fitting, single-breasted, slightly baggy coat with small collar, short lapels, a fastened top button close to the neck and plenty of pockets.

Sari Long draped fabric worn by Indian women. Often highly decorated or patterned material is used.

Sarong Malaysian wrapped, calf-length skirt. Worn by footballer David Beckham.

Shell suit Supposedly athletic wear made of a shiny material worn by certain men and women alike.

Snood A type of hairnet, gathering the hair into a bag, that became popular during the Elizabethan era. In the 1980s snoods were launched as a type of loose Balaclava helmet or scarf covering the head and neck except for the face. Snoods have long been worn by factory girls to keep their hair away from machinery, and by both men and women in food industry, sometimes attached to a cap for smarter protection.

Socks Woven or knitted foot protection, usually worn with shoes. The earliest known socks were discovered in Egyptian graves in Antinoe, dating to about 500 BCE.

Spats A shoe covering made of cloth or leather, fastened with a strip passing under the sole of the shoe, and buttoned down one side.

Spencer A long-sleeved, short jacket worn by women in the early part of the C19. In modern-day Australia, a spencer is an undervest, and in England a long-sleeved vest.

Stole Neck wrapping developed from the Roman toga, which over time became smaller and smaller.

Thong According to fashion legend, the thong was invented in 1939 during the World Fair in New York, when the New York mayor ruled that the city's nude dancers could no longer dance naked. The G-string or thong was their way of obeying the letter of the law.

Tights Also known as pantihose, a one-piece garment fitting tightly from waist to toe introduced in the 1960s; vital with miniskirts. C16 men wore such garments with the doublet (doublet and hose) and present-day (Shakespearean) actors also don tights.

Tracksuits Along with jogging pants and shell suits typified the introduction of sports clothes for everyday wear. Endured because of the sheer comfort of the style.

Trainers or **Sneakers** Padded, comfortable sports shoes which became ubiquitous from the 1980s. Companies like Nike and Reebok contributed towards the branding of everyday wear.

Turban Male headdress, common in parts of Asia and the Middle East, consisting of a long piece of cloth wound around the head.

Tuxedo American name for a dinner jacket, named after a country club in New York state.

Twinset A cardigan and matching top; has become a symbol of British (female) conservatism, often with a pearl necklace.

UFO trousers Fashion trousers for the younger wearer with numerous ribbon-like tags, said to create a whirling effect when dancing.

Urban street wear The sports and work clothes worn by working class urban youth translated into fashion items from the late 1980s onwards.

Musical instruments and the composition of the Orchestra
Musical instruments are divided into families or groups, distinguished by
how the sound is generated:

Strings produce sound by plucking, slapping, strumming of strings.

Aeolian harp	Komungo
Balalaika	Kora
Banjo	Koto
Biwa	Lute
Bouzouki	Lyre
'Cello (Violoncello)	Mandolin
Crwth	Mbira
Double bass	Musical bow
Dulcimer	Psaltery
Gayageum	Samisen (Shamisen)
Geomungo	Sitar
Guitar:	Ukulele
Acoustic guitar	Vieille
Bass guitar	Vihuela
Classical guitar	Viol
Electric Guitar	Viola
Slide guitar	Viola d'amore
Steel guitar	Violin (fiddle)
Hardanger fiddle	Violotta
Harp	Washtub bass
Hurdy gurdy	Xalam (Khalam)
Jew's harp	Zither

Woodwind instruments produce sound by vibration of air inside the
instrument, after air is blown into or across the mouth of the instrument.
They do not have to be made of wood, and most have a reed fixed into the
mouthpiece.

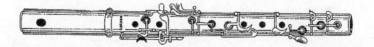

Bagpipes	Ocarina
Bassoon	Pan pipes (panflute, syrinx,
Bombarde	quills)
Clarinet	Piccolo
Contrabassoon	Recorder
Cor Anglais (English horn)	Saxophone
Crumhorn	Shakuhachi
Flute	Shawm
Heckelphone	Slide whistle (swanee whistle,
Nose flute	piston flute, jazz flute)
Oboe	Tromboon

Brass instruments produce sound when the players lips vibrate or 'buzz' into a cup- or funnel-shaped mouthpiece, making air inside the instrument vibrate. They do not have to be made of brass.

Alpenhorn	Mellophone
Baritone horn	Ophicleide
Bazooka	Quinticlave
Bugle	Sackbut
Conch	Serpent
Cornet	Shofar
Cornett (Cornetto)	Sousaphone
Didgeridoo	Trombone
Euphonium	Trumpet
Flugelhorn	Tuba
French horn	Wagner tuba

Free reed instruments produce sound by using blowing, bellows or striking to make variously sized and shaped reeds vibrate.

Accordion	Melodica
Concertina	Pipe organ (some pipes; others
Harmonica	are woodwind)
Harmonium	Sheng
Kobing	

Percussion instruments produce sound when struck, scraped or shaken.

Bell	Taiko
Castanets	Tambourine
Chimes	Timpani (Kettledrums)
Cymbals	Tom-Tom
Drum	Tsuzumi
Abïa drum	Water drum
African drum	Gong
Bass drum	Guiro
Bodhran	Glockenspiel
Bongo drum	Maracas
Conga	Marimba
Djembe	Metallophone
O Daiko	Steelpan
Octaban	Triangle
Octapad	Vibraphone
Snare	Washboard
Steel drum	Xylophone
Tabla	Xylorimba

Keyboard instruments produce sound when the keys of a keyboard are struck, either hitting strings or forcing air through through pipes.

Accordion	Clavichord
Calliope (steam organ)	Harpsichord
Carillon	Organ (pipe organ)
Celesta	Piano

Electronic instruments use electronic means to produce sound.

Drum machine	Synthesizer
Mellotron	Moog
Rhodes piano	Teleharmonium
Sampler	Theremin
Synclavier	

Others

Bull-roarer	Musical Saw
Hardart	Suikinkutsu (Japanese water
Kazoo	zither)
Lasso d'amore	

The human voice

Alto This term, the Italian for 'high', is used to describe a male voice higher than that of any tenor. Mostly it now refers to the lower range of female voice or, in church choirs, the voices of boys and women.

Baritone In male singers this is the nearest to normal speech, being an intermediate range of voice.

Bass Among male voices, the lowest – though not necessarily the most limited.

Basso profundo An even deeper bass.

Castrato In a woman the equivalent would be either soprano or contralto. In males it was produced by castration, practised for this purpose in C17 and C18 Europe, mostly in the interests of church music.

Coloratura soprano An extravagantly styled form of soprano voice.

Contralto Among types of female voice, this is the lowest.

Counter-tenor An adult male soloist singing unusually high, *ie* as an alto.

Falsetto Usually this term describes an adult male alto, but with less full-ness than the voice of a counter-tenor.

Heldentenore German expression describing a 'hero tenor', one who can sing above the volume of a full orchestra.

Mezzo-soprano This voice falls between the ranges of soprano and alto. Its potential richness is useful for operatic roles.

Soprano Among female singers, the highest type of voice, with a wide dramatic range.

Tenor Apart from castrato, this is the highest male voice; like sopranos, tenors can produce a variety of sounds, from light to dramatically profound.

Orchestras

The word orchestra derives from ancient Greek drama, where the orchestra was a space set aside for the musicians and chorus between the auditorium and the stage. Nowadays the word is applied to a group of musicians usually playing Western classical music. A small orchestra is called a chamber orchestra, whereas a larger one is usually called a symphony or philharmonic orchestra.

The typical symphony orchestra consists of only four groups of instruments: strings, woodwinds, brass and percussion. While the size of an orchestra varies, a larger orchestra will average more than 90 instruments. A fairly typical composition would be:

	Small orchestra	Medium orchestra	Large orchestra
Strings			
First violins	8	12	16
Second violins	8	12	16
Violas	6	10	12
'Cellos	4	8	10
Basses	2	4	8
Woodwinds			
Flutes	2	2	2
Piccolo	–	1	1
Oboes	2	2	3
English horn	–	1	1
Clarinets	2	2	3
Bass clarinet	–	1	1
Bassoons	2	2	3
Contrabassoon	–	1	1
Brass			
Trumpets	2	3	4
French horns	2	4	6
Trombones	–	2	3
Tuba	–	1	1
Percussion			
Timpani	1	1	1
Other	–	2	4
Total	**41**	**71**	**96**

Medicine

Bones of the human body

Skull	Occipital	1	001	001
Skull	Parietal (one pair)	2	002	002
Skull	Sphenoid	1	003	003
Skull	Ethmoid	1	004	004
Skull	Inferior nasal conchae (1 pair)	2	005	005
Skull	Frontal (1 pair, fused)	1	006	006
Skull	Nasal (1 pair)	2	007	007
Skull	Lacrimal (1 pair)	2	008	008
Skull	Temporal (1 pair)	2	009	009
Skull	Maxilla (1 pair)	2	010	010
Skull	Zygomatic (1 pair)	2	011	011
Skull	Vomer	1	012	012
Skull	Palatine (1 pair)	2	013	013
Skull	Mandible (1 pair, fused)	1	014	014
Skull	**Skull total**	**22**	**T01**	**015**
Inner ears	Malleus	2	015	016
Inner ears	Incus	2	016	017
Inner ears	Stapes	2	017	018
Inner ears	**Inner ears total**	**6**	**T02**	**019**
Vertebrae	Cervical (neck)	7	018	020
Vertebrae	Thoracic (chest)	12	019	021
Vertebrae	Lumbar (back)	5	020	022
Vertebrae	Saccral (5 fused = sacrum)	1	021	023
Vertebrae	Coccyx (tail; 3–5 fused)	1	022	024
Vertebrae	**Vertebrae total**	**26**	**T03**	**025**
Vertebral ribs	'True' ribs (7 pairs)	14	023	026
Vertebral ribs	'False' ribs (5 pairs of which 2 float)	10	024	027
Vertebral ribs	**Vertebral ribs total**	**24**	**T04**	**028**
Sternum	Manubrium	1	025	029
Sternum	Sternebrae	1	026	030
Sternum	Xiphisternum	1	027	031
Sternum	**Sternum total**	**3**	**T05**	**032**
Hyoid	**Hyoid (in the throat)**	**1**	**T06**	**033**
Pectoral girdle	Clavicle (1 pair)	2	028	034
Pectoral girdle	Scapula (including Coracoid, 1 pair)	2	029	035
Pectoral girdle	**Pectoral girdle total**	**4**	**T07**	**036**
Arm (2 of)	Humerus	2	030	037
Arm (2 of)	Radius	2	031	038
Arm (2 of)	Ulna	2	032	039
Arm (2 of)	Carpus: Scaphoid	2	033	040
Arm (2 of)	Lunate	2	034	041

Arm (2 of)	Triquetral	2	035	042
Arm (2 of)	Pisiform	2	036	043
Arm (2 of)	Trapezium	2	037	044
Arm (2 of)	Trapezoid	2	038	045
Arm (2 of)	Capitate	2	039	046
Arm (2 of)	Hamate	2	040	047
Arm (2 of)	Metacarpals	10	041	048
Arm (2 of)	Phalanges: First digit	4	042	049
Arm (2 of)	Second digit	6	043	050
Arm (2 of)	Third digit	6	044	051
Arm (2 of)	Fourth digit	6	045	052
Arm (2 of)	Fifth digit	6	046	053
Arm (2 of)	**Arm (2 of) total**	**60**	**T08**	**054**
Pelvic girdle	Ilium, Ischium and Pubis (combined) 1 pair of hip bones, innominate	1	047	055
Leg (2 of)	Femur	2	048	056
Leg (2 of)	Tibia	2	049	057
Leg (2 of)	Fibula	2	050	058
Leg (2 of)	Tarsus: Talus	2	051	059
Leg (2 of)	Calcaneus	2	052	060
Leg (2 of)	Navicular	2	053	061
Leg (2 of)	Cuneiform, medial	2	054	062
Leg (2 of)	Cuneiform, intermediate	2	055	063
Leg (2 of)	Cuneiform, lateral	2	056	064
Leg (2 of)	Cuboid	2	057	065
Leg (2 of)	Metatarsals	10	058	066
Leg (2 of)	Phalanges: First digit	4	059	067
Leg (2 of)	Second digit	6	060	068
Leg (2 of)	Third digit	6	061	069
Leg (2 of)	Fourth digit	6	062	070
Leg (2 of)	Fifth digit	6	063	071
Leg (2 of)	**Leg (2 of) total**	**58**	**T09**	**072**
	Grand total	**204**	**GT**	**073**

Medical specialties and scientific studies concerned with the human body

With our knowledge of medicine improving all the time, the number of medical branches or specialties is constantly growing. This list of branches of study to do with the human body or with medicine includes some areas that are no longer accepted as scientific, such as phrenology, as well as some, such as nuclear medicine, that are so new that they are likely to divide into sub-groups.

Medical specialities – ordered by name

Name	Professional speciality / study of
Aceology	therapeutics
Acology	medical remedies
Adenology	glands
Aerospace medicine	astronauts, pilots
Allergology	allergies
Anesthesiology	anaesthetics
Angiology	blood, lymphatic system
Arthrology	joints
Astheniology	aging diseases
Audiology	hearing
Auxology	the science of growth
Bacteriology	bacteria
Biology	life
Biometrics	biological measurement
Cardiology	heart
Chiropody	feet
Craniology	skull
Critical care	emergencies
Cryobiology	effects of very cold conditions
Cytology	living cells
Dactylography	fingerprints
Dactylology	sign language
Dentistry	teeth
Dermatology	skin
Desmology	ligaments
Diving medicine	deep sea divers
Eccrinology	excretion
Embryology	embryos
Emetology	vomiting
Emmenology	menstruation
Endemiology	local diseases
Endocrinology	glands
Enzymology	enzymes
Ephebiatrics	adolescence
Epidemiology	diseases, epidemics
Etiology	causes of disease
Forensic medicine	applying medical knowledge to the law
Gastroenterology	stomach, intestines

Genealogy	relationships and descent
Genesiology	reproduction and heredity
Geriatrics	diseases of elderly people
Gerontology	aging and elderly people
Glossology	language, tongues
Gynaecology	diseases of women
Hedonics	pleasure
Hematology	blood
Hepatology	liver
Histology	organic tissues
Hydropathy	treating diseases with water
Hygienics	health and sanitation
Hypnology	hypnosis, sleep
Iatrology	treatment
Immunogenetics	genetic relationship of immunity
Immunology	immunities
Karyology	cell nuclei
Kinesiology	movement and posture
Laryngology	larynx
Leprology	leprosy
Mereology	ecology
Midwifery	birth
Microbiology	effect of micro-organisms
Myology	muscles
Nasology	the nose
Neonatology	newborn babies
Nephrology	kidneys
Neurobiology	anatomy of the nervous system
Neurology	nervous system
Noology	science of the intellect
Nosology	diseases
Nostology	senility
Nuclear medicine	applies radioactive substances for scanning or treatment
Obstetrics	midwifery
Occupational therapy	therapeutic use of hobbies, crafts
Oncology	tumours
Ophthalmology	eye diseases
Optology	sight
Optometry	examination of eyes
Osmology	smells and olfactory processes

Osphresiology	the sense of smell
Osteology	bones
Otology	the ear
Otorhinolaryngology	ear, nose and throat
Paedology	children
Pain management	pain
Palliative care	caring for the dying
Parasitology	parasites
Pathology	disease
Paediatrics (pediatrics)	children
Periodontics	gums
Pharmacology	drugs
Pharyngology	the throat
Phenology	how climate affects organisms
Phoniatrics	speech defects
Phrenology	bumps on the head*
Physiology	processes of an organism
Physiotherapy	therapeutic use of movement, exercises
Podiatry	feet
Podology	feet
Proctology	rectum
Prosthetics	artificial body parts
Psychiatry	mental diseases
Psychobiology	biology of the mind
Psychogenetics	mental states
Psychology	mind
Psychopathology	mental illness
Pulmonary medicine	lungs
Pyretology	fevers
Radiology	X-rays
Radiotherapy	radiation or radioactive substances used in treatment
Reflexology	reflexes
Rheumatology	rheumatism
Rhinology	the nose
Sarcology	fleshy parts of the body
Sexology	sexual behaviour
Sociobiology	biological basis of human behaviour
'Special' clinic	sexually transmitted diseases
Sphygmology	the pulse
Splanchnology	entrails

Stomatology	the mouth
Suicidology	suicide
Symptomatology	symptoms of illness
Syphilology	syphilis
Teratology	malformations or abnormal growths
Threpsology	science of nutrition
Tocology	obstetrics, midwifery
Toxicology	poisons
Trichology	hair and its disorders
Trophology	nutrition
Typhlology	blindness
Urology	urinary tract
Venereology	venereal disease
Victimology	victims
Virology	viruses

Medical specialities – ordered by area of study

Speciality / study of	*Name*
Adolescence	ephebiatrics
Aging and elderly people	gerontology
Aging diseases	astheniology
Allergies	allergology
Anaesthetics	anesthesiology
Artificial body parts	prosthetics
Astronauts; pilots	aerospace medicine
Bacteria	bacteriology
Behaviour, biological basis of	sociobiology
Biological measurement	biometrics
Birth	midwifery
Blindness	typhlology
Blood	hematology
Blood, lymphatic system	angiology
Bones	osteology
Bumps on the head*	phrenology
Causes of disease	etiology
Cell nuclei	karyology
Children	paedology, paediatrics (pediatrics)
Climate, effects of	phenology
Cold, effects of extreme	cryobiology
Disease	pathology

Diseases	nosology
Diseases of women	gynaecology
Diseases, epidemics	epidemiology
Divers, deep sea	diving medicine
Drugs	pharmacology
Dying	palliative care
Ear	otology
Ear, nose and throat	otorhinolaryngology
Ecology	mereology
Elderly people	geriatrics
Embryos	embryology
Emergencies	critical care
Entrails	splanchnology
Enzymes	enzymology
Excretion	eccrinology
Eye diseases	ophthalmology
Eyes, examination of	optometry
Feet	chiropody, podiatry, podology
Fevers	pyretology
Fingerprints	dactylography
Fleshy parts of the body	sarcology
Glands	adenology, endocrinology
Growth, science of	auxology
Gums	periodontics
Hair and its disorders	trichology
Health and sanitation	hygienics
Hearing	audiology
Heart	cardiology
Hobbies, therapeutic use of	occupational therapy
Hypnosis, sleep	hypnology
Immunity, genetic relationship of	immunogenetics
Immunities	immunology
Intellect, science of	noology
Joints	arthrology
Kidneys	nephrology
Language; the tongue	glossology
Law, application of medical knowledge to	forensic medicine
Larynx	laryngology

Leprosy	leprology
Life	biology
Ligaments	desmology
Liver	hepatology
Living cells	cytology
Local diseases	endemiology
Lungs	pulmonary medicine
Malformations or abnormal growths	teratology
Medical remedies	acology
Menstruation	emmenology
Mental diseases	psychiatry
Mental illness	psychopathology
Mental states	psychogenetics
Microorganisms, effect of	microbiology
Midwifery	obstetrics
Mind	psychology
Mind, biology of	psychobiology
Mouth	stomatology
Movement and posture	kinesiology
Movement, therapeutic use of	physiotherapy
Muscles	myology
Nervous system	neurology
Nervous system, anatomy	neurobiology
Newborn babies	neonatology
Nose	nasology
Nose	rhinology
Nutrition	trophology
Nutrition, science of	threpsology
Obstetrics, midwifery	tocology
Organic tissues	histology
Pain	pain management
Parasites	parasitology
Pleasure	hedonics
Poisons	toxicology
Processes of an organism	physiology
Pulse	sphygmology

Radiation or radioactive substances used in treatment	radiotherapy
Radioactive substances for scanning or treatment	nuclear medicine
Rectum	proctology
Reflexes	reflexology
Relationships and descent	genealogy
Reproduction and heredity	genesiology
Rheumatism	rheumatology
Senility	nostology
Sexual behaviour	sexology
Sexually transmitted diseases	'special' clinic
Sight	optology
Sign language	dactylology
Skin	dermatology
Skull	craniology
Smell, sense of	osphresiology
Smells and olfactory processes	osmology
Speech defects	phoniatrics
Stomach, intestines	gastroenterology
Suicide	suicidology
Symptoms of illness	symptomatology
Syphilis	syphilology
Teeth	dentistry
Therapeutics	aceology
Throat	pharyngology
Treating diseases with water	hydropathy
Treatment	iatrology
Tumours	oncology
Urinary tract	urology
Venereal disease	venereology
Victims	victimology
Viruses	virology
Vomiting	emetology
X-rays	radiology

* The 'bumps' referred to here are the detailed contours of the skull; it was once thought that 'reading the bumps' would enable a practitioner to interpret the strengths and weaknesses of the brain beneath.

Medical prefixes and suffixes

The following forms may be used to interpret many medical terms, or to devise new ones. It may be necessary to insert a vowel before a combining consonant (or vice versa) to aid pronunciation.

Prefix/suffix	Meaning
a-, an-	not, without
acr-	top, height, extremity
aden-	gland, glandular
adip-	fat, fatty tissue
-aemia	pertaining to the blood
aesthesio-	see **esthesio-**
aetio-	see **etio-**
-algia	pain
all-	other, different, atypical
alveol-	alveolus, alveolar – pertaining to a small cavity
ambly-	connected with amblyopia – lazy eyes
amyl-	starch
ana-	upward
anchyl-	see **ankyl-**
angi-	blood or lymph vessel
anhydr-	lacking water
ankyl-	stiffness, immobility
ante-	anterior, prior to, in front of
antero-	anterior, from front to
anti-	opposing in effect or activity
arteri-	artery, arterial
arthr-	joint
bio-	life, living organisms or tissue
-biosis	mode of life
-blast	formative unit esp. of living matter, germ, cell layer
blast-	bud, budding, germ
blephar-	eyelid, cilium, flagellum
brachy-	short
brady-	slow
bronch-	bronchial tube, bronchial
bronchi-	bronchial tubes

bucco-	buccal
carcin-	tumor, cancer
cardi-	heart, cardiac
-cardium, -cardia	heart action or location
cata-	down
cephal-	head
cerebr-	brain, cerebrum
cervic-	neck, cervix of an organ, cervical
chem-	chemical, chemistry
chir-	hand
chlor-	green
chol-	bile, gall
chondr-	cartilage
chromat-	colour, chromatin
cin-	see kin-
-coccus	berry-shaped organism
col-	colon, colon bacillus
copr-	feces
cortico-	cortex, cortical
crani-	cranium, cranial
cry-	cold, freezing
crypt-	hidden, covered
-cyst	bladder, sac
cyst-	bladder
cyt-	cell, cytoplasm
-cyte	cell
dactyl-	finger, toe, digit
dent-	tooth, teeth, dental
-derm	skin, covering
derm-	skin
-derma	skin or skin ailment of a type
dermat-	skin
-dermis	layer of skin or tissue
desm-	connective tissue
dextr-	right, dextrorotatory
dys-	abnormal, difficult, impaired
ect-	outside, external
-ectomy	surgical, removal
-emia	condition of having blood, condition of having in the blood

encephal-	brain
-encephalia	condition of having a brain
-encephaly	condition of having a brain
end-	within, taking in
ent-	inner, within
enter-	intestine
epi-	upon, besides, attached to, outer, after
episio-	vulva
-ergic	exhibiting or stimulating activity
eroto-	sexual desire
erythr-	red, erythrocyte
esthesio-	sensation
etio-	cause, formed by chemical degradation of a compound
eu-	well, true
exo-	outside, turning out
extra-	outside, beyond
feto-	fetus
fibr-	fiber, fibrous tissue, fibrous
foeto-	see feto-
fore-	occuring earlier, situated at the front, front part of
-fuge	one thing that drives away
galact-	milk, related to galactose
gastr-	belly, gastric
-genic, -genetic	producing, produced by
geront-	aged one, old age
gingiv-	gum, gums
gloss-	tongue
glyc-	sugar, glycine
-gnathous	having a jaw
gon-	sexual, generative, semen, seed
-gram	drawing, writing, record
-graph	something written, instrument for making or transmitting records
gynec-	woman
haem-	see hem-
haemat-	see hemat
-haemia	see -emia
helminth-	flatworm
hem-, hema-, hemat-	blood
hemi-	half

-hemia	see -emia
hemo-	blood
hepat-	liver, hepatic
herpet-	reptile or reptiles, herpes
heter-	other than usual, other, different
hist-	tissue
hol-	complete, completely
hom-	one and the same, similar, alike
home-	like, similar
hy-, hyo-	connecting with the hyoid bone, hyoid
hyal-	glass, glassy, hyaline
hydr-	water, liquid
hyper-	excessively, excessive
hypn-	sleep, hypnotism
hypo-	under, less than normal or normally
hypothalamico-	hypothalamus, hypothalamic
hyps-	high
hyster-	womb, hysteria
-iatric	of or relating to medical treatment or healing
-iatrics	medical instrument
-iatrist	physician, healer
iatro-	physician, medicine, healing
-iatry	medical treatment, healing
ichthy-	fish
-ics	study, characteristic actions or activities, characteristic qualities operations or phenomena
icter-	jaundice
-id	skin rash caused by
-id	structural element of a lower molar or premolar, structure body or particle of a kind
-ida	animals that are or have the form of
-idae	members of the family of in names of zoological families
idio-	one's own, self-produced
-idrosis	a specific form of sweating
il-	see in-
ile-	ileum, ileal
illio-	iliac
im-	see in-
immuno-	physiological immunity, immunologic
-in	neutral chemical compound, enzyme, antibiotic, pharmaceutical product

in-	before
in-	within, into, toward, on, before
infra-	below, within, below in a scale or series
ino-	fibrous
intra-	within, during, between layers of
intro-	in, inward
ir-	see in-
irid-	iris of the eye
is-	equal, for or from different individuals of the same species
-ism	act, a state condition or property, abnormal state or condition resulting from excess of a thing, abnormal state or condition characterised by resemblance to a person or thing
-ite	substance produced through some process, segment or constituent part of a body or of a bodily part
-itic	of, resembling or marked by
-itis	disease, inflammation of
jejun-	jejunum, jejunal
kary-	nucleus of a cell
kerat-	cornea
kin-	motion, action
kinet-	movement, motion
klept-	stealing, theft
lact-	milk, lactic acid
laev-	see lev-
-lalia	speech disorder
laryng-	larynx, laryngeal
leio-	smooth
-lepsy	taking, seizure
lept-	small, weak, thin, fine
leuk-	white, leukocyte, white matter of the brain
leukocyt-	leukocyte
lev-	left, on the left side, to the left
-lexia	reading of a kind or with an impairment
lingu-	tongue
lip-	fatty tissue
-lith	calculus
lob-	lobe
-logy	doctrine, theory, science, discipline
lumb-	lumbar

lute-	corpus luteum
lymph-	lymph, lymphatic tissue
-lysis	decomposition, disintegration
-lyte	substance capable of undergoing decomposition
-lytic	of, relating to, or effecting decomposition
mal-	bad, abnormal, abnormally, inadequate, inadequately
mamm-	breast
mast-	breast, nipple, mammary gland
-mastia	condition of having breasts or mammary glands
medi-	middle
-megaly	abnormal enlargement
mening-	meninges
mes-	mid, intermediate
mesio-	mesial
meta-	occuring later than or in succession to, situated behind or beyond
micr-	small, using microscopy, abnormally small
mon-	one, affecting a single part
-morph	one having a form
morph-	form, shape, structure, type
-morphic	having a form
-morphism	quality or state of having a form
-morphy	qaulity or state of having a form
muc-	mucus, mucous
multi-	many, having more than two, affecting many parts
muscul-	muscle, muscular
my-, myo	muscle, myoma
myc-, mycet	fungus
-mycete	fungus
-mycin	substance obtained from a fungus
myel-	marrow, bone marrow, spinal cord
-myelia	a condition of the spinal cord
myx-	mucus, myxoma
nan-	dwarf
narc-	numbness, narcosis, deep sleep
nas-	nose, nasal
ne-	new, an abnormal new formation
necr-	those that are dead, death
nemat-	thread, nematode
nephr-	kidney
-nephros	kidney

nerv-, neur-	nerve, neural
neutro-	neutral, neutrophil
noci-	pain
norm-	normal
nos-	disease
not-	back, back part
nucle-	nucleus, nucleic acid
o-, oo-	egg, ovum
ocul-	eye, ocular
-odont	having teeth of a nature
odont-	tooth
-odontia	form, condition, or mode of treatment of the teeth
-odynia	pain
oesophag-	see esophag-
oestr-	see estr-
olig-	few, deficiency, in-sufficiency
-oma	tumor
omphal-	umbilicus, umbilical
onco-	tumor, bulk
onych-	nail of the finger or toe
-onychia	conditions of the nails of the fingers or toes
-onychium	fingernail, toenail, region of the fingernail or toenail
oophor-	ovary, ovarian
-opia	condition of having vision, condition of having a visual defect
opisth-	dorsal, posterior
-opsia	vision of a kind or condition
-opsy	examination
ophthalm-	eye, eye-ball
-ophthalmia	condition of having eyes
opto-	vision, optic
-orchism, -orchidism	a form or condition of the testes
-orexia	appetite
organ-	organ
oro-	mouth, oral
orth-	straight, perpendicular, correct
-osis	action, abnormal or diseased condition, increase
osm-	odour, smell
osmo-	osmosis, osmotic
osse-	bone

osteochondr-	bone and cartilage
-ostosis	ossification of a part or to a degree
ot-	ear
-otic	of, relating to, or characterised by an action, process or condition, showing an increase or a formation
-otic	having a relationship to the ear
ov-	egg, ovum
paed-	see ped-
-pagus	congenitally united twins with a type of fixation
phag	eating, phagocyte
palat-	palate, palatal
pale-	early, old
pan-	all, whole
papill-	papilla, papillary
-para	woman delivered of children
-parous	giving birth to
-path	practitioner of a system of medicine that emphasises one aspect of disease or its treatment, one suffering from a disorder
path-	pathological, pathological state
-pathic	feeling or affected in a way, affected by a disease of a part or kind, relating to therapy based on a unitary theory of disease or its treatments
patho-	feeling, disease of a part or kind, therapy or system of therapy based on a unitary theory of disease or its treatment
-pathy, -pathia	
ped-	foot, feet; child, children
-pellic	having a pelvis of such and such a type
-penia	deficiency of
-pepsia	digestion
peri-	surrounding
-pexy	fixation, making fast
phac-, phak-	lens
-phage	one that eats
-phagia, -phagy	eating, eating of a type or substance
phall-	penis
pharmaco-	medicine, drug
pharyng-	pharynx, pharyngeal
-phasia	speech disorder

-phemia	speech disorder relating to the articulation or fluency of speech sounds
-phile	lover, one having an affinity for or a strong attraction to
-philia	tendency toward, abnormal appetite or liking for
-philiac	one having a tendency toward, one having an abnormal appetite or liking for
-philic	having an affinity for, loving
-philous	loving, having an affinity for
phleb-	vein
-phobe	one fearing or averse to
-phobia	abnormal fear
-phobic	having an aversion for or fear of, lacking affinity for
-phonia	speech disorder
-phoria	bearing, state, tendency
phot-	light, radiant energy
-phrasia	speech disorder
phren-	mind, diaphragm
-phrenia	disordered condition of mental functions
phthisio-	phthisis
physi-	physical, physiological
phyt-	plant
-phyte	plant having a characteristic or habitat, pathological growth
pil-	hair
-plasia, -plasy	development, formation
-plasm	formative or formed material
-plastic	developing, of or relating to
-plasty	plastic surgery
-plegia	paralysis
pleur-	pleura
-ploid	having or being a chromosome number that bears a relationship to or is times the basic chromosome number characteristic of a given plant or animal group
-pnea	breath, breathing
pneum-	air, lung, respiration, pneumonia
pneumat-	air, respiration
pneumon-	lung
-pnoea	see -pnea
-poiesis	production, formation
-poietic	productive, formative
poly-	many, excessive

post-	after, behind
postero-	posterior
-praxis	therapeutic treatment by a system or agency
pre-	earlier than, in front of
presby-	old age
pro-	earlier than, front
proct-	rectum, anus
pros-	in front
prosop-	face
prot-	beginning, principal
prote-	protein
pseud-	false, spurious
psych-	mind, psychological methods, brain, mental
-ptysis	spewing, expectoration
pulmon-	lung
py-, pyo-	pus
pyel-	renal pelvis
pyl-	portal vein
pyr-	fire, fever
pyret-	fever
pytal-	saliva
rachi-	spine
radi-	radiant energy, radioactive, radium, radioactive isotopes esp as produced artificially
rect-	rectum, rectal
reni-	kidney, renal
retin-	retina
retro-	backward, situated behind
rhabd	rodlike structure
rheo	current
rhin-	nose, nasal
rhod-	rose, red
-rrhachis	spine
-rrhagia	abnormal or excessive discharge or flow
-rrhaphy	suture, sewing
-rrhea	flow, discharge
-rrhexis	rupture, splitting
-rrhoea	see -rrhea
sacr-	sacrum, sacral
salping-	fallopian tube, eustachian tube
sapr-	rotten, dead or decaying organic matter

sarc-	flesh, striated muscle
scapul-	scapula, scapular
scat-	excrement
-schisis	breaking up of attachments or adhesions, fissure
schisto-	cleft, divided
schiz-	characterised by or involving cleavage, schizophrenia
scler-	hard, sclera
-scope	means for viewing or observing
-scopic	viewing or observing
-scopy	viewing, observation
sial-	saliva
sider-	iron
somat-	body, somatic
-somia	condition of having a body
somni-	sleep
sperm-	seed, germ, sperm
spermat-	seed, spermatozoon
splen-	spleen
spondyl-	vertebra, vertebrae
spor-	seed, spore
staphyl-	uvulva, staphylococci
-stat	agent causing inhibition of growth without destruction
steat-	fat
stomat-	mouth
-stomy	surgical operation establishing a usually permanent opening into a part
strepto-	twisted, streptococcus
sub-	under, subordinate portion of, less than completely or perfectly
super-	greater than normal, situated or placed above
supra-	transcending
syn-	with, at the same time
syndesm-	ligament, connection
tachy-	rapid, accelerated
taen-, ten-	tapeworm
talo-	astragalar
tel-	end
terat-	monster
thanat-	death
therm-	heat
-thermia	state of heat, generation of heat

thorac-	chest, thorax, thoracic
-thrix, -triches	pathological condition of having hair
thromb-	blood clot, marked by association with thrombosis
-thymia	condition of mind and will
-tome	part, cutting instrument
-tomy	incision, section
-tonia, -tony	condition or degree of tonus
tonsill-	tonsil
tox-	toxic, toxin
toxic-	poison
trache-	trachea, tracheal
trachel-	neck, uterine cervix
trans-	through, so as to change or transfer
-trema	hole, orrifice, opening
trich-	hair, filament
-trichia	condition of having hair
troph-	nutritive
-trophic	of, relating to, or characterised by nutrition or growth
-trophy	nutrition, nurture, growth
-tropia	condition of a deviation in the line of vision
-tropic	turning, attracted to or acting upon
-tropin	hormone
tubercul-	tubercle, tubercle bacillus, tuberculosis
ultra-	beyond in space, beyond the range or limits of
ur-, urin-, uro-	urine, urinary tract, urinary, urea
uran-	palate
uretero-	ureter, ureteral
urethr-	urethra
-uria	presence of in urine, condition of having urine
uric-	uric acid
uter-	uterus, uterine
vag-	vagus nerve
vagin-	vagina
valvul-	small valve, valvule, fold
varic-	varix
vas-	vessel, vascular
vascul-	vessel, blood vessel
ven-	vein
ventr-	abdomen, ventral
vermi-	worm
vesico-	of or relating to the urinary bladder

vesicul-	vesicle, vesicular
vulv-	vulva, vulvular
xer-	dry, arid
xiph-	sword-shaped, xiphoid
-zoic	having an animal mode of existence
-zyme	enzyme

Matters mystical, spiritual, philosophical, religious

Beasts heraldic and mythical

Amphisbaena The body of a bird with an extended reptilian tail, and a head on each end of the body with glowing eyes. It can move rapidly in either direction, and may grasp the neck of one head with the teeth of the other and thus bowl along like a hoop.

Basilisk More is known about its effects than its characteristics; it can ignite birds as they overfly it, and can kill by its glance, by its smell, by its bite, and by the sound of its hiss. Its lethal glance is of some concern; it is suggested that you might kill a basilisk by looking at it first, but the procedure obviously carries an inherent risk. If you are likely to meet one, it is wise to carry a weasel, for weasels are immune to the venom; thus the basilisk may be a variety of serpent. The basilisk may be hatched by a toad from the egg of an elderly cockerel; alternative names are basilicoc and cockatrice.

Bonnacon Large, hairy, beast, whose horns were rendered safe by curling upon themselves – but watch out for the rear end whence it could expel a 'voluminous and acrid discharge' that would spread over three acres, ignite trees and even singe the hunting dogs.

Caladrius An all-white bird, said to be popular because it could cure jaundice (in an unspecified way), and its dung could cure blindness. Moreover, when presented to a sick man, it would avert its eyes if he were destined to die, but look him in the face if he was going to get better, the very look being the cure.

Centaur Half man (the head), half horse (the body); the man's waist merges into the horse's neck.

Cerberus The three-headed dog that guards the entrance to hell.

Cinomolgus An Arabian bird that nests in cinnamon shreds in trees so tall that they cannot be plundered by man.

Cockatrice See **Basilisk**.

Dipsa A very tiny but lethal creature; even as you die, you may not realise that you have been bitten by a dipsa.

Dragon Comes in many varieties; characteristics include a scaly body, sagittal tail, one or more pairs of wings, and the ability to breathe fire.

Griffin A beast whose front end and forelegs are those of an eagle, complete with wings, and its rear end that of a lion; thus it combines the King of Birds and the King of Beasts.

Hydrus A serpent whose ploy is to coat itself with mud, slither into the mouth of a sleeping crocodile, and expand itself so as to burst the crocodile open. The effects of its painful bite may be alleviated with cow-dung.

Jaculus Lies in wait in a tree; launches itself (as the flying jaculus) and buries its fatal fangs in the neck of its prey. Refer to A A Milne *The House at Pooh Corner* Ch IV: In Which It Is Shown That Tiggers Don't Climb Trees, wherein Tigger does in fact climb a tree (with Roo on his back) and is misidentified by Pooh (on the ground) as a Jagular: 'They hide in the branches of trees and drop on you as you go underneath,' said Pooh.

Leucrota The result of a union between a hyena and a lioness; the huge mouth in its horselike head opens right back to the ears, and is furnished with strips of bone instead of teeth; it is supposed to chatter like a human, but whether anyone can make sense of what it utters is not known.

Manticora A beast with the head of a man bearing three rows of teeth, the body of a lion, and the stinging tail of a scorpion; it has a shrill voice and eats human flesh.

Mermaid Maid of the sea; the top half a beautiful girl with long hair that she is wont to comb incessantly while gazing into a mirror; the bottom half the scaly hinder end and tail of a fish. Possibly based on the real-life manatee or sea-cow. The Belgian artist René Magritte turned the mermaid concept on its head (so to speak) by showing a creature formed from the front end of a scaly fish and the rear end of (presumably) a beautiful girl – nothing like so attractive.

Monceros Distinct from the unicorn; larger, and much less delicate, with an armour-piercing horn and (unlike the unicorn) no interest whatever in virgins.

Onocentaur The horse-body of the centaur is replaced by the body of an ass.

Parandus A beast the size of an ox, with large antlers and a shaggy coat and the ability when frightened to become invisible by assuming the colour of its background.

Phoenix A unique bird that lived in India; on attaining the age of 500 years, it flew to Heliopolis and sat on a specially-prepared aromatic pyre which it ignited by striking its beak against a stone, and promoted by fanning it with its wings, whereupon the bird rapidly became a pile of ash from which soon emerged a worm which rapidly grew to an adult phoenix and flew back to India.

Scitalis A small, slithering beast which may catch you as you admire its beautiful patterns.

Seps A small but extremely unpleasant snake whose venom will destroy flesh and bone, leaving nothing of its prey.

Siren A bird with a woman's head and a sweet voice to lure sailors to their doom; alternatively, a type of mermaid with wings.

Tragelaphe The 'goatbuck', a type of stag with a goat's beard and shoulder hair.

Unicorn Reputedly a small animal, very strong, that can kill an elephant with its single horn. It can run so fast that no hunter can catch it, so send a virgin to lie in wait for the unicorn; it will leap into her lap and embrace her, when it may readily be caught. It has been suggested that a pair of unicorns missed Noah's Ark, consoling themselves that there would be another along in a minute.

Yale A black beast the size of a horse, with two horns, one of which can be folded down its back so that the other can be used solo, and the folded one brought back into play if the other is damaged.

Books of the Holy Bible

OT	Old Testament	No of chapters
Gen	The First Book of Moses, called Genesis	50
Exod	The Second Book of Moses, called Exodus	40
Lev	The Third Book of Moses, called Leviticus	27
Num	The Fourth Book of Moses, called Numbers	36
Deut	The Fifth Book of Moses, called Deuteronomy	34
Josh	The Book of Joshua	24

Judg	The Book of Judges	21
Ruth	The Book of Ruth	4
I Sam; 1 Sam	The First Book of Samuel, otherwise called The First Book of the Kings	31
II Sam; 2 Sam	The Second Book of Samuel, otherwise called The Second Book of the Kings	24
I Kgs; 1 Kgs	The First Book of Kings, commonly called The Third Book of the Kings	22
II Kgs; 2 Kgs	The Second Book of Kings, commonly called The Fourth Book of the Kings	25
I Chr; 1 Chr	The First Book of the Chronicles	29
OII Chr; 2 Chr	The Second Book of the Chronicles	36
Ez, Ezra	Ezra	10
Neh	The Book of Nehemiah	13
Est, Esther	The Book of Esther	10
Job	The Book of Job	52
Ps	The Book of Psalms	150
Prov	The Proverbs	31
Eccles	Ecclesiastes; or, the Preacher	12
SS, S of Sol	The Song of Solomon	8
Isa	The Book of the Prophet Isaiah	66
Jer	The Book of the Prophet Jeremiah	52
Lam	The Lamentations of Jeremiah	5
Ezek	The Book of the Prophet Ezekiel	48
Dan	The Book of Daniel	12
Hos	Hosea	14
Joel	Joel	3
Am, Amos	Amos	9
Obad	Obadiah	1
Jonah	Jonah	4
Mic	Micah	7
Nah, Nahum	Nahum	3
Hab	Habakkuk	3
Zeph	Zephaniah	3
Hag	Haggai	2
Zech	Zechariah	14
Mal	Malachi	4
Apoc	**Apocrypha (15 Books)**	
I Esd; 1 Esd	I Esdras	9
II Esd; 2 Esd	II Esdras	16
Tob, Tobit	Tobit	14
Jud, Judith	Judith	16
Rest of Est	The Rest of the Chapters of the Book of Esther	
Wis of Sol	The Wisdom of Solomon	19
Ecclus	The Wisdom of Jesus the Son of Sirach, or Ecclesiasticus	51

Bar	Baruch	6
Pr of Az	The Prayer of Azariah and the Song of the Three Jews	1
S of Three	The Song of the Three Holy Children	1
Sus	The History of Susanna	1
B&D, Bel & Sn	The History of the Destruction of Bel and the Dragon Daniel	1
Pr of Man	The Prayer of Manasses, King of Judah	1
I Macc; 1 Macc	The First Book of the Maccabees	16
II Macc; 2 Macc	The Second Book of the Maccabees	15
NT	**New Testament (27 Books)**	
Matt	The Gospel According to Saint Matthew	28
Mark	The Gospel According to Saint Mark	16
Luke	The Gospel According to Saint Luke	24
John	The Gospel According to Saint John	21
Acts	The Acts of the Apostles	28
Rom	The Epistle of Paul the Apostle to the Romans	16
I Cor; 1 Cor	The First Epistle of Paul the Apostle to the Corinthians	16
II Cor; 2 Cor	The Second Epistle of Paul the Apostle to the Corinthians	13
Gal	The Epistle of Paul the Apostle to the Galatians	6
Eph	The Epistle of Paul the Apostle to the Ephesians	5
Phil	The Epistle of Paul the Apostle to the Philippians	4
Col	The Epistle of Paul the Apostle to the Colossians	4
I Thess; 1 Thess	The First Epistle of Paul the Apostle to the Thessalonians	5
II Thess; 2 Thess	The Second Epistle of Paul the Apostle to the Thessalonians	3
I Tim; 1 Tim	The First Epistle of Paul the Apostle to Timothy	6
II Tim; 2 Tim	The Second Epistle of Paul the Apostle to Timothy	4
Titus	The Epistle of Paul to Titus	3
Phil, Philem	The Epistle of Paul to Philemon	1
Heb	The First Epistle of Paul the Apostle to the Hebrews	8
Jas	The General Epistle of James	5
I Pet; 1 Pet	The First Epistle General of Peter	5
II Pet; 2 Pet	The Second Epistle General of Peter	3
I John; 1 John	The First Epistle General of John	1
II John; 2 John	The Second Epistle of John	1
III John; 3 John	The Third Epistle of John	1
Jude	The General Epistle of Jude	1
Rev	The Revelation of St John the Divine (not 'Revelations')	22

Fortune telling or divination

Many words for telling the future derive from the Greek word *manteia*, meaning divination. As such they often end in 'mancy'. Some of these techniques reach back into antiquity, and would hardly be popular – or indeed legal – nowadays. For example, few people today would choose to sacrifice an animal in a public place, rip out its entrails or internal organs and seek meaning in their colour, shape and arrangement, even if they were allowed to get away with it. On the other hand, ringing premium-rate telephone lines to seek an astrological or tarot reading is a symptom of the modern world.

Name	Fortune telling by means of
Aeromancy	the weather, especially clouds
Alectryomancy	bird and grains
Alomancy	salt
Amniomancy	examining an afterbirth
Anthomancy	flowers
Apantomancy	random meetings with animals
Arithmancy	numbers
Astragalomancy	dice or knucklebones
Astrology	stars
Astromancy	stars
Austromancy	wind
Automatic writing	writing in a trance
Belomancy	arrows
Bibliomancy	opening a book at random
Botanomancy	burning branches or plants
Capnomancy	smoke patterns
Cartomancy	playing cards
Causimancy	fire
Ceroscopy	wax
Chiromancy	palmistry or palm-reading
Conchomancy	shells
Crystalomancy	crystal ball gazing
Cubomancy	throwing dice
Enoptromancy	mirrors
Geomancy	throwing earth
Graphology	handwriting
Halomancy	salt
Haruspicy	examining animal entrails
Hematomancy	blood

Hepatoscopy	inspecting animal livers
Hieroscopy	entrails
Hydromancy	water, especially ripples
I-Ching	Chinese hexagrams
Lecanomancy	water in a basin or pool
Libanomancy	incense smoke
Lithomancy	precious stones
Logomancy	words
Metoposcopy	lines of the forehead
Numerology	numbers
Oneiromancy	dreams
Oomancy	eggs
Ophidiomancy	snakes
Ornithomancy	birds in flight
Osteomancy	bones
Ouija board	'spirit' messages
Pedomancy	soles of the feet
Pessomancy	pebbles
Phyllomancy	leaves
Physiognomancy	face
Pyromancy / pyroscopy	fire
Rhabdomancy	a stick or rod
Runes	Norse letters
Scapulomancy	inspecting burnt shoulder blades
Scrying	gazing into crystal, mirrors, flames, bowl of water, or ink
Selenomancy	the moon
Sortilege	drawing lots
Spheromancy	a crystal ball
Spodomancy	ashes, cinders or soot
Stercomancy	studying seeds in faeces
Tarot cards	special cards
Tasseography	tea leaves
Theomancy	oracles

Ordered by object used

Object	Name
Afterbirth	amniomancy
Animal entrails	haruspicy

Animals, random meetings with	apantomancy
Arrows	belomancy
Ashes, cinders or soot	spodomancy
Bird and grains	alectryomancy
Birds in flight	ornithomancy
Blood	hematomancy
Bones	osteomancy
Book, opening at random	bibliomancy
Burning branches or plants	botanomancy
Chinese hexagrams	I-Ching
Crystal ball gazing	crystalomancy; spheromancy
Dice or knucklebones	astragalomancy
Dice, throwing	cubomancy
Drawing lots	sortilege
Dreams	oneiromancy
Earth, throwing	geomancy
Eggs	oomancy
Entrails	hieroscopy
Face	physiognomancy
Fire	causimancy
Fire	pyromancy / pyroscopy
Flowers	anthomancy
Gazing into crystal, mirrors, flames, bowl of water, or ink	scrying
Handwriting	graphology
Incense smoke	libanomancy
Leaves	phyllomancy
Lines of the forehead	metoposcopy
Livers, animal	hepatoscopy
Mirrors	enoptromancy
Moon	selenomancy
Norse letters	runes
Numbers	arithmancy
Numbers	numerology
Oracles	theomancy

Palmistry or palm-reading	chiromancy
Pebbles	pessomancy
Playing cards	cartomancy
Precious stones	lithomancy
Salt	alomancy
Salt	halomancy
Seeds in faeces	stercomancy
Shells	conchomancy
Shoulder blades, burnt	scapulomancy
Smoke patterns	capnomancy
Snakes	ophidiomancy
Soles of the feet	pedomancy
'Spirit' messages	ouija board
Stars	astrology; astromancy
Stick or rod	rhabdomancy
Tarot cards	tarot cards
Tea leaves	tasseography
Water in a basin or pool	lecanomancy
Water, especially ripples	hydromancy
Wax	ceroscopy
Weather, especially clouds	aeromancy
Wind	austromancy
Words	logomancy
Writing in a trance	automatic writing

Schools of philosophy

Derived from Greek, the word philosophy means love of wisdom. The foundation of modern western philosophy lies in the different schools of thought, approaching wisdom in different ways, that were established in ancient Greece. During the early centuries of Christianity the only permitted philosophy was religious, and it was not until the Renaissance (around C15) that classical philosophies were revived in western Europe. Modern western philosophy did not, however, really begin until the C18 Enlightenment, when thinkers began to distance themselves from religious philosophy, and to ask different sorts of questions about the world, reality and methods of thinking. Eastern philosophical movements are different in nature, being mainly concerned with exploring spiritual traditions. Developed mainly in India, China, and Japan, these include Confucianism, Taoism, Buddhism, Zen Buddhism, Hinduism and Shinto. Other movements in eastern philosophy include Maoism and Legalism.

Some major philosophical schools in Classical Greece

	Summary	*Key figures*
Epicureanism	The ultimate good is the absence of pain from body and soul.	Epicurus (341–270BCE)
Pythagoreanism	Reality is mathematical in nature at its deepest level.	Pythagoras (?580–?500BCE)
Realism	Objects have reality and independent existence, even when people are not thinking about them.	Plato (?427–?347BCE) Aristotle (384–322BCE)
Socratic Method	Careful application of reasoned questions approaches truth. Taught through questioning.	Socrates (?470–399BCE)
Stoicism	Reason is all. Reacting to the world with intellectual detachment rather than emotional passion.	Zeno of Citium (C3BCE)

Branches or divisions in modern western philosophy

Metaphysics The study of existence and other basic categories of things, such as causality, objects, properties.

Epistemology The study of knowledge: its nature and justification.

Ethics The study of what makes actions right or wrong, and the application of ethical theories to moral problems.

Logic The study of reason, is sometimes included as a division.

Philosophy in the modern world

	Summary	Key figures
Empiricism	A theory of knowledge. Beliefs need to be confirmed by experience.	Thomas Hobbes (1588–1679) David Hume (1711–76)
Cartesianism (critical philosophy)	Reason, not experience, is the main source and test of knowledge. 'I think, therefore I am.' Introduced doubt and critique about truth. Sought secure, indubitable foundation for knowledge by casting aside the insecure. Inspired rationalism as main philosophical doctrine on continental Europe.	René Descartes (1596–1650)
French Materialism	Matter is the only true reality. Thoughts and emotions are just functions of matter.	Julien Offray de la Mettrie (1709–51)
Continental philosophy/ continental idealism	Thoughts are the basis of reality. The world is an idea/thought.	Immanuel Kant (1724–1804) Georg Wilhelm Friedrich Hegel (1770–1831)
Utilitarianism	Effects of an action define its ethics. Ethical actions promote happiness.	Jeremy Bentham (1748–1831) John Stuart Mill (1806–73)
Existentialism	Subjective existence is all. Humans are free agents, responsible for constructing their own existences.	Søren Kierkegaard (1813–55) Jean-Paul Sartre (1905–80) Simone de Beauvoir (1908–1986)
Marxism	Economic basis of society determines its culture. Change comes about because of class struggle.	Karl Marx (1818–83)
Analytic philosophy	Logic-based analysis of the world. Directly opposed to Continental Philosophy/ Idealism/ Existentialism.	Gottlob Frege (1848–1925), William van Orman Quine (1908–2000)
Structuralism	Rules and relationship between elements of a structure is all-important for meaning.	Ferdinand de Saussure (1857–1913) Noam Chomsky (1928–)

Phenomenology	The study of phenomena – things that appear to us – using intuition and imagination.	Edmund Husserl (1859–1938), Martin Heidegger (1889–1976)
Logical positivism	Logic exemplifies truth and the world. Examines how logic relates to the world. Rejects metaphysics. Sub-branches: Logical Atomism, Ideal Language Philosophy.	Bertrand Russell (1872–1970) Ludwig Wittgenstein (1889–1951)
Modernism	Primarily an early C20 literary/artistic movement with wider influence. Rejection of previous (Victorian and Edwardian) conventions and traditions. Experimental and innovative.	
Postmodernism	Late C20 artistic trend questioning and exploring definite meanings and ideals. Rejects idea of objective reality or single world view in favour of irony and irrationalism. Sub-branches: Deconstuctionism.	Michel Foucault (1926–84), Jacques Derrida (1930–)

Some mainly Christian religious -isms

-ism	Doctrine or belief
Adamitism	religious justification of nakedness
Adoptionism	Christ was not the natural son of God but the adopted son of God
Agnosticism	we cannot know anything or be certain of anything except that which we experience on the material plane
Albigensianism	a dualist universe, individual experience of God, rejection of priestly authority (a sect in southern France from C11 to C13)
Anglicanism	the doctrine of the Church of England
Animalism	humans do not have a spiritual nature
Animism	inanimate objects have spirits or souls
Anthropotheism	gods are only humans raised to divine status
Antidisestablish-mentarianism	opposition to the movement to remove the official religious status of the Church of England
Antilapsarianism	denial that humanity fell from grace
Antipedobaptism	infant baptism is not valid
Apocalypticism	the end of the world is nigh
Arianism	Christ was not originally part of God but was raised to divine status

Atheism	there is no god
Autosoterism	individuals can obtain salvation through themselves
Autotheism	conviction that one is Christ or God incarnate
Bitheism	there are two gods
Calvinism	the Protestant ideology of John Calvin (1509–64), stressing predestination
Casualism	chance rules the universe
Catabaptism	infant baptism is wrong
Catholicism or Roman Cathol-icism	the doctrines and practices of the Roman Catholic church
Collegialism	the church should be independent from the state
Cosmotheism	God is the cosmos
Creationism	the Biblical story of God's creation of the universe is literal truth, or, God creates an individual soul at the time of conception or birth
Deism	belief in God through reason rather than religious teaching
Disestablishment-arianism	movement to remove the official religious status of the Church of England
Dogmatism	belief that one's own doctrines and dogma are the only authoritative ones
Dualism	there is one good force or God and one evil force or God
Egotheism	identification of the self with God
Evangelism	spreading the Christian message
Fatalism	human beings are powerless to determine their fates: all events are pre-determined
Fundamentalism	interpreting every word of one's holy book as literal truth
Gnosticism	individuals can find knowledge of God within themselves without need for an interceding priest. The spiritual element of humanity can be released from its prison within matter
Holobaptism	baptism requires total immersion in water
Humanism	people can establish moral rules and a just society without reference to a god
Illuminism	special enlightenment or illumination can come from within without the need for teachings of a priest
Immanentism	God is permanently present or immanent throughout the universe

Immaterialism	there is no material substance
Indifferentism	all religions are equally valid or invalid
Kenotism	in becoming human, Christ was no longer divine in any way
Laicism	opposition to priests and the clergy
Latitudinarianism	freedom of thought and belief
Legalism	salvation depends on strictly following the law
Lutheranism	the Protestant ideology of Martin Luther (1483–1546), stressing plain faith
Malism	the world is essentially evil
Messianism	there will be a messiah or saviour
Methodism	the Nonconformist ideology of John Wesley (1702–91), stressing simple worship
Millenarianism	there will be 1,000 glorious years of Christ's reign after the Second Coming
Modalism	unity of Father, Son and Holy Spirit
Monopsychism	individuals have a single eternal soul
Monotheism	there is only one God
Mortalism	the soul is mortal
Nomism	the law or laws take on religious meaning
Numenism	there are local deities or spirits of place
Paedobaptism	infant baptism is essential
Paganism	a nature religion; any religion that is not Christian
Panentheism	the world is only part, but not all, of God's being
Pantheism	there are many gods; God is the material universe and forces of nature
Perfectibilism	humans are capable of becoming perfect
Pessimism	the universe is essentially evil
Polytheism	there are many gods and goddesses
Predestinarianism	events are fixed and fated to happen; there is no free will
Protestantism	doctrines of churches which separated from the Roman Catholic church
Psychism	there is a universal soul
Psycho-pannychism	souls sleep from death to resurrection
Psychotheism	God is a purely spiritual entity
Puritanism	C16 and C17 movement of extreme, sober Protestantism
Quietism	enlightenment comes through mental tranquillity
Reincarnationism	at death, the soul is reborn in another body

Sacerdotalism	priests are needed to mediate and intercede between God and humankind
Salvationism	God will deliver one from sin and from the penalties for sinning
Sectarianism	adherence to the division of religion into separate sects or groups, with overtones of bigotry and narrow-mindedness
Scepticism or Skepticism	questioning religious beliefs
Solarism	emphasis on solar myths
Spiritualism	souls or spirits of the dead can communicate with the living on earth
Synergism	salvation results from the human will and divine spirit co-operating
Terminism	an individual only has a specific time within which to repent for past sins
Thanatism	the soul dies with the body
Theism	belief in the existence of God without the need for special revelation
Theocentrism	God is the central fact of existence
Theopantism	God is the only reality
Theopsychism	the soul is divine
Tolerationism	tolerance of religious differences
Totemism	a kinship group has a special relationship with an object or animal
Transcendentalism	God exists outside the physical world in a way which transcends ordinary perception; there are supernatural or mystical events and experiences
Transmigrationism	at death, the soul passes into another body
Tritheism	the three members of the Trinity are separate gods
Triumphalism	one particular religious creed is superior to all others
Ubiquitarianism	Christ is everywhere
Unitarianism	there is no trinity, God is one being
Universalism	universal salvation
Vitalism	there is a vital force behind life
Zoomorphism	representing gods in animal form
Zootheism	giving divine qualities to animals

Who's who in the major religions of the world

Judaism

Judaism, the world's oldest monotheistic religion, was founded by **Abraham**, from whom all the Jewish people are descended. It was first formalised after the Jews were taken into exile in Babylon in 586 BCE.

The near descendants of Abraham founded twelve tribes, each named after their ancestor among the sons of **Jacob**, as follows:

Reuben, **Simeon**, Levi, **Judah**, **Issachar**, **Zebulun**, **Dan**, **Napthali**, **Gad**, **Asher**, Joseph, and **Benjamin**. No tribe is named after **Joseph**; instead, two are each named after his sons, **Manasseh** and **Ephraim**. The tribe of **Levi** is not reckoned among the twelve, but has been associated with ceremonial functions.

The Bible records figures from both the legends and history of the Jewish people, or Hebrews, according to which the first man was **Adam**, father of all humanity. **David** (c1001–968 BCE), the first king of Israel, captured Jerusalem and made it his capital. **Deborah** was a prophetess, whose song of triumph on defeating the Canaanites (Judges, 5) is considered one of the finest pieces of early Hebrew literature. The prophet **Elijah** (C9 BCE) defended Judaism against the cult of the god Baal. **Esther**, queen of Persia, risked her life to save the Jews from massacre. **Eve**, the mother of humankind, was created by God from a rib taken from her husband Adam. **Gideon** saved Israel from an invasion by the Midianites, with an army of three hundred. **Herod** 'the Great', allied himself with the occupying Romans; he was the rebuilder of the Temple in Jerusalem. **Isaiah**, prophet and statesman, was a denunciator of the rich. **Jeremiah**, as a prophet of Israel, suffered many wrongs including persecution by his own people; as a result he is associated with the deepest pessimism. **Job** was assailed by God with all sorts of trouble as a test, and was rewarded in this life for not losing his faith. **Jonah**, having disobeyed God's instruction to become a missionary, survived being swallowed by a great fish and repented. **Joshua** was commanded by God to settle in the lands between the Mediterranean and the Euphrates river; he saw to it that the Promised Land was divided between the tribes of Israel. **Judith**, memorably recorded in paintings of the Renaissance, saved many of her fellow Jews by cutting off the head of the Babylonian general Holofernes while he slept. **Moses**, greatest of Hebrew prophets, led his people from slavery to the Promised Land. **Samson**, who came to be a personification of physical strength, was unmanned by Delilah, who found that he was made weak when his hair was cut off. **Zephaniah** (C7 BCE) was a prophet who led an impassioned denunciation of the Judean establishment.

Christianity

Christianity grew out of the teachings of **Jesus Christ**, who was put to death by the Romans in about 30 CE. His first followers, the Twelve Apostles, each has his own emblem:

Peter: the key to the Kingdom of Heaven; **Andrew**: a decussate or diagonal cross; **Thomas**: a spear or arrow; **James the Less**: a fuller's bat, as used in cloth manufacture; **John**: chalice and dragon; **Jude**: a club or cross or carpenter's square; **Matthew**: a purse or money box, or a spear or axe; **Matthias**: an axe, halberd, lance or a book; **Bartholomew**: a butcher's knife; **Philip**: a cross, or loaves and fishes; **James**: scallop shells; **Simon**: a saw, or sometimes fishes.

The Christian Church eventually divided into three main denominations: **Roman Catholic**, **Protestant**, and **Eastern Orthodox**. Of these in turn, Protestantism has shown most readiness to form flourishing subsects; its main groups, mostly active internationally, are:

Baptists, founded in England (1609) and Rhode Island (1638); **Church of England** (1534); **Episcopal Church** (1784), an American offshoot of the Church of England; **Presbyterian Church** (1557), founded in Scotland; **Quakers** (mid C17), first established in England; **Unitarians** (1560s), founded in northern and eastern Europe.

Within Christianity there are many orders of monks, friars, and nuns living in groups together under vows of poverty, chastity and obedience. Hermits – monks living in solitude – are an exception. The following orders are each given with their date of foundation.

Monks and friars

Pachomian monks: 318
Basilian monks: 360
Augustinian monks: 388
Benedictine monks: 529
Constitutions of Theodore: c 800
Camaldulian monks: c 970
Vallombrosan monks: c 1038
Augustinian canons: c 1060
Carthusian monks: 1080
Cluniac monks: 1090
Cistercian monks: 1098
Fontevrault monks: c 1100
Order of St Gilbert of Sempringham: 1148
Carmelite friars: c 1155
Trinitarian order: 1198

Premonstratensian canons: 1200
Franciscan friars: 1209
Dominican friars: 1215
Monks of Our Lady of Ransom: 1223
Silvestrine monks: 1231
Servite monks: 1233
Austinian hermits: 1256
Celestine monks: c 1260
Olivetan monks: 1319
Ambrosian monks: c 1370
Hieronymite friars: 1374
Franciscan Observant friars: 1415
Minim brothers: 1435
Capuchin friars: 1525
Hospitaller friars of St John of God: 1537
Discalced Carmelite friars: 1562
Augustinian recollect friars: 1588
Trappist monks: 1664
Mekhitarist monks: 1702
Marist brothers: 1817
Society of St John the Evangelist: 1866
Priests of the Sacred Heart: 1878
The Taizé Community: 1948

Nuns

Benedictine nuns: 529
Fontevrault nuns: c 1100
Beguine nuns: c 1180
Poor Clare nuns: 1214
Carthusian nuns: 1229
Bridgettine nuns: 1344
Carmelite nuns: 1452
Ursuline nuns: 1535
Discalced Carmelite nuns: 1562
Theatine nuns: 1583
Sisters of the Institute of the Blessed Virgin Mary: 1609
Sisters of Charity of St Vincent de Paul: 1629
Servite nuns: 1640
Redemptorist nuns: 1750
Passionist nuns: 1770
Sisters of Mercy: 1827

Little Sisters of the Poor: 1840
Nuns of the Community of St Mary: 1865
Society of the Sacred Heart of Jesus: 1880
Sisters of Our Lady of Charity of the Good Shepherd: 1883
Sisterhood of St John the Divine: 1884
Poor Clares of Reparation: 1922

The Old Testament, in roughly the same form, is common to both Judaism and Christianity; only Christians acknowledge the New Testament as a sacred text. This part of the Bible covers the life of Christ, and the establishment of Christianity, up to about the year 125.

Within the New Testament, the Apostle **Matthew** figures largely, along with **Mark**, **Luke** and **John**, as the authors of the four Gospels making up most of this part of the Bible. **Barnabas**, who is also referred to as Joseph, was a Cypriot who worked with St Paul to spread Christianity. **Judas Iscariot**, originally one of the Apostles, became a byword for treachery of any kind following his betrayal of Jesus to the Roman authorities. **John the Baptist** initiated Jesus' life as a preacher by baptising him; later he was beheaded by King Herod of Galilee. **Joseph** was the husband of Jesus' mother Mary. He was a descendant of King David, and a carpenter from the village of Nazareth. **Mary**, as mother of Jesus, is described as the Virgin Mary, on account of the doctrine that Jesus was conceived by a miracle while she was still a virgin. She is revered, in particular among Roman Catholics, as a symbol of maternal virtues. **Mary Magdalene** was a follower of Jesus, often seen as a figure of repentance. **Paul**, originally named Saul, was at first a persecutor of the early Christians. However, while on his way to Damascus one day he was temporarily struck blind and heard a message from God as a result of which he became a leading member of the infant Church. The Romans eventually beheaded him. As a Roman governor with responsibility for Judaea, **Pontius Pilate** is conspicuous in Christian doctrine for his part, however reluctant, in Jesus' crucifixion. Among religious groupings dominant in Judaea during the lifetime of Jesus, the **Pharisees** had both religious and political influence, exercised in support of an inflexible traditionalism much criticised by Jesus. Their enemies the **Sadducees** were also concerned with politics as well as religious belief, and were drawn largely from the local governing class. Strongly connected with the Pharisees were the **Scribes**, the traditional students and interpreters of the Torah.

Islam

The foundations of Islam lie in ancient times: the first Muslim, according to the Koran, was **Ibrahim**, the Abraham of the Jewish and Christian religions, who was divinely guided to see God as the only deity and to reject all pagan beliefs. Islam was established as an organised religion by **Muhammad**, whose name means 'Praised One'. Other spellings of Muhammad are Mohammed, Mahomet, and Mohomed. Muslims believe that he was the last of the prophets, completing the teachings of **Moses** and **Jesus**.

The anti-idolatry of Muhammad's teachings is reflected in the fact that the representation of people in art is forbidden; consequently most historical figures or movements within Islam are known mainly through written records. From within Muhammad's own lifetime, **Abu Bakr** was a wealthy follower of the Prophet who became the first leader or caliph to succeed him. **Abu Talib** was Muhammad's uncle and guardian. **Aisha** was the daughter of Abu Bakr and Muhammad's wife. **Fatima**, Muhammad's daughter, became the wife of Abu Talib's son **Ali. Ismail**, Ibrahim's son, was traditionally the ancestor of the Arab peoples. **Khadja**, Muhammad's first wife, was originally his employer and subsequently his earliest follower. **Omar**, or Umar Ibn al-Khattab, initially persecuted Muhammad, but became a convert and, after Muhammad's death, the second caliph to succeed him. Among the northern tribes of Arabia, the **Quraysh** was the one to which Muhammad belonged.

Muslim sects

Nearly thirty years after the death of Muhammad, the world of Islam divided into two main factions. Of these, the **Sunni** Muslims are the more conservative group and make up a large majority, who acknowledge leadership exercised by caliphs from Muhammad's own tribe. The **Shi'ites** consider the only lawful Muslim authority to come from **imams**, descendants of Muhammad through his daughter Fatima and Ali, her husband. They are a minority throughout Islam except in Iran.

Later schisms produced a number of smaller sects. The Baha'i faith, which grew out of the Shi'ite sect, was established by **Mirza Husaynali** in Iran in 1863; it believes in the unification of all faiths. **Wahhabis** predominate in Saudi Arabia and comprise a movement founded in C18 by **Muhammad bin' Abd al-Wahhab**, who sought a return to the simplicity of early Islam. Their influence currently means holding off such western influences as the use of alcohol. **Sufis** represent the continuing search for closer contact with God, through mysticism and indifference to material wealth. **Black Muslims** are a movement generated in C20 America. Under the name the Nation of Islam it was established by **Elijah Muhammad**, following on from the ideas of **Wallace D. Fard**, and was further developed by **Malcolm X**. One of its main objects was to declare black people as superior to any other; however some white people are now included among its members.

Hinduism

The earliest forms of Hinduism lie in prehistoric times, when they were already practised in the Indus Valley. There was no one founding figure, and Hindu gods are many and various. But the different forms of Hinduism share certain beliefs: in reincarnation, in rules of behaviour, in given forms of ceremony, and in the caste system. This last has been officially outlawed, but still has an influence. It determines the social standing of everyone from birth and divides them into four main classes: at the top, **brahmins**, or priests; then **kshatriyas**, warriors and rulers; **viasyas**, traders and minor officials; and unskilled workers, or **sudras**. Below all these is the **pariah** class, the 'untouchables'.

The numerous gods of Hinduism are seen as parts of one divine entity. This universal spirit is known as **Brahman**, whose most important aspects are the many-armed gods **Brahma**, **Vishnu** and **Shiva**.

The good side of Brahma, the creator, is Vishnu, who traditionally has appeared on earth so far in nine incarnations. These have been: **Matsya** – fish; **Kurma** – tortoise; **Varaha** – boar; **Narasimha** – man–lion; **Vamana** – dwarf; **Parashurama** – Rama with the axe; **Rama** – prince; **Krishna** – young hero and lover; and the **Buddha**. One incarnation, **Kalki**, is still to come. The attributes of Vishnu are: disk, mace, conch shell, lotus, seven-headed cobra, caste mark, and garland of forest flowers.

The other side of this 'trinity' is Brahma's destructive aspect, which takes the form of Shiva, also known as Nataraja, Lord of the Dance. In this form he is also shown with several typical features: as he dances, he crushes the demon of ignorance; he holds a drum and the flame of destruction; a surrounding arch of fire stands for the circle of life and death; a cobra represents fertility; a leopard skin signifies strength; he wears a look of concentration, and his several hands are raised in blessing.

There are few temples to Brahma himself, but he is depicted in many others, where he is shown to have: four faces, one for each part of the universe; a sacrificial ladle; prayer beads; four scriptures; a jar of water from the sacred Ganges river; and a lotus throne. Paradoxically, as the One and the All he tends not to be an object of worship.

Other gods

Aditi was the mother of all the gods; **Agni**, the god of fire and sacrifice. The Bhakta saints were members of the **Vaisnava Bhakti** movement, which flourished in the C11 and early C12. Though they considered God to be inaccessible to all understanding, they held him nonetheless to be the only reality. Their faith expressed itself in doing good, and in seeking God by chanting and singing. **Ganesha** is the elephant-headed deity, protector of scribes and traders. **Hanuman** is the monkey god. The black deity **Kali** is Shiva's bloodthirsty wife; as Uma or Parvati she is also the goddess of motherhood. Krishna, one of the incarnations of Vishnu, is worshipped as a lover and as a dragon-slayer. Vishnu's wife **Lakshmi** is the goddess of wealth, beauty, and good fortune. **Saravasti**, the wife of Brahma, is a river deity. As goddess of knowledge and truth, she is also protector of writers. **Sati** was the first wife of Shiva. By tradition it was through her that the practice of suttee was established whereby widows (without unborn or young children) died on their husband's funeral pyre; a practice forbidden in British India in 1829, though it continued in Nepal until 1877.

Buddhism

The founder of Buddhism, known as 'the **Buddha**', or 'the enlightened', was born Siddhartha Gautama, c 563 BCE in what is now the kingdom of Nepal. He grew up in the household of his father, **Prince Suddodhana**, rajah of the **Sakya** tribe, and subsequently married the beautiful **Princess Yasodhara**.

In about his thirtieth year Gautama had a succession of visions. These showed him an old man; a sick man; a dead body; and an encounter between himself and an itinerant holy man. The first three of these visions confirmed in him a view of life as governed by suffering; as a response to these, and to his perceived meeting with the holy man, he left a life of courtly luxury, together with his wife and his son **Rahula**, to seek enlightenment.

This he did by living a dismal life of self-denial as a wandering monk for six years, during which time his search met with no success. Coming to a village one day, he decided to stay, sitting beneath a bodhi tree until an answer to his quest might come to him. Here he was suddenly shown that the perfect way lay in a life of contemplation, based upon the fact that the route to avoidance of suffering lay through rejection of selfish desires. Much of Buddhism is a radical development of Hinduism, rather than an original religion. Its heritage includes the **sangha**, or order of Buddhist monks and nuns. This word is sometimes also used to describe an ideal community of those who have reached a higher state of spiritual awareness.

Buddha died c 483 BCE, having spent about forty years preaching his message of dharma, or the truth of salvation, throughout northern India. Subsequently Buddhism spread widely throughout southern and eastern

Asia. In the middle years of the C3 BCE the Indian emperor **Ashoka** made it a national religion. During the C7 CE it became widely established in Japan; one large Buddhist sect, founded here by the dogmatically inclined **Nichiren** (1222–82), still flourishes. The C14 and C15 saw the rise of Tibetan Buddhism or Lamaism, whose current leader, the **Dalai Lama**, has lived in exile since 1959.

Confucianism

Confucius is the Latinised name by which the West usually refers to the Chinese philosopher K'ung-fu-tzu (551–479 BCE), a descendant through the dukes of **Sung** to the kings of the **Shang** dynasty. The code of belief and behaviour founded by him comprises a system of moral behaviour without religion; its most famous tenet was, 'What you do not wish done to yourself, do not do to others.' In 517 BCE he met **Lao-Tzu**, whose teachings were to lead much later to the development of Taoism. Confucius gained many followers over a lifetime in senior government and as a teacher. After his death the philosopher **Mencius**, properly Meng-tse (372–298 BCE), the Second Sage, strove to show officialdom how it should govern following practical rules derived from Confucianism. The rationalist **Hsun Tzu** (298–230 BCE) differed from Mencius' belief in man's innate virtue; he spread the doctrine that humankind was born without virtue, but that it can benefit from the right moral teaching. Over the following centuries the spread of Confucianism was accompanied by support from various rulers. In the second century BCE it became the Chinese state ideology; during this time it was the Confucians who educated the **Emperor Wu Ti** (140–87 BCE). The **Emperor Ming** decreed in 59 BCE that sacrifices should be made to Confucius in every public school. During the Sung dynasty, Neo-Confucianism developed as a reaction to Taoist and Buddhist doctrines. Some centuries after the spread of Confucius' teachings to Japan, it was Neo-Confucianism that became adopted by that country's **Tokugawa** shoguns.

Politics

Some political -isms

The suffix -ism is often used to create a new noun to describe a political or religious system of belief, even though in some cases, such as anarchy, a perfectly good noun already exists. The suffix was first used in C17, but there are now so many -isms one wonders how people in earlier periods of history managed to express themselves. Perhaps they had fewer political ideologies or religious beliefs to discuss.

-ism	Doctrine or belief
Absolutism	autocracy or despotism; government by a ruler who has total, absolute power
Altruism	unselfish concern for the welfare of others
Anarchism	government should be abolished and society should be organised through individual responsibility
Authoritarianism	support for a domineering dictatorial form of government
Benthamism	utilitarianism first expounded by Jeremy Bentham (1748–1832)
Bolshevism	Russian communism; literally 'majority'
Capitalism	means of production should be in private ownership with few or no state controls
Causalism	the universe and human affairs are governed by chance
Centrism	middle-of-the-road political views
Collectivism	communal control of means of production
Communism	classless society with communal ownership of means of production
Conservatism	opposition to radical change; preservation of the best of existing political and social traditions (sometimes 'with a small c')
Despotism	rule by an autocratic, absolute ruler, usually a tyrannical one
Determinism	choices and events are predetermined by preceding events
Egalitarianism	all people should have equal rights and social, economic and political privileges
Egoism	putting one's own interests and welfare above all; pursuit of self-interest is the highest good
Egotism	excessive self-centredness

Elitism	society should be ruled by a small, elite group of talented or intellectual individuals
Entryism	joining a group in order to change it from within (possibly a triumph of hope over experience)
Fascism	authoritarian right-wing, nationalistic ideology opposed to liberalism and democracy; specifically in Mussolini's Italy and Hitler's Nazi Germany
Humanism	solutions should be sought using human reason and compassion
Immoralism	rejection of moral rules
Imperialism	taking over other countries
Individualism	individual interests and independence are paramount
Internationalism	countries should co-operate and work together
Leftism	support of left-wing co-operative, socialist or communist political views
Leninism	or Marxism–Leninism, communist ideology emphasising imperialism as the developed form of capitalism. After Soviet leader Vladimir Ilyich Lenin né Ulyanov (1870–1924)
Liberalism	supports social change and reform, tolerance, individual liberty
Libertarianism	the state should never be involved in restricting personal liberty and freedom of choice
Maoism	Marxist–Leninist ideology emphasising revolutionary potential of peasantry and advocating guerrilla warfare. After Chinese leader Mao Ze dong or Tse-tung (1893–1976)
Marxism	economics determines culture; historical change comes about through class struggle; after political philosopher Karl Marx (1818–83)
Materialism	placing more importance on acquiring material goods and possessions than spiritual or ethical values
McCarthyism	making unsubstantiated allegations, mainly of membership of communist organisations and 'un-American activities'; after American politician Joseph McCarthy (1908–57)
Meliorism	the world can become better through human effort
Millenarianism	an ideal society will be created in the future
Monarchism	society should be ruled by an hereditary monarch – king, queen, emperor, etc

Mutualism	social symbiosis: the individual and society are mutually dependent
Nationalism	devotion to one's country's interests, sometimes to the point of racism
Nazism	extreme, right-wing fascist view involving white supremacy and a willingness to use violence to achieve its aims; after Adolf Hitler's National Socialist German Worker's Party in Germany
Nihilism	denial of all established government and authority
Patriotism	love of one's country
Racism	view that a particular human 'race' is superior and should be politically and socially dominant
Radicalism	there should be extreme changes in society
Reactionism	opposition to significant social or political change
Republicanism	government should be a republic, with power in the hands of the people or their elected representatives
Revolutionism	overthrow of existing government, usually by violent means
Rightism	support of right-wing reactionary, conservative or traditional politics
Socialism	state control of wealth and property
Stalinism	totalitarian, bureaucratic state communism; after Soviet leader Joseph Stalin né Josif Vissarionovitch Dzhugashvili (1879–1953)
Syndicalism	a revolutionary movement advocating syndicates of workers seizing control of the means of production
Thatcherism	a particular brand of free-market British conservatism associated with prime minister Margaret Thatcher (1935–)
Totalitarianism	a single-party, dictatorial state where the government has powers over every area of life
Trotskyism	advocation of worldwide revolution by workers. After Soviet politician Leon Trotsky (1879–1940)
Utilitarianism	an action's morality is determined by its effect
Utopianism	ideal of a perfect society

Science and technology

Some computer programming languages

There are hundreds of programming languages in use, some highly specialised or used within just one company or institution. These are some of the major languages used around the world.

Language	Full name / named after	Most common use
A+	—	Business
ABC	—	Personal computing
Ada	Named after Ada, Lady Lovelace, who worked with Charles Babbage and whose notes have been invaluable in our understanding of Babbage's works.	Real-time systems control, *eg*: military use
AED	ALGOL Extended for Design	Computer-aided design
ALGOL	Algorithmic Language	Mathematical or logical processing; *eg* with FORTRAN and LISP, one of the three major 'classic' languages
AMPL	A Mathematical Programming Language	Maths
APL	Array Programming Language	Education, maths
APT	Automatically Programmed Tools	
B	—	Operating systems
BASIC	Beginners All-purpose Symbolic Instruction Code	Games, education
BCPL	B Combined Programming Language	Systems programming, maths, science
Blue	—	Teaching programming
C	—	Operating systems, games, business, science
C++	—	Operating systems, games, business, science, personal computer applications
CHILL	CCITT High Level Language	Telecommunications
COBOL	Common Business Oriented Language	Business data processing
COMAL	Common Algorithmic Language	Games, education
CORAL	Computer On-line Real-time Application Language	Military applications
DCL	Digital Command Language	Operating systems
Euphoria	–	Personal computer applications

FORTH	Fourth-generation computer language	Science, industry, business
FORTRAN	*Formula Trans*lation	Maths, engineering, science; with ALGOL and LISP, one of the three major 'classic' languages
GPSS	General Purpose Systems Simulation	
HTML	Hypertext Mark-up Language	Web pages
Java	The Java coffee its writers consumed in enormous quantities.	Internet applications
LISP	List Processing	Micro-computer applications, artificial intelligence developments. With ALGOL and FORTRAN, one of the three major 'classic' languages
Logo	—	Teaching programming
ML	Meta Language	Internet applications. Dynamic applications
Oberon	—	Personal computer applications
Occam	William of Occam, or Ockham (c1285–c1349), responsible for 'Occam's Razor' *Entia non slunt multiplicanda practer neccessitatem* or, in modern parlance, 'Keep it simple, stupid'	Programs running processes in parallel
Pascal	The mathematican Blaise Pascal (1623–62)	Education
Perl	—	Scripting for Internet applications
PL1	Programming Language 1	Science, engineering, business, systems
PL/B	Programming Language B	Business
Postscript	—	Printing
PROLOG	*Programming in Logic*	Systems, Artificial Intelligence
RPG	Report Program Generator	Business
SGML	Standard Generalised Mark-up Language	Databases
SIMULA	*Simulation Language*	Simulation applications
SNOBOL	String Oriented Symbolic Language	Text editors
SQL	Structured Query Language	Databases
Visual Basic	—	Personal computer applications
XML	Extensible Mark-up Language	Databases, Web pages

Weights and measures

SI units

The Système International d'Unités (SI) is an international and coherent system of units devised to meet all known needs for measurement in science and technology. The system was adopted by the eleventh Conférence Générale des Poids et Mesures (CGPM) in 1960.

There are seven base units and a number of derived and supplementary units formed as products or quotients of powers of the base units.

Base units

metre (m) = unit of length
kilogram (kg) = unit of mass
second (s) = unit of time
Ampere (A) = unit of electric current
Kelvin (K) = unit of thermodynamic temperature
mole (mol) = unit of amount of substance
candela (cd) = unit of luminous intensity

Derived units

There are special names and symbols for some of the derived SI units; those approved by the CGPM are as follows:

Hertz (Hz) = unit of frequency
Newton (N) = unit of force
Pascal (Pa) = unit of pressure, stress
Joule (J) = unit of energy, work, quantity of heat
Watt (W) = unit of power, radiant flux
Coulomb (C) = unit of electric charge, quantity of electricity
Volt (V) = unit of electric potential, potential difference, electromotive force
Farad (F) = unit of electric capacitance
Ohm (Ω) = unit of electric resistance
Siemens (S) = unit of electric conductance
Weber (Wb) = unit of magnetic flux
Tesla (T) = unit of magnetic flux density
Henry (H) = unit of inductance
Degree Celsius (°C) = unit of celsius temperature
Lumen (lm) = unit of luminous flux
Lux (lx) = unit of illuminance
Becquerel (Bq) = unit of activity (of a radionuclide)
Gray (Gy) = unit of absorbed dose, specific energy imparted, kerma, absorbed dose index
Sievert (Sv) = unit of dose equivalent, dose equivalent index

Supplementary units

The derived units include, as a special case, the supplementary units which may be treated as dimensionless within the SI.

Radian (rad) = unit of plane angle
Steradian (sr) = unit of solid angle

Other units are expressed in terms of base units and/or supplementary units. Some of the more commonly used are the following:

Unit of area = square metre (m^2)
Unit of volume = cubic metre (m^3)
Unit of velocity = metre per second (ms^{-1})
Unit of acceleration = metre per second squared (ms^{-1})
Unit of density = kilogram per cubic metre ($kg\ m^{-3}$)
Unit of momentum = kilogram metre per second ($kg\ ms^{-1}$)
Unit of magnetic field strength = ampere per metre ($A\ m^{-1}$)
Unit of surface tension = newton per metre (Nm^{-1})
Unit of dynamic viscosity = pascal second (Pa s)
Unit of heat capacity = joule per kelvin ($J\ K^{-1}$)
Unit of specific heat capacity = joule per kilogram kelvin ($J\ kg^{-1}\ K^{-1}$)
Unit of heat flux density, irradiance = watt per square metre ($W\ m^{-2}$)
Unit of thermal conductivity = watt per metre kelvin ($W\ m^{-1}\ K^{-1}$)
Unit of electric field strength = volt per metre ($V\ m^{-1}$)
Unit of luminance = candela per square metre ($cd\ m^{-2}$)

SI prefixes – orders of magnitude
These are as follows:

multiples			*submultiples*		
yotta	(Y)	$\times 10^{24}$	deci	(d)	$\times 10^{-1}$
zetta	(Z)	$\times 10^{21}$	centi	(c)	$\times 10^{-2}$
exa	(E)	$\times 10^{18}$	milli	(m)	$\times 10^{-3}$
peta	(P)	$\times 10^{15}$	micro	(μ)	$\times 10^{-6}$
tera	(T)	$\times 10^{12}$	nano	(n)	$\times 10^{-9}$
giga	(G)	$\times 10^{9}$	pico	(p)	$\times 10^{-12}$
mega	(M)	$\times 10^{6}$	femto	(f)	$\times 10^{-15}$
kilo	(k)	$\times 10^{3}$	atto	(a)	$\times 10^{-18}$
hecto	(h)	$\times 10^{2}$	zepto	(z)	$\times 10^{-21}$
deca	(da)	$\times 10^{1}$	yocto	(y)	$\times 10^{-24}$

Derived units

The table below shows the derived units and their dimensions in more detail.

Quantity	Unit	Symbol	Equivalent
area	square metre	m^2	—
volume	cubic metre	m^3	—
velocity	metre per second	$m \cdot s^{-1}$	
angular velocity	radian per second	$rad\ s^{-1}$	
acceleration	metre per second squared	$m \cdot s^{-2}$	
angular acceleration	radian per second squared	$rad\ s^{-2}$	
frequency	hertz	Hz	s^{-1}
density	kilogram per cubic metre	$kg \cdot m^{-3}$	
momentum	kilogram metre per second	$kg \cdot m \cdot s^{-1}$	
angular momentum	kilogram metre squared per second	$kg \cdot m^2 \cdot s^{-1}$	
momentum of inertia	kilogram metre squared	$kg \cdot m^2$	
force	newton	N	$kg \cdot m \cdot s^{-2}$
pressure, stress	pascal	Pa	$N \cdot m^{-2} = kg \cdot m^{-1} \cdot s^{-2}$
work, energy, quantity of heat	joule	J	$N \cdot m = kg \cdot m^2 \cdot s^{-2}$
power	watt	W	$J \cdot s^{-1} = kg \cdot m^2 \cdot s^{-3}$
surface tension	newton per metre	$N \cdot m^{-1}$	$kg \cdot s^{-2}$
dynamic viscosity	newton second per metre squared	$N \cdot s \cdot m^{-2}$	$kg \cdot m^{-1} \cdot s^{-1}$
kinematic viscosity	metre squared per second	$m^2 \cdot s^{-1}$	
temperature	degree Celsius	°C	
thermal coefficient of linear expansion	per degree Celsius, or per kelvin	$°C^{-1}, K^{-1}$	
thermal conductivity	watt per metre degree C	$W \cdot m^{-1} \cdot °C^{-1}$	$kg \cdot m \cdot s^{-3} \cdot °C^{-1}$
heat capacity	joule per kelvin	$J \cdot k^{-1}$	$kg \cdot m^2 \cdot s^{-2} \cdot K^{-1}$
specific heat capacity	joule per kilogram kelvin	$J \cdot kg^{-1} \cdot K^{-1}$	$m^2 \cdot s^{-2} \cdot K^{-1}$
**specific latent heat	joule per kilogram	$J \cdot kg^{-1}$	$m^2 \cdot s^{-2}$
electric charge	coulomb	C	$A \cdot s$

electromotive force, potential difference	volt	V	$W \cdot A^{-1} =$ $kg \, m^2 s^{-3} \cdot A^{-1}$
electric resistance	ohm	Ω	$V \cdot A^{-1} =$ $kg \, m^2 s^{-3} \cdot A^{-2}$
electric conductance	siemens	S	$A \cdot V^{-1} =$ $kg^{-1} \cdot m^{-2} s^3 \cdot A^2$
electric capacitance	farad	F	$A \cdot s \cdot V^{-1} =$ $kg^{-1} \cdot m^{-2} s^4 \cdot A^2$
inductance	henry	H	$V \cdot s \cdot A^{-1} =$ $kg \, m^2 s^{-2} \cdot A^{-2}$
magnetic flux	weber	Wb	$V \cdot s =$ $kg \, m^2 s^{-2} \cdot A^{-1}$
magnetic flux density	tesla	T	$Wb \cdot m^{-2} =$ $kg \, s^{-2} \cdot A^{-1}$
magnetomotive force	ampere	A	
luminous flux	lumen	lm	$cd \cdot sr$
illumination	lux	lx	$lm \cdot m^{-2} =$ $cd \cdot sr \, m^{-2}$
radiation activity	becquerel	Bq	s^{-1}
radiation absorbed dose	gray	Gy	$J \cdot kg^{-1} = m^2 s^{-2}$

Metric and Imperial units and conversions (* = exact)

This table shows Imperial (foot–pound–second) units in the first column, and SI units in the third. It also gives the factors by which any chosen unit in one system has to be multiplied to convert it to its equivalent in the other.

Column 1	Equivalent	Column 2	Col 2 > Col 1 x	Col 1 > Col 2 x
Length				
inch (in)	—	centimetre (cm)	0.39370078	2.54*
foot (ft)	12 in	metre	3.280840	0.3048*
yard (yd)	3 ft; 36 in	metre	1.09361	0.9144*
mile	1760 yd	kilometre (km)	0.6213711	1.609344*
fathom	6 ft	metre	0.54680	1.8288*
chain	22 yd	metre	0.04970	20.1168
UK nautical mile	6080 ft	kilometre	0.5396118	1.853184*
International nautical mile	6076.1 ft	kilometre	0.5399568	1.852*
angstrom unit (Å)	10^{-10} m	micron	10^4	10^{-4}

Area

square inch		square centimetre	0.1550	6.4516*
square foot	144 sq in	square metre	10.7639	0.092903*
square yard	9 sq ft	square metre	1.19599	0.836127*
acre	4840 sq yd	hectare (ha; 10^4 m^2)	2.47105	0.404686*
square mile	640 acres	square kilometre	0.38610	2.589988*

Volume

cubic inch		cubic centimetre	0.061024	16.3871*
cubic foot	1728 cu in	cubic metre	35.31467	0.028317*
cubic yard	27 cu ft	cubic metre	1.30795	0.764555*

Capacity

litre	100 centilitres	cubic centimetre or millimetre	0.001*	1000*
pint	4 gills	litre	1.759753	0.568261
UK gallon	8 pints; 277.4 in^3	litre	0.219969	4.546092
barrel (for beer)	36 gallons	hectolitre	0.611026	1.63659
US gallon	0.0832675 UK gallons	litre or dm^3	0.264172	3.785412
fluid ounce	0.05 pint	millilitre	0.035195	28.413074

Velocity

feet per second (ft/s)		metres per second	3.280840	0.3048
miles per hour (mph)		kilometres per hour	0.621371	1.609344
UK (1.00064 Int.Knots)	nautical mile/hour	kilometres per hour	0.5396118	1.853184

Acceleration

foot per second per second (ft/s^2)		metres per second per second (m/s^2)	3.280840	0.3048*

Mass

grain (gr)	a 1/480th of an oz troy	milligram (mg)	0.0154324	64.79891
dram (dr)	27.3438 gr	gram	0.564383	1.77185

ounce (avoirdupois)	16 drams	gram	0.0352740	28.349523125
pound (avoirdupois)	16 ounces	kilogram	2.20462*	0.45359237*
stone	14 pounds	kilogram	0.15747304	6.35029318
quarter	28 pounds	kilogram	0.0787375	12.70058636*
hundred weight (cwt)	112 pounds	kilogram	0.0196841	50.80234544*
ton (long)	2240 pounds	tonne (=1000 kg)	0.9842065	1.0160469088

Note: a pound troy consists of 12 ounces troy each of 480 grains

Density

pounds per cubic inch		grams per cubic centimetre	0.0361272	27.6799
pounds per cubic foot		kilograms per cubic metre	0.0624280	16.0185

Force

dyne (dyn)	10^{-5} Newton	Newton	10^5	10^{-5}
poundal (pdl)		Newton	7.23301	0.138255
pound-force (lbf)		Newton	0.224809	4.44822
tons-force		kilonewton (kN)	0.100361	9.96402
kilogram-force (kgf) (or kilopond)		Newton	0.101972	9.80665

Energy (Work, Heat)

erg	10^{-7} Joule	Joule	10^7	10^{-7}
horse-power (hp) (550 ft/lbf/sec)		Kilowatt (kW)	1.34102	0.745700
therm		mega joule (MJ)	0.00947817	105.506
kilowatt hour (kWh)		mega joule (MJ)	0.277778	3.6
calorie (international)		Joule	0.238846*	4.1868*
British thermal unit (Btu)		Kilo-Joule (kJ)	0.947817	1.05506

Pressure, stress

millibar (mbar or mb)	1000 dynes/cm^2	Pa	0.01*	100*
standard atmosphere (atm)	760 torrs	kPa	0.0098692	101.325
pounds per square inch (psi)		Pa	0.000145038	6894.76
pounds per square inch (psi)		kilogram-force per cm^2	14.2233	0.0703070

ISO paper sizes

An A0 sheet is 1m^2 in area.

The sides of a sheet of an ISO size are in the ratio 1:$\sqrt{2}$, so if a sheet is cut in half on the long side, the ratio of the sides of the halves remains the same.

A-sizes – magazines and books

Size	mm x mm
4A	3364 x 4756
3A	2378 x 3364
2A	1682 x 2378
1A	1189 x 1682
A0	841 x 1189
A1	594 x 841
A2	420 x 594
A3	297 x 420
A4	210 x 297
A5	148 x 210
A6	105 x 148
A7	74 x 105
A8	52 x 74
A9	37 x 52
A10	26 x 37

B-sizes – for use when there is no suitable size in the A series; for posters, wall charts and the like

Size	mm x mm
B0	1000 x 1414
B1	707 x 1000
B2	500 x 707
B3	353 x 500
B4	250 x 353
B5	176 x 250
B6	125 x 176
B7	88 x 125
B8	62 x 88
B9	44 x 62
B10	31 x 44

C-sizes – for envelopes

C4	324 x 229
C5	229 x 162
C6	114 x 162

DL or long sizes.

DL	110 x 220

Writing and drawing papers – by size

Name	in x in
Pott	15 x 12.5
Brief	16.5 x 13.25
Double Demy	31 x 20
Double Large Post	33 x 21
Double Post	30.5 x 19
Double Foolscap	26.5 x 16.5
Sheet and ½ Foolscap	24.5 x 13.5
Sheet and ⅓ Foolscap	22 x 13.5
Foolscap	17 x 13.5
Pinched Post	18.5 x 14.75
Post	19 x 15.25
Demy	20 x 15.5
Copy or Draft	20 x 16

Large Post	21 x 16.5
Medium	22 x 17.5
Royal	24 x 19
Super Royal	27 x 19
Cartridge	26 x 21
Elephant	28 x 23
Imperial	30 x 22
Colombier	34.5 x 23.5
Atlas	34 x 26
Grand Eagle	42 x 28.75
Double Elephant	40 x 26.75
Antiquarian	53 x 31
Emperor	72 x 48

Writing and drawing papers – by name

Name	in x in
Antiquarian	53 x 31
Atlas	34 x 26
Brief	16.5 x 13.25
Cartridge	26 x 21
Colombier	34.5 x 23.5
Copy or Draft	20 x 16
Demy	20 x 15.5
Double Demy	31 x 20
Double Elephant	40 x 26.75
Double Foolscap	26.5 x 16.5
Double Large Post	33 x 21
Double Post	30.5 x 19
Elephant	28 x 23
Emperor	72 x 48
Foolscap	17 x 13.5
Grand Eagle	42 x 28.75
Imperial	30 x 22
Large Post	21 x 16.5
Medium	22 x 17.5
Pinched Post	18.5 x 14.75
Post	19 x 15.25
Pott	15 x 12.5
Royal	24 x 19
Sheet and ½ Foolscap	24.5 x 13.5

Sheet and ⅓ Foolscap	22 x 13.5	
Super Royal	27 x 19	

Bound books – by size

Size	in x in	cm x cm
Crown 32mo	3.75 x 2.5	6 x 9
Crown 16mo	5 x 3.75	9 x 13
Demy 16mo	5.625 x 4.375	11 x 14
Demy 18mo	5.75 x 3.75	
Foolscap Octavo (8vo)	6.75 x 4.25	17 x 11
Crown 8vo	7.5 x 5	19 x 13
Large Crown 8vo	8 x 5.25	
Demy 8vo	8.375 x 5.625	22 x 14
Medium 8vo	9.5 x 6	23 x 15
Royal 8vo	10 x 6.25	25 x 16
Super Royal 8vo	10.25 x 6. 75	25 x 17
Imperial 8vo	11 x 7.5	28 x 19
Foolscap Quarto (4to)	8.5 x 6.75	22 x 17
Crown 4to	10 x 7.5	25 x 19
Demy 4to	11.25 x 8.75	29 x 22
Royal 4to	12.5 x 10	31 x 25
Super Royal 4to	13.5 x 10	34 x 25
Crown Folio	15 x 10	38 x 25
Demy Folio	15.5 x 11.25	
Royal Folio	20 x 12.5	
Music	14 x 10.25	
Imperial Folio	15 x 11	38 x 28

Bound books – by name

Crown 16mo	5 x 3.75	9 x 13
Crown 32mo	3.75 x 2.5	6 x 9
Crown 4to	10 x 7.5	25 x 19
Crown 8vo	7.5 x 5	19 x 13
Crown Folio	15 x 10	38 x 25
Demy 16mo	5.625 x 4.375	11 x 14
Demy 18mo	5.75 x 3.75	
Demy 4to	11.25 x 8.75	29 x 22
Demy 8vo	8.375 x 5.625	22 x 14
Demy Folio	15.5 x 11.25	

Foolscap Octavo (8vo)	6.75 x 4.25	17 x 11
Foolscap Quarto (4to)	8.5 x 6.75	22 x 17
Imperial 8vo	11 x 7.5	28 x 19
Imperial Folio	15 x 11	38 x 28
Large Crown 8vo	8 x 5.25	
Medium 8vo	9.5 x 6	23 x 15
Music	14 x 10.25	
Royal 4to	12.5 x 10	31 x 25
Royal 8vo	10 x 6.25	25 x 16
Royal Folio	20 x 12.5	
Super Royal 4to	13.5 x 10	34 x 25
Super Royal 8vo	10.25 x 6. 75	25 x 17

Brown paper – by size

Name	in x in
Kent Cap	21 x 18
Bag Cap	24 x 19.5
Haven Cap	26 x 21
Imperial Cap	29 x 22
Double Four Pound	31 x 21
Elephant	34 x 24
Double Imperial	45 x 29
Casing	46 x 36

Brown paper – by name

Name	in x in
Bag Cap	24 x 19.5
Casing	46 x 36
Double Four Pound	31 x 21
Double Imperial	45 x 29
Elephant	34 x 24
Haven Cap	26 x 21
Imperial Cap	29 x 22
Kent Cap	21 x 18

The natural world

Chemical elements

By atomic number

Atno	Symbol	Name	State	Discov	Atomic weight	By (nationality)
1	H	hydrogen	G	1766	1.0079	H Cavendish (E)
2	He	helium	G	1868	4.0026	J Lockyer (E) and P-J-C Jannsen (F)
3	Li	lithium	M	1817	6.941	JA Arfwedson (S)
4	Be	beryllium (was Gl glucinium)	M	1798	9.0122	N-L Vauquelin (F)
5	B	boron	NM	1808	10.81	L-J Gay-Lussac and L-J Thennard (F), H Davy (E)
6	C	carbon	NM	—	12.011	
7	N	nitrogen	G	1772	14.0067	D Rutherford (E)
8	O	oxygen	G	1772	15.9994	CW Scheele (S), J Priestley (E)
9	F	fluorine	G	1886	18.9984	H Moissan (F)
10	Ne	neon	G	1898	20.179	W Ramsay and MW Travers (E)
11	Na	sodium (Latin: natrium)	M	1807	22.98977	H Davy (E)
12	Mg	magnesium	M	1808	24.305	H Davy (E)
13	Al	aluminium; aluminum	M	1825	26.98154	HC Oerstedt (D), F Wöhler (G)
14	Si	silicon	NM	1824	28.0855	JJ Berzelius (S)
15	P	phosphorus	NM	1669	30.97376	H Brand (G)
16	S	sulfur (sulphur)	NM	—	32.06	
17	Cl	chlorine	G	1774	35.453	CW Scheele (S)
18	Ar	argon	G	1894	39.948	W Ramsay and Lord Rayleigh (E)
19	K	potassium (Latin: kalium)	M	1807	39.0983	H Davy (E)
20	Ca	calcium	M	1808	40.08	H Davy (E)
21	Sc	scandium	M	1879	44.9559	LF Nilson (S)
22	Ti	titanium	M	1795	47.88	MH Klaproth (G)
23	V	vanadium	M	1830	50.9415	MG Sefström (S)
24	Cr	chromium	M	1798	51.996	N-L Vauquelin (F)
25	Mn	manganese	M	1774	54.9380	JG Gahn (S)

26	Fe	iron (Latin: ferrum)	M	c–4000	55.847	
27	Co	cobalt	M	1737	58.9332	G Brandt (S)
28	Ni	nickel	M	1751	58.69	AF Cronstedt (S)
29	Cu	copper (Latin: cuprum)	M	c–8000	63.546	
30	Zn	zinc	M	1746	65.38	AS Marggraf (G)
31	Ga	gallium	M	1875	69.72	L de Boisbaudran (F)
32	Ge	germanium (once eka-silicon)	M	1886	72.59	CA Winkler (G)
33	As	arsenic	NM	c1220	74.9216	Albertus Magnus (G)
34	Se	selenium	M	1818	78.96	JJ Berzelius (S)
35	Br	bromine	L	1826	79.904	A-J Balard (F)
36	Kr	krypton	G	1898	83.80	W Ramsay and MW Travers (E)
37	Rb	rubidium	M	1861	85.4678	RW Bunsen and GR Kirchoff (G)
38	Sr	strontium	M	1787	87.62	W Cruikshank (Sc)
39	Y	yttrium	M	1794	88.9059	J Gadolin (Fin)
40	Zr	zirconium	M	1789	91.22	MH Klaproth (G)
41	Nb	niobium (was columbium)	M	1801	92.9064	C Hatchett (E)
42	Mo	molybdenum	M	1781	95.94	PJ Hjelm (S)
43	Tc	technetium (was masurium)	M	1937	97.9072	C Perrier (F) and E Segré (I/USA)
44	Ru	ruthenium	M	1844	101.07	KK Klaus (Est)
45	Rh	rhodium	M	1804	102.9055	WH Wollaston (E)
46	Pd	palladium	M	1803	106.42	WH Wollaston (E)
47	Ag	silver	M	c–4000	107.868	
48	Cd	cadmium	M	1817	112.41	F Stromeyer (G)
49	In	indium	M	1863	114.82	F Reich and HT Richter (G)
50	Sn	tin (Latin: stannum)	M	c–3500	118.69	
51	Sb	antimony (Latin: stibium)	M	c–1000	121.75	
52	Te	tellurium	NM	1783	127.60	FJ Muller (Baron von Reichenstein A)
53	I	iodine	NM	1811	126.9045	B Courtois (F)
54	Xe	xenon	G	1898	131.29	W Ramsay and MW Travers (E)
55	Cs	caesium	M	1860	132.9054	RW von Bunsen and GR Kirchhoff (G)
56	Ba	barium	M	1808	137.33	H Davy (E)
57	La	lanthanum	M	1839	138.9055	CG Mosander (S)
58	Ce	cerium	M	1803	140.12	JJ Berzelius and W Hisinger (S)
59	Pr	praseodymium	M	1885	140.9077	C Auer von Welsbach (A)

Atno	Symbol	Name	State	Discov	Atomic weight	By (nationality)
60	Nd	neodymium	M	1885	144.24	C Auer von Welsbach (A)
61	Pm	promethium (was illinium)	M	1945	144.9128	J Marinsky, LE Glendenin and CD Coryell (US)
62	Sm	samarium	M	1879	150.36	L de Boisbaudrin (F)
63	Eu	europium	M	1901	151.96	EA Demarçay (F)
64	Gd	gadolinium	M	1880	157.25	J-C-G de Marignac (Sw)
65	Tb	terbium	M	1843	158.9254	CG Mosander (S)
66	Ds	dysprosium (alt symbol Dy)	M	1886	162.50	L de Boisbaudrin (F)
67	Ho	holmium	M	1878	164.9304	J-L Soret (F) and PT Cleve (S)
68	Er	erbium	M	1843	167.26	CG Mosander (S)
69	Tm	thulium	M	1879	168.9342	PT Cleve (S)
70	Yb	ytterbium	M	1878	173.04	J-C-G de Marignac (Switz)
71	Lu	lutetium; lutecium	M	1907	174.967	G Urbain (F)
72	Hf	hafnium	M	1923	178.49	D Coster (N) and GC de Hevesy (H/S)
73	Ta	tantalum	M	1802	180.9479	AG Ekeberg (S)
74	W	tungsten (alias wolfram)	M	1783	183.85	JJ and F de Elhuyar (Sp)
75	Re	rhenium	M	1925	186.207	W Noddack, Fr I Tacke and O Berg (G)
76	Os	osmium	M	1804	190.2	S Tennant (E)
77	Ir	iridium	M	1804	192.22	S Tennant (E)
78	Pt	platinum	M	1748	195.08	A de Ulloa (Sp)
79	Au	gold (Latin: aurum)	M	—	196.9665	
80	Hg	mercury (Greek: hydrargyrum)	LM	c–1600	200.59	
81	Tl	thallium	M	1861	204.83	W Crookes (E)
82	Pb	lead (Latin: plumbum)	M	—	207.2	
83	Bi	bismuth	M	1753	208.9084	C-F Geoffroy (F)
84	Po	polonium	M	1898	208.9824*	Mme M Curie (P/F)
85	At	astatine (was alabamine)	M	1940	209.9870*	DR Corson, KR Mackenzie (US) and E Segré (I/US)
86	Rn	radon	G	1900	222.0176*	FE Dorn (G)
87	Fr	francium (was virginium)	M	1939	223.0197*	Mlle M Perey (F)
88	Ra	radium	M	1898	226.0254*	P and Mme M Curie (Pol/F) and MG Bemont (F)
89	Ac	actinium	M	1899	227.0278*	A Debierne (F)
90	Th	thorium	M	1829	232.0381	JJ Berzelius (S)
91	Pa	prot(o)actinium	M	1917	231.03588	O Hahn (G), Fr L Meitner (A); F Soddy and JA Cranston (E)

92	U	uranium	M	1789	238.0289	MH Klaproth (G)
93	Np	neptunium		1940	237.0482*	
94	Pu	plutonium		1940	244.0642*	
95	Am	americium		1944	243.0614*	
96	Cm	curium		1944	247.0703*	
97	Bk	berkelium		1949	247.0703*	
98	Cf	californium		1950	231.0796*	
99	Es	einsteinium		1953	252.0828*	
100	Fm	fermium		1953	257.0951*	
101	Md	mendelevium			258.0984*	
102	No	nobelium			259.1010*	
103	Lr	lawrencium (formerly Lw)			262.1097*	
104	Rf	rutherfordium			261.1088*	
105	Db	dubnium			262.1141*	
106	Sg	seaborgium			266.1219*	
107	Bh	bohrium			264.1247*	
108	Hs	hassium			267.1318*	
109	Mt	meitnerium			268.1388*	
110	Uun	ununnilium			271.1461*	
111	Uuu	unununium			272.1535*	
112	Uub	ununbium			277.1641*	

*AW of isotope with longest-known half-life.
State: M – metal; NM – non-metal; L – liquid; LM – liquid metal; G – gas
Nationality of discoverer: A – Austrian; E – English; F – French; Fin – Finnish; G – German;
H – Hungarian; I – Italian; N – Netherlands; P – Polish; S – Swedish; Sc – Scottish; Sp – Spanish;
Sw – Swiss; US – American.

By symbol

At no	Symbol	Name	State
89	Ac	actinium	M
47	Ag	silver	M
13	Al	aluminium; aluminum	M
95	Am	americium	
18	Ar	argon	G
33	As	arsenic	NM
85	At	astatine (was alabamine)	M
79	Au	gold (Latin: aurum)	M
5	B	boron	NM
56	Ba	barium	M
4	Be	beryllium (was Gl glucinium)	M
107	Bh	bohrium	
83	Bi	bismuth	M
97	Bk	berkelium	

At no	Symbol	Name	State
35	Br	bromine	L
6	C	carbon	NM
20	Ca	calcium	M
48	Cd	cadmium	M
58	Ce	cerium	M
98	Cf	californium	
17	Cl	chlorine	G
96	Cm	curium	
27	Co	cobalt	M
24	Cr	chromium	M
55	Cs	caesium	M
29	Cu	copper (*Latin: cuprum*)	M
105	Db	dubnium	
66	Ds	dysprosium (*alt symbol Dy*)	M
68	Er	erbium	M
99	Es	einsteinium	
63	Eu	europium	M
9	F	fluorine	G
26	Fe	iron (*Latin: ferrum*)	M
100	Fm	fermium	
87	Fr	francium (*was virginium*)	M
31	Ga	gallium	M
64	Gd	gadolinium	M
32	Ge	germanium (once eka-silicon)	M
1	H	hydrogen	G
2	He	helium	G
72	Hf	hafnium	M
80	Hg	mercury (*Greek: hydrargyrum*)	LM
67	Ho	holmium	M
108	Hs	hassium	
53	I	iodine	NM
49	In	indium	M
77	Ir	iridium	M
19	K	potassium (*Latin: kalium*)	M
36	Kr	krypton	G
57	La	lanthanum	M
3	Li	lithium	M
103	Lr	lawrencium (*formerly Lw*)	
71	Lu	lutetium; lutecium	M
101	Md	mendelevium	
12	Mg	magnesium	M
25	Mn	manganese	M
42	Mo	molybdenum	M
109	Mt	meitnerium	

7	N	nitrogen	G
11	Na	sodium (Latin: natrium)	M
41	Nb	niobium (was columbium)	M
60	Nd	neodymium	M
10	Ne	neon	G
28	Ni	nickel	M
102	No	nobelium	
93	Np	neptunium	
8	O	oxygen	G
76	Os	osmium	M
15	P	phosphorus	NM
91	Pa	prot(o)actinium	M
82	Pb	lead (Latin: plumbum)	M
46	Pd	palladium	M
61	Pm	promethium (was illinium)	M
84	Po	polonium	M
59	Pr	praseodymium	M
78	Pt	platinum	M
94	Pu	plutonium	
88	Ra	radium	M
37	Rb	rubidium	M
75	Re	rhenium	M
104	Rf	rutherfordium	
45	Rh	rhodium	M
86	Rn	radon	G
44	Ru	ruthenium	M
16	S	sulfur (sulphur)	NM
51	Sb	antimony (Latin: stibium)	M
21	Sc	scandium	M
34	Se	selenium	M
106	Sg	seaborgium	
14	Si	silicon	NM
62	Sm	samarium	M
50	Sn	tin (Latin: stannum)	M
38	Sr	strontium	M
73	Ta	tantalum	M
65	Tb	terbium	M
43	Tc	technetium (was masurium)	M
52	Te	tellurium	NM
90	Th	thorium	M
22	Ti	titanium	M
81	Tl	thallium	M
69	Tm	thulium	M
92	U	uranium	M
112	Uub	ununbium	

At no	Symbol	Name	State
110	Uun	ununnilium	
111	Uuu	unununium	
23	V	vanadium	M
74	W	tungsten *(alias wolfram)*	M
54	Xe	xenon	G
39	Y	yttrium	M
70	Yb	ytterbium	M
30	Zn	zinc	M
40	Zr	zirconium	M

By name

At no	Symbol	Name	State
89	Ac	actinium	M
13	Al	aluminium; aluminum	M
95	Am	americium	
51	Sb	antimony *(Latin: stibium)*	M
18	Ar	argon	G
33	As	arsenic	NM
85	At	astatine *(was alabamine)*	M
56	Ba	barium	M
97	Bk	berkelium	
4	Be	beryllium *(was Gl glucinium)*	M
83	Bi	bismuth	M
107	Bh	bohrium	
5	B	boron	NM
35	Br	bromine	L
48	Cd	cadmium	M
55	Cs	caesium	M
20	Ca	calcium	M
98	Cf	californium	
6	C	carbon	NM
58	Ce	cerium	M
17	Cl	chlorine	G
24	Cr	chromium	M
27	Co	cobalt	M
29	Cu	copper *(Latin: cuprum)*	M
96	Cm	curium	
105	Db	dubnium	
66	Ds	dysprosium *(alt symbol Dy)*	M
99	Es	einsteinium	
68	Er	erbium	M
63	Eu	europium	M

100	Fm	fermium	
9	F	fluorine	G
87	Fr	francium (was virginium)	M
64	Gd	gadolinium	M
31	Ga	gallium	M
32	Ge	germanium (once eka-silicon)	M
79	Au	gold (Latin: aurum)	M
72	Hf	hafnium	M
108	Hs	hassium	
2	He	helium	G
67	Ho	holmium	M
1	H	hydrogen	G
49	In	indium	M
53	I	iodine	NM
77	Ir	iridium	M
26	Fe	iron (Latin: ferrum)	M
36	Kr	krypton	G
57	La	lanthanum	M
103	Lr	lawrencium (formerly Lw)	
82	Pb	lead (Latin: plumbum)	M
3	Li	lithium	M
71	Lu	lutetium; lutecium	M
12	Mg	magnesium	M
25	Mn	manganese	M
109	Mt	meitnerium	
101	Md	mendelevium	
80	Hg	mercury (Greek: hydrargyrum)	LM
42	Mo	molybdenum	M
60	Nd	neodymium	M
10	Ne	neon	G
93	Np	neptunium	
28	Ni	nickel	M
41	Nb	niobium (was columbium)	M
7	N	nitrogen	G
102	No	nobelium	
76	Os	osmium	M
8	O	oxygen	G
46	Pd	palladium	M
15	P	phosphorus	NM
78	Pt	platinum	M
94	Pu	plutonium	
84	Po	polonium	M
19	K	potassium (Latin: kalium)	M
59	Pr	praseodymium	M
61	Pm	promethium (was illinium)	M

At no	Symbol	Name	State
91	Pa	prot(o)actinium	M
88	Ra	radium	M
86	Rn	radon	G
75	Re	rhenium	M
45	Rh	rhodium	M
37	Rb	rubidium	M
44	Ru	ruthenium	M
104	Rf	rutherfordium	
62	Sm	samarium	M
21	Sc	scandium	M
106	Sg	seaborgium	
34	Se	selenium	M
14	Si	silicon	NM
47	Ag	silver	M
11	Na	sodium *(Latin: natrium)*	M
38	Sr	strontium	M
16	S	sulfur (sulphur)	NM
73	Ta	tantalum	M
43	Tc	technetium *(was masurium)*	M
52	Te	tellurium	NM
65	Tb	terbium	M
81	Tl	thallium	M
90	Th	thorium	M
69	Tm	thulium	M
50	Sn	tin *(Latin: stannum)*	M
22	Ti	titanium	M
74	W	tungsten *(alias wolfram)*	M
112	Uub	ununbium	
110	Uun	ununnilium	
111	Uuu	unununium	
92	U	uranium	M
23	V	vanadium	M
54	Xe	xenon	G
70	Yb	ytterbium	M
39	Y	yttrium	M
30	Zn	zinc	M
40	Zr	zirconium	M

Rocks

Minerals and metals

Minerals are naturally occurring, inorganic, solid substances with an internal crystal structure and a definite chemical composition. Most minerals are chemical compounds: only one group has just one chemical in the molecular structure. Minerals are the building blocks of rocks, which are aggregates of different minerals, and of many other natural objects such as jewels or gemstones, metals and metal ores, which we tend to think of as separate substances, are really nothing but minerals.

There are over 3,000 known minerals, grouped into nine classes according to their chemical composition.

Some native non-metals and semi-metals from Mineral Class I

Element	Chemical symbol
Antimony	Sb
Arsenic	As
Bismuth	Bi
Chaoite	C
Diamond	C
Graphite	C
Rosickyite	S
Selenium	Se
Silicon	Si
Sulphur	S
Tellurium	Te

Metals

Metals are defined by the following properties:

1 solid at room temperature (with the exception of mercury)
2 shiny when their surfaces are fresh (but often becoming dull with oxidation)
3 high melting points (with very few exceptions)
4 good conductors of heat and electricity
5 malleable (can be beaten and shaped)

Class	Name	Categories	Chemical composition	Examples	Comments
I	Elements	metals, semi-metals, non-metals, metallic and semi-metallic alloys	'Native' elements, which are composed of just one chemical; compound alloys of metallic or semi-metallic elements, chemically bonding in the same way as elements	Diamond Gold and Platinum (neither ever 100% pure in their natural form)	Many rare minerals in this group, eg lead as a native element, not in an ore, is highly uncommon. Metals have very similar properties, but non-metals vary widely
II	Sulphides	sulphides, antimonides, arsenides, bismuthinides, selenides, sulphosalts, tellurides	Compounds of one or more metallic elements combined with the non-metallic element sulphur or the semi-metals antimony, arsenic, selenium, and tellurium, or sulphur and either antimony, arsenic, or bismuth	Cubanite Galena (lead ore) Marcasite Pyrite	
III	Halides	fluorides, bromides, chlorides, iodides	One or more metallic elements combined with a halogen of the halogen elements (chlorine, bromine, fluorine, or iodine)	Fluorite Rock salt	
IV	Oxides	oxides, hydroxides	One or more metallic elements combined with oxygen, water or the hydroxyl ion (OH)	Corundum (emery, ruby, sapphire) Haematite (iron ore) Magnetite Opal Quartz	

V	Carbonates	carbonates, borates, nitrates	One or more metallic elements plus the free radical carbonate compound, or with borate or nitrate radical compounds	Borax Dolomite Malachite Soda	Apart from some borates, most Class V minerals are soft and brittle or fragile. Nitrates are mostly soluble in water so are only found in arid areas
VI	Sulphates	sulphates, sulphites, chromates, molybdates, selenates, selenites, tellurates, tellurites, tungstates (wolframates)	One or more metallic elements plus the free radical sulphate compound or, more rarely, a different free radical compound such as chromate, molybdate, etc	Epsomite Gypsum	All soft and fragile
VII	Phosphates	phosphates, arsenates, vanadates	One or more metallic elements associated with the free radical phosphate, arsenate or vandate compounds	Apatite Turquoise	
VIII	Silicates	cyclosilicates, inosilicates, nesosilicates, phyllosilicates, sorosilicates, tectosilicates,	Compounds of Silicon and oxygen. Subdivisions are by molecular structure	Beryl Chlorite Feldspars Garnets Mica Rhodonite Talc Topaz	The largest class

6 ductile (can be drawn into wire)

Native metals – from the Mineral Class I

Element	Chemical symbol
Aluminum	Al
Cadmium	Cd
Chromium	Cr
Copper	Cu
Gold	Au
Indium	In
Iridium	(Ir, Os, Ru)
Iron	Fe
Lead	Pb
Mercury	Hg
Nickel	Ni
Palladium	Pd
Platinum	Pt
Rhodium	(Rh, Pt)
Silver	Ag
Tellurium	Te
Tin	Sn
Titanium	Ti
Zinc	Zn

The greatest difference between pure metals is their colour. Some have highly useful properties such as being magnetic; or the ability to conduct heat, *eg* copper, aluminium and iron, which means they can be used for cooking implements; or the ability to conduct electricity *eg* copper, silver and gold. The last two are less often used for this purpose than copper because they are much, much more expensive. Aluminium is light as well as being strong, so it is a useful lightweight structural metal, and is used in suspended HV electrical conductors where lightness is more important than cost. Rocks in which metal is found are called ores, and mixtures of metals are alloys. Metal alloys often have even more advantages than one metal on its own, for example, steel is stronger than iron, stainless steel does not rust, titanium alloys are strong but light.

Main metallic alloys

Name	Alloy of
Brass	copper and zinc
Bronze	copper and tin

Gold jewellery	usually gold and nickel
Iron-nickel	Iron and nickel
Stainless steel	iron, carbon, chromium, nickel, and manganese
Steel	iron and carbon
Titanium alloys	titanium, aluminium and vanadium

Jewels and gemstones

Known as the 'flowers of the mineral kingdom', all gemstones are beautiful enough to be used as adornment; are relatively rare and therefore precious; are relatively hard so they will not scratch too easily; and have a high index of refraction so that they sparkle (the higher the index, the more they sparkle). A very few – amber, coral, pearl – are organic in origin; all the others are minerals. Diamond is the only gem which is made of a single element (carbon), while the others are mineral compounds.

The hardness of a mineral is measured in **Mohs' scale** of scratch hardness, which was developed by Friedrich Mohs (1773–1839). The higher the number, the harder the material.

Mohs' number	Classification	Sample mineral for comparative measurement	Simple test
1	soft	talc (softest)	can be scratched with a fingernail
2	soft	gypsum	can be scratched with a fingernail
3	medium hard	calcite	can be scratched with a copper coin
4	medium hard	fluorite	can be scratched with a knife
5	medium hard	apatite	can be scratched with a knife
6	hard	orthoclase	can be scratched with a steel file
7	hard	quartz	scratches window glass
8	hard	topaz	—
9	hard	corundum (ruby, sapphire)	—
10	hard	diamond (hardest)	—

Weights used by Gemsmiths

Carat The word derives from either *qirat* (Arabic) or *keration* (Greek), for the seed of the carob bean; or from *kuara*, African for the seed of the coraltree. The modern metric carat is the equivalent of 0.2g, or 200mg. For diamonds, one-hundredth of a carat is a point. Other parts of a carat are described simply in fractions or decimals. Note that this is not the same carat measurement used to describe the purity of gold.

Gram Used to measure rough stones and less-precious gems.

Grain The equivalent of one quarter of a carat or 0.05g, an old-fashioned measure for pearls.

Main gemstones in descending order of hardness:

Stone	Mohs' hardness	Refractive index in n
Diamond	10	2.42
Ruby (corundum)	9	1.76–1.77
Sapphire (corundum)	9	1.76–1.77
Cubic zirconia (artificial)	8.5	2.17
Chrysoberyl (includes alexandrite and cat's-eye)	8.5	1.74–1.75
YAG (artificial)	8.25	1.83
Noble spinel	8	1.71
Topaz (blue and colourless)	8	1.61–1.62
Topaz (yellow-brown and pink)	8	1.63–1.64
Aquamarine (beryl)	7.5–7.8	1.56–1.60
Emerald (beryl)	7.5–7.8	1.57–1.60
Beryl (precious)	7.5–7.8	1.56–1.60
'High' zircon	7.5	1.96–2.01
Rhodolite (garnet)	7–7.5	1.76
Pyrope (garnet)	7–7.5	1.73–1.75
Andalusite	7–7.5	1.63–1.64
Cordierite	7–7.5	1.53–1.55
Spessartine (garnet)	6.5–7.5	1.80
Tsavolite (garnet)	6.5–7.5	1.74
Almandine (garnet)	6–7.5	1.76–1.83
Tourmaline	7	1.62–1.64
Agate (quartz)	7	1.53–1.54
Amethyst (quartz)	7	1.54–1.55
Chalcedony	7	1.53–1.54
Chrysoprase (quartz)	7	1.53–1.54
Citrine (quartz)	7	1.54–1.55
Cornelian (quartz)	7	1.53–1.54
Rock crystal (quartz)	7	1.54–1.55
Tiger's eye (quartz)	7	1.53–1.54
Olivine (chrysolite or peridot)	6.5–7	1.65–1.69
Jadeite jade	6.5–7	1.66–1.67
Spodumene	6–7	1.65–1.68
Demantoid (garnet)	6.5–7	1.88
Hessonite (garnet)	6.5–7	1.74
GGG (artificial)	6.5	2.02
Zoisite	6.5	1.69–1.70
Chalcedony	6.5	1.53

Hematite	6.5	2.94–3.22
Pyrite	6–6.5	–
Labradorite (feldspar)	6–6.5	1.56–1.57
Moonstone (feldspar)	6–6.5	1.53–1.54
Rhodonite	5.5–6.5	1.73–1.74
Opal	5.5–6.5	1.45
'Low' zircon	6	1.79–1.81
Noble orthoclase (feldspar)	6	1.52–1.53
Amazonite (feldspar)	6	1.52–1.53
Diopside	5.5.6	1.68–1.71
Turquoise	5–6	1.61
Nephrite jade	5–6	1.61
Lapis lazuli	5–5.5	1.50
Serpentine	2–5	1.55–1.56
Pearl	2.5–4.5	—
Malachite	4	1.66–1.91
Rhodochrosite	4	1.60–1.82
Coral (calcareous)	3.5–4	—
Amber	2.5	1.54

The main gemstones in descending order of 'sparkle'

	Refractive index in n	Mohs' hardness
Hematite	2.94–3.22	6.5
Diamond	2.42	10
Cubic zirconia (artificial)	2.17	8.5
GGG (artificial)	2.02	6.5
'High' zircon	1.96–2.01	7.5
Demantoid (garnet)	1.88	6.5–7
YAG (artificial)	1.83	8.25
Spessartine (garnet)	1.80	6.5–7.5
'Low' zircon	1.79–1.81	6
Almandine (garnet)	1.76–1.83	6–7.5
Ruby (corundum)	1.76–1.77	9
Sapphire (corundum)	1.76–1.77	9
Rhodolite (garnet)	1.76	7–7.5
Chrysoberyl (includes alexandrite and cat's-eye)	1.74–1.75	8.5
Hessonite (garnet)	1.74	6.5–7
Tsavolite (garnet)	1.74	6.5–7.5
Pyrope (garnet)	1.73–1.75	7–7.5
Rhodonite	1.73–1.74	5.5–6.5
Noble spinel	1.71	8

Zoisite	1.69–1.70	6.5
Diopside	1.68–1.71	5.5.6
Malachite	1.66–1.91	4
Jadeite jade	1.66–1.67	6.5–7
Olivine (chrysolite or peridot)	1.65–1.69	6.5–7
Spodumene	1.65–1.68	6–7
Andalusite	1.63–1.64	7–7.5
Topaz (yellow-brown and pink)	1.63–1.64	8
Tourmaline	1.62–1.64	7
Topaz (blue and colourless)	1.61–1.62	8
Nephrite jade	1.61	5–6
Turquoise	1.61	5–6
Rhodochrosite	1.60–1.82	4
Emerald (beryl)	1.57–1.60	7.5–7.8
Aquamarine (beryl)	1.56–1.60	7.5–7.8
Beryl (precious)	1.56–1.60	7.5–7.8
Labradorite (feldspar)	1.56–1.57	6–6.5
Serpentine	1.55–1.56	2–5
Amethyst (quartz)	1.54–1.55	7
Citrine (quartz)	1.54–1.55	7
Rock crystal (quartz)	1.54–1.55	7
Amber	1.54	2.5
Cordierite	1.53–1.55	7–7.5
Agate (quartz)	1.53–1.54	7
Chalcedony	1.53–1.54	7
Chrysoprase (quartz)	1.53–1.54	7
Cornelian (quartz)	1.53–1.54	7
Moonstone (feldspar)	1.53–1.54	6–6.5
Tiger's eye (quartz)	1.53–1.54	7
Chalcedony	1.53	6.5
Amazonite (feldspar)	1.52–1.53	6
Noble orthoclase (feldspar)	1.52–1.53	6
Lapis lazuli	1.50	5–5.5
Opal	1.45	5.5–6.5
Coral (calcareous)	–	3.5–4
Pearl	–	2.5–4.5
Pyrite	–	6–6.5

The main gemstones grouped by colour
See table opposite.

Colourless or off-white	Yellow, brownish yellow, greenish-yellow, brown, orange	Green	Blue, blue-gray	Red, pink	Violet	Gray, black
Beryl (precious)	Amber	Alexandrite chrysoberyl	Amazonite (feldspar)	Almandine (garnet)	Almandine (garnet)	Hematite
Chalcedony	Andalusite	Amazonite (feldspar)	Aquamarine	Beryl (precious)	Amethyst (quartz)	Jadeite jade
Coral	Beryl (precious)	Andalusite	Chalcedony	Chalcedony	Cordierite	Labradorite (feldspar)
Sapphire (corundum)	Chalcedony	Aquamarine	Coral	Coral	Sapphire (corundum)	Moonstone (feldspar)
Cubic zirconia (artificial)	Chrysoberyl	Chalcedony	Cordierite	Fire opal	Jadeite jade	Nephrite jade
Diamond	Citrine quartz	Emerald	Sapphire (corundum)	Hessonite (garnet)	Noble spinel	Opal
GGG (artificial)	Common opal	Sapphire	Diamond	'High' zircon	Rhodolite (garnet)	Quartz
'High' zircon	Moonstone (feldspar)	Demantoid (garnet)	'High' zircon	Jadeite jade	Topaz	Star diopside
Jadeite jade	Sapphire (corundum)	Diamond	Jadeite jade	Noble spinel	Zircon	Tourmaline
Moonstone (feldspar)	Diamond	Diopside	Labradorite (feldspar)	Pyrope (garnet)	Zoisite (tanzanite variety)	
Nephrite jade	Hessonite (garnet)	'High' zircon	Lapis lazuli	Rhodochrosite		
Opal	Jadeite jade	Jadeite jade	Moonstone (feldspar)	Rhodolite (garnet)		
Pearl	Noble orthoclase (feldspar)	'Low' zircon	Noble spinel	Rhodonite		
Rock crystal (quartz)	Olivine	Malachite	Opal	Rose quartz		
Serpentine	Pyrite	Nephrite jade	Tourmaline	Ruby (corundum)		
Strontium titanate (artificial)	Serpentine	Olivine	Topaz	Spessartine (garnet)		
Topaz	Tiger's eye	Serpentine	Turquoise	Spodumene (kunzite variety)		
Tourmaline	Topaz	Spodumene (hiddenite variety)	Zoisite (tanzanite variety)	Topaz		
YAG (artificial)	Tourmaline	Tourmaline		Tourmaline (rubellite variety)		
	YAG (artificial)	Tsavolite (garnet)				
	Zircon	YAG (artificial)				

Colours of Diamonds

International Diamond Council grade	Old name
Exceptional white	River
Rare white	Top Wesselton
White	Wesselton
Slightly tinted white	Top Crystal
Tinted white	Crystal
Tinted colour 1	Top Cape
Tinted colour 2	Cape
Tinted colour 3	Light Yellow
Tinted colour 4	Yellow

Wedding anniversary	Jewels
12th	Agate
13th	Moonstone
17th	Amethyst
18th	Garnet
30th	Pearl
35th	Coral
40th	Ruby
45th	Sapphire
55th	Emerald
60th	Diamond

Meteorology

Cloud formations

When water droplets in the air condense, they form clouds of various shapes and heights, according to the conditions. Like biological specimens, clouds are given Latin names, and are arranged in a hierarchy of genus, species, and variety. There are 10 genera, although in reality there are only three main forms: cirrus, cumulus and stratus. All other clouds, even the other seven main types, are variations of or a combination of one or more of the three. At one time meteorologists named a fourth basic type, nimbus, which just means 'rain-bearing', but this has been dropped as a separate genus of cloud, no doubt because so many clouds bring or harbinger rain. The genus describes the type of cloud, the species describes its structure and shape, and the variety describes how transparent it is and how its elements are arranged.

The three major cloud forms

Cloud name	Abbr	Name means	Shape	Conditions for formation	Height	Composition	Weather	Comments
Cirrus	Ci	Tuft of hair	Delicate, feathery and wispy, like a beard	Ice crystals	High; Never less than 18,000 ft	Ice crystals	Fair. No rain or snow. But, build-up of dense clouds might mean storm is on its way	Crystals are so fine sunlight passes through them. Appears white, except sometimes at sunset or sunrise
Cumulus	Cu	Heap	A pile of puffy cotton wool balls with flat bottoms. The size depends on the force of the upwards movement	Usually when moist, warm air is forced upwards and cools	Low through to High. 5–6,000 ft ranging up to 39,000 ft	Mostly water	Fair except when forced to giant, towering cumulonimbus formations	Rainbows occasionally associated with large cumulus clouds
Stratus	St	Layer	Horizontal layers stretched out across the sky	Often when a layer of warm air cools and condenses when it passes over a layer of cooler air	Low	Water	Occasionally drizzle, fog, mist, light snow	Can make the sky appear grey

The other way of grouping clouds is by the height of their base from the earth – low, medium and high – with their composition depending on their height. This, of course, is almost impossible to gauge correctly from the earth without the help of measuring instruments.

Apart from helping in day-dreaming, clouds aid in weather prediction; most are associated with particular weather and also indicate what wind patterns and movements of different air masses are on their way, bringing changes in temperature or precipitation. One particular cloud type falls outside classical classification: contrails, which are clouds formed when water vapour left in the path of aircraft condenses.

Height specifications

Classification	Height above earth	Composition	Name prefix
Low	No more than 6,500 feet (2,000 m)	Water droplets	—
Medium	6,500–20,000 ft (2,000 to 6,000 m)	Mainly water, some ice crystals	Alto-
High	20,000 ft (6,000 m)	Ice crystals	Cirr-

The 14 species of cloud

Example full names are Altocumulus castellatus, Cumulonimbus mammatus, but Fractocumulus and Fractonimbus.

Species	Abbr	Description	Applies to
Calvus	cal	Bald or smooth tops	Cb
Capillatus	cap	'having hair'; fibrous or plumed masses	Cb
Castellatus	cas	Castle-like battlements, sometimes in lines	Ac, Cc, Ci, Sc
Congestus	con	Piled up and growing	Cu
Fibratus	fib	Only just curving	Ci, Cs
Floccus	flo	Tufted	Ac, Cc, Ci
Fractus	fra	Broken and ragged	Cu, St
Humilis	hum	Flattened	Cu
Lenticularis	len	Lens-shaped or almond-shaped	Ac, Cc, Sc,
Mediocris	med	Medium; small bulges on the tops	Cu
Nebulosus	neb	Thin veil or layer	Ca, St,
Spissatus	spi	Dense; appears grey	Ci
Stratiformis	str	Large flat sheet	Ac, Cc, Sc,
Uncinus	unc	Hooked or comma-shaped	Ci

The other seven major cloud forms

Cloud name	Abbr	Appearance	Height	Associated weather	Weather prediction	Comments
Altocumulus	Ac	Lumps or rippled effect; 'mackerel' sky	Medium	Often bad	Poor weather on its way	Is sometimes thought to be a UFO
Altostratus	As	Grey sheet	Medium	Often light rain	Continuous rain on its way	Sun shines through dimly
Cumulonimbus	Cb	Very large, towering cauliflower-like cumulus formations, with the tops of the clouds forced very high from earth, up to 60,000 ft; top sometimes anvil-shaped	High	'Thunderhead' clouds; thunder and lightning or summer thunderstorms. If towering shapes forced to swirl, associated with extreme bad weather such as hurricanes		Rainbows are nearly always associated with these clouds
Cirrocumulus	Cc	Small, white shapes		No rain	Storms are on their way	
Cirrostratus	Cs	Thin, high sheets	High	No rain	Rain on its way	
Nimbostratus	Ns	Thick, shapeless, dark	Medium	Heavy rain or snow		
Stratocumulus	Sc	Nearly full sky cover in large, layered heaps	Low	Usually drizzle		

Some cloud varieties

Variety	Abbr	Description	Applies to
Duplicatus	du	Layered	Ac, As, Ci, Cs, Sc
Intortus	in	Twisted	Ci
Lacunosus	la	Holed like a net	Ac, Cc
Opacus	op	Covers moon or sun	Ac, As, Sc, St
Perlucidus	pe	Patchy with small spaces	Ac, Sc
Radiatus	ra	Parallel strips	Ac, As, Ci, Cu, Sc
Translucidus	tr	Translucent enough for moon or sun to be seen	Ac, As, Sc, St
Undulatus	un	Waves	Ac, As, Cc, Cs, Sc
Vertebratus	ve	Like vertebrae or ribs	Ci

Accessory clouds form in association with one of the ten main types:

Accessory cloud	Description	Types
Pannus	Shreds of cloud	Cu, Cb, As, Ns
Pileus	Cap cloud	Cu, Cb
Velum	Veil	Cu, Cb

Some other features of clouds

Name	Description
Arcus	Arch
Incus	Anvil
Mamma	Pouches hanging from upper cloud
Tuba	Funnels
Virga	Fallstreaks

Beaufort scale

The Beaufort Scale describes the strength of a wind. The scale was devised by Francis Beaufort (1774–1857; later Rear-Admiral Sir Francis Beaufort) when he was a Commander in 1805. The US Weather Bureau added the worst hurricanes in 1955.

Force	Description	mph	kph	knots
0	Calm	0–1	0–1.6	0–1
1	Light Air	1–3	1.6–5	1–3
2	Light Breeze	4–7	5–11	4–6
3	Gentle Breeze	8–12	11–20	7–10
4	Moderate Breeze	13–18	20–30	11–16
5	Fresh Breeze	19–24	30–39	17–21
6	Strong Breeze	25–31	39–50	22–27
7	Near Gale	32–38	50–60	28–33
8	Gale	39–46	60–74	34–40
9	Strong Gale	47–54	74–87	41–47
10	Storm	55–63	87–100	48–55
11	Violent Storm	64–75	100–120	56–65
12	Hurricane	76–82	120–132	66–71
13	Hurricane	83–92	132–148	72–80
14	Hurricane	93–103	148–166	81–89
15	Hurricane	104–114	166–183	90–99
16	Hurricane	115–125	183–201	100–108
17	Hurricane	126–136	201–220	109–118

Names of hurricanes

Hurricanes are given approved names, repeated every six years. The first hurricane of the year begins with A, the next with B, and so on. It is not expected that there will be more than 23 hurricanes in any year. To determine which set of names is to be used, divide the year by six; the remainder (R) indicates the column to use.

R=0	R=1	R=2	R=3	R=4	R=5
1992, 1998, 2004	1993, 1999, 2005	1994, 2000, 2006	1995, 2001, 2007	1996, 2002, 2008	1997, 2003, 2009
Alex	Arlene	Alberto	Allison	Arthur	Ana
Bonnie	Bret	Beryl	Barry	Bertha	Bill
Charley	Cindy	Chris	Chantal	Cristobal	Claudette
Danielle	Dennis	Debby	Dean	Dolly	Danny
Earl	Emily	Ernesto	Erin	Edouard	Erika
Frances	Floyd	Florence	Felix	Fay	Fabian
Gaston	Gert	Gordon	Gabrielle	Gustav	Grace
Hermine	Harvey	Helene	Humberto	Hanna	Henri
Ivan	Irene	Isaac	Iris	Isidore	Isabel
Jeanne	Jose	Joyce	Jerry	Josephine	Juan
Karl	Katrina	Keith	Karen	Kyle	Kate
Lisa	Lenny	Leslie	Lorenzo	Lili	Larry
Matthew	Maria	Michael	Michelle	Marco	Mindy

Nicole	Nate	Nadine	Noel	Nana	Nicholas
Otto	Ophelia	Oscar	Olga	Omar	Odette
Paula	Philippe	Patty	Pablo	Paloma	Peter
Richard	Rita	Rafael	Rebekah	Rene	Rose
Shary	Stan	Sandy	Sebastien	Sally	Sam
Tomas	Tammy	Tony	Tanya	Teddy	Teresa
Virginie	Vince	Valerie	Van	Vicky	Victor
Walter	Wilma	William	Wendy	Wilfred	Wanda

Winds and earthquakes

US Torro Force (tornado strength)

FC funnel cloud

 0 light

 1 mild

 2 moderate

 3 strong

 4 severe

 5 intense

 6 moderately devastating

 7 strongly devastating

 8 severely devastating

 9 severely devastating

10 intensely devastating

11 intensely devastating

12 super tornado

Two scales are used to measure earthquake strength: the Richter Scale and the Mercalli Scale

Mercalli	Richter	
1	<3	felt only by seismographs
2	3.0–3.4	feeble (just noticeable by some people)
3	3.5–4.0	slight (similar to passing of heavy lorries)
4	4.0–4.4	moderate (rocking of loose objects)
5	4.5–4.8	quite strong (felt by most people even when sleeping)
6	4.9–5.4	strong (trees rock and some structural damage caused)
7	5.5–6.0	very strong (walls crack)
8	6.1–6.5	destructive (weak buildings collapse)
9	6.6–7.0	ruinous (houses collapse and ground pipes crack)
10	7.1–7.3	disastrous (landslides, ground cracks and buildings collapse)
11	7.4–8.1	very disastrous (few buildings remain)
12	>8.1	catastrophic (ground rises and falls in waves)